ORGANIZATIONAL BEHAVIOR IN SCHOOLS

 Robert G. Owens

BROOKLYN COLLEGE

PRENTICE-HALL, INC., Englewood Cliffs, N. J.

To Barbara, who understood

13–641027–8
Library of Congress Catalog Card Number: 78–86521

Current printing (last digit):

10 9 8 7 6 5 4

Prentice-Hall International, Inc., *London*
Prentice-Hall of Australia Pty. Ltd., *Sydney*
Prentice-Hall of Canada Ltd., *Toronto*
Prentice-Hall of India Private Ltd., *New Delhi*
Prentice-Hall of Japan, Inc., *Tokyo*

Printed in the United States of America

preface

This is a book for educational administrators or for those who want to become educational administrators. It deals with knowledge, theory, and research of the behavioral sciences and is intended to serve as a concise guide to some of the achievements of behavioral research which school administrators can use in professional practice.

This book was written for superintendents of schools and school principals, as well as for the all-important "middle management" administrators from whose ranks the candidates for "top management" jobs come. Directors of programs such as Physical Education and Health Education, Instruction, and Pupil Services, department chairmen, coordinators, and others with administrative responsibilities in education will find much of value in these pages. It is hoped that they will also find practical professional assistance.

Rather than compiling a catalog of research or a review of the literature, the author has organized related concepts and theories under specific functional headings such as *decision making, leadership,* and *change in an organizational setting.* Each chapter provides the reader with three important perspectives on the topic covered:

 1. A general description of the "state of the art" in the area covered by the chapter
 2. Emphasis on certain particularly significant ideas or studies that have provided powerful breakthroughs in the search for knowledge and understanding
 3. Implications for the professional practice of administration in schools and school systems

The goal has been to provide the school administrator with a useful working tool for responding to contemporary demands for effective action—a tool that will enable him to grasp quickly the new behavioral knowledge that is transforming school administration, and grasp it in such a way that he can begin to use it immediately in coping with professional problems.

A spiral plan of development, familiar to those acquainted with techniques of curriculum construction, has been used in the exposition of important concepts. Motivation theory, for example, is introduced in Chapter 1 and is then enlarged upon in Chapters 2 through 9. A similar approach has been used for other important topics such as social systems theory, role theory, and feedback.

Since organizational behavior is concerned with the ways in which individuals and groups behave in *all kinds* of organizations, not just schools, material has been drawn from many fields, particularly business, industry, public administration, and the military. The implication is, of course, that, as organizations, schools have much in common with other organizations. The theme of the book is that there is a body of knowledge and theory which is applicable to the behavior of individuals and groups of individuals in all kinds of organizations and that educational administrators can profit from an awareness of it. That body of knowledge and theory is, of course, the discipline known as *organizational behavior.*

I am indebted to many friends and colleagues who encouraged and helped me in this project. Professor Carl R. Steinhoff of New York University provided wise counsel when I was first developing the book and after he read a preliminary draft of the manuscript. Professor Thomas J. Sergiovanni of the University of Illinois provided insightful suggestions and comments after he read successive drafts of the manuscript. A special debt of gratitude is owed to Professor Stephen H. Lockwood of Brooklyn College whose unflagging encouragement and confidence buoyed me in moments of uncertainty and difficulty.

To Louis E. Rosenzwieg, Dean of Teacher Education at Brooklyn

College, and to my colleagues in the Education Department there I express appreciation—not only for their encouragement, but for contributing to a climate which fostered scholarly endeavor.

Special thanks are due to Mrs. Edna Bartlett for preparing drafts of the manuscript and to Mrs. Elaine Goldman, who skillfully and patiently saw to the preparation of the final manuscript.

Finally, I wish to acknowledge the very valuable help of Mrs. Nancy B. Flanders, Senior Clerk of the Babylon (New York) Public Library, in tracking down many needed references—a task to which she brought not only her considerable professional skills but her personal enthusiasm as well.

R. G. O.

contents

❧ 1 ❧

recent developments in
educational administration

Revolutions generally occur when threads of the past are consciously loomed into a serviceable fabric by master weavers whose arts are in tune with the time.

—William W. Wayson[1]

It is probably an exaggeration to say that recent developments in educational administration constitute a revolution, but it is no exageration to say that the last decade or two have witnessed profound changes which seem to forecast more extensive developments in the near future. Although it is true that, until the mid-1960's, the impact of the "new" developments had been felt most keenly by university professors of educational administration and by a small number of school district superintendents, by that time increasing numbers of school principals and others in administrative positions began to be aware of what was occurring. Much of the "new" in educational administration involves new knowledge which leads to new insights into administrative behavior with consequent hope for increasing the professional capability of school administrators to meet the challenges that lie ahead in American education.

I

Recent developments in educational administration, taken as a whole, have been given various labels; none has yet achieved universal acceptance. Some refer to the "revolution" in educational administration while others speak of a "new ferment" in educational administration and still others discuss "the new Administration." Each of these labels—and all of them are currently in wide use in the literature of educational administration—suggests more than a superficial "fad," something more fundamental than another new "in" gimmick, for educational administration has been part of a long process of historical development, and the current emphasis on the "new ferment" signifies an important breakthrough in that history. We can best set the stage for understanding this breakthrough by taking at least a quick look at the recent history of educational administration. But, as all school administrators know, educational administration is a profession of recent vintage, a newcomer to systematic study and research. Its roots are to be found in the older fields of administration and, particularly, public administration. To gain a reasonably accurate perspective, we must look at some of the highlights of the development of the field of administration itself as distinct from educational administration.

Administration and Educational Administration

In a typical university administration is not generally regarded as an academic discipline. For example, *business administration* is usually taught in a school or college devoted to business with its own specialized faculty. *Public administration* is also usually organized as a distinct unit in a university, such as a college, school, or—in the case of a small institution—a department. *Hospital administration* is under the aegis of the medical school. We do not often find a school in a university devoted to the professional practice of administration, as such.

Educational administration is, generally, taught within the framework of the school of education—sometimes comprising a department of the school, but often being less formally structured and known simply as a "program." In colleges of education and schools of education, the teaching of administration is commonly even further fragmented and diffused: the school guidance and counseling faculty may offer courses in the administration of guidance programs, the physical education faculty may do the same, and so with each of many "special fields" in the school of education. In fact, in a school or college of education, many faculty members may be found teaching administration in a wide variety of unrelated courses. The content of these courses, and the ways in which they are taught, are usually developed independently with little or no reference to each other. More than likely, there is virtually no contact between the faculty teaching administration courses in the school of education and faculty members in other parts of the institution who are also preparing students for administrative responsibilities.

This arrangement is the typical and traditional way in which administration is studied and taught. It is based on some time-honored and generally held viewpoints, three of which are:

1. *The administrator of an organization must have a high level of technical knowledge of the area to be administered.* For example, to be successful as an elementary school principal it is assumed that one must possess considerable knowledge about the teaching of young children. And a director of athletics must have a high level of competence in teaching physical education. Moreover, we might suppose, the top administrator of a great scientific and technical university must himself be a competent scientist or technical person.

2. *Whatever the art or science of administration includes, it is best taught and learned in practical application to specific situations.* This viewpoint suggests that, to a large extent, the tasks that administrators face are quite different in various specialized fields. This view would hold that the tasks and functions of, say, a hospital administrator are uniquely and distinctively different from those of the principal of a large high school.

3. *Administration, as a body of knowledge and practice, is neither an academic discipline nor a profession.* This viewpoint considers the knowledge content of administration, and its professional manifestations in terms of organized practice, too inadequate to warrant it a place with the recognized academic disciplines and the professions.

These views are slowly changing—reflecting fundamental developments that have already effected major changes in the practice of administration in and out of education, and forecasting still further changes.

Public Administration as a Beginning

The study of *Cameralism* is a reasonable starting place in the search for a systematic definition of administration.[2] In the 1700's the Cameralists of Austria and Germany developed an administrative technology which was concerned with the functions and activities of particular governing systems.

---

[2] For a discussion of Cameralism see Roald F. Campbell and Russell T. Gregg, eds., *Administrative Behavior in Education* (New York: Harper & Row, Publishers, 1957), pp. 85–90.

Nearer to us in time, and better known to most of us, are the ideas and concepts that underlay the establishment of the reputable civil services of Europe and Great Britain in the nineteenth century. Two key notions provided the essential rationale for the Civil Services:

1. *The idea that administration is an activity that can be studied and taught separately from the content of what is being administered.* For example, a postman need not administer a postal service, nor must tax attorneys administer the collection of taxes.
2. *The belief that decisions about the policies and purposes of government belong to the realm of political action but that these decisions are best implemented by civil servants whose jobs are not dependent on the whims of politics and who are free to develop good administrative procedures.* This includes much more than the mere creating of a civil service as an alternative to corruption and the "spoils system." This belief is based on the concept that a disinterested administrative organization can become more effective than one which is involved in the policy making process. In the twentieth century, the Secretariat of the United Nations and the Foreign Service of the United States State Department are good illustrations of this concept in action.

In the United States in the nineteenth century, the term "administration" was also used in the context of government and the ideas it represented gave rise to the growth of public administration, although "civil service" in America tended to connote a system designed to insure honesty and fairness rather than the expertness associated with the European and British systems. Woodrow Wilson was the catalyst who crystalized early thinking about the professionalization of administration with the publication of his now-famous essay, "The Study of Administration," in 1887. He felt that the improvement of administrative techniques depended on scholarly study and learning in the specialized field of administration itself. "The object of administrative study," he wrote in an often quoted statement, "is to rescue executive methods from the confusion and costliness of empirical study and set them upon foundations laid deep in stable principle."[3] A 31-year-old assistant professor at the time he published this article, Wilson was far ahead of his time in arguing earnestly for the inclusion of the study of administration as a subject fit for universities to deal seriously with. It is interesting to note that 40 years were to pass before the first textbook of the principles in public administration which he called for was published (1927). The search for principles was essential to the development of an administrative science, as differentiated from administrative folklore or custom.

---

[3] Woodrow Wilson, "The Study of Administration," *Political Science Quarterly*, II, No. 2 (June, 1887), 197–222.

Impact of the Industrial Revolution

At about the close of the nineteenth century—the time of Woodrow Wilson's scholarly contributions—western European and American businessmen were stepping up their efforts to increase profits from industry. The best way to obtain greater profits in that burgeoning era of industry was generally felt to be to lower the unit cost of producing goods. One way to do this, of course, was to step up mass production through the use of innovations such as the assembly line. The leadership of pioneering industrial giants such as Henry Ford is widely recognized in connection with such technological breakthroughs. In this era of industrial expansion, the key men then—as they are in our own day of technological revolution—were the engineers and technically oriented scientists. These were the men who could build the machines and then combine them into assembly line units. This was the era of the engineering consultant and the drive for efficiency.

Frederick W. Taylor is a name well known to many students of administration. He had a scientific and engineering background and, in the early 1900's, was one of the top engineering consultants in American industry. We know that Taylor had read Wilson's essay and had been influenced by it. From about 1900 to 1915, as he worked to solve practical production problems in factories all over America, Taylor developed what later became known as his "principles of scientific management." These became enormously popular, not only in industry, but in the management of all kinds of organizations, including the family. A best seller of a few years ago, *Cheaper by the Dozen*, vividly recounts how "efficiency" invaded every corner of the family life of Frank B. Gilbreth, one of Taylor's closest colleagues. Taylor's "principles of scientific management" were aimed primarily at lowering the unit cost of factory production, although he and his followers claimed that these principles could be applied universally [4]; they became a virtual mania in the press and throughout our society.[5] Briefly, Taylor saw management problems as consisting of thirteen key steps, two of which are especially important:

1. *Distributing minute, specialized tasks*, which when taken together would get a job done

---

[4] Frederick Taylor, *The Principles of Scientific Management* (New York: Harper & Row, Publishers, 1911), p. 8.

[5] For a vivid description of this period and the power of business and industrial leaders to force their values on school administrators, see Raymond E. Callahan, *Education and the Cult of Efficiency* (Chicago: The University of Chicago Press, 1962).

2. *Coordinating or ordering these numerous small specialized tasks* to accomplish the entire job

In practice, Taylor's ideas led to time-and-motion studies, rigid discipline on the job, concentration on the tasks to be performed with minimal interpersonal contacts between workers, and strict application of incentive pay systems.[6]

At the same time that Taylor's ideas and their application were having such enormous impact on American life, a French industrialist was working out some powerful ideas of his own. Henri Fayol had a background quite different from Taylor's, which helps to account for some of the differences in perception of the two men. Whereas Taylor was essentially a technician whose first concern was the middle-management level of industry, Fayol had the background of a top-management executive. It would be useful to mention briefly some of the ideas Fayol advanced to give us a better perspective of what he contributed to the growth of thought in administration:

1. Unlike Taylor, who tended to view men as extensions of factory machinery, Fayol focused his attention on the manager rather than the worker.
2. He clearly separated the processes of administration from other operations in the organization, such as production.
3. He emphasized the common elements of the processes of administration in different organizations.

Fayol believed that a trained administrative group was essential to improving the operations of organizations which were becoming increasingly complex. As early as 1916, Fayol wrote that administrative ability "can and should be acquired in the same way as technical ability, first at school, later in the workshop." [7] He added that we find good and bad administrative methods existing side by side "with a persistence only to be explained by lack of theory." [8]

Fayol advanced the search for the principles of administration, which Wilson had called for, when he defined administration as comprising five "elements": (1) to plan, (2) to organize, (3) to command, (4) to coordinate, and (5) to control.[9] He went further by identifying a list of fourteen "principles," among which were: (1) unity of command,

---

[6] Amitai Etzioni, *Modern Organizations* (Englewood Cliffs, N. J.: Prentice-Hall, Inc., 1964), p. 21.

[7] Henri Fayol, *General and Industrial Management*, trans. Constance Storrs (London: Sir Isaac Pitman & Sons, 1949), p. 14.

[8] *Ibid.*, p. 15.

[9] *Ibid.*, Chap. 5.

(2) authority, (3) initiative, and (4) morale. Avoiding a rigid and dogmatic application of his ideas to the administration of organizations, Fayol emphasized that flexibility and a sense of proportion were essential for managers who adapted principles and definitions to particular situations—quite a different interpretation than that of Taylor, who held firmly to uniform, emphatic application of principles.

By the time of Fayol and Taylor it was clear that the Western world was becoming an "organizational society." As giant industrial organizations grew in the early 1900's, so did government and other organizational aspects of life grow. The relatively simple social and political structures of the pre-industrial era seemed inherently inadequate in an urban industrial society. Life was not always completely happy in this new social setting, and a great deal of friction—social, political, and economic—resulted. The increasing sense of conflict between men and organizations became a major factor in the struggle of learning to live successfully with this new kind of world, this industrial world where the individual was a part of some organization at every turn. The years before World War I were punctuated by frequent outbursts of this conflict such as labor unrest, revolution, and the rise of communism. In this setting, a German sociologist, Max Weber, produced some of the most useful, durable, and brilliant work on an administrative system that seemed promising at that time and has since proven indispensable: *bureaucracy*.

At a period when men and organizations were dominated by the whims of authoritarian industrialists and entrenched political systems, Weber saw hope in bureaucracy. Essentially, the hope was that well-run bureaucracies would become fairer, more impartial, and more predictable—in general, more rational—than organizations subject to the caprice of powerful individuals. Weber felt that well-run bureaucracies would be efficient, in fact, the most efficient form of organization yet invented. Such a viewpoint may not reflect modern experiences with bureaucracies, but Weber was convinced that in a *well-run* bureaucracy efficiency would be high for a number of reasons, especially because bureaucrats are highly trained, technical specialists, each skilled in his own portion of an administrative task. According to Weber, the bureaucratic apparatus would be very impersonal, minimizing irrational personal and emotional factors and leaving bureaucratic personnel free to work with a minimum of friction or confusion. This, he concluded, would result in expert, impartial, and unbiased service to the organization's clients. In the ideal bureaucracy Weber envisioned certain characteristics which are, in a sense, principles of administration:

1. A division of labor based on functional specialization
2. A well-defined hierarchy of authority

3. A system of rules covering the rights and duties of employees
4. A system of procedures for dealing with work situations
5. Impersonality of interpersonal relations
6. Selection and promotion based only on technical competence [10]

Part of Weber's genuis lay in his sensitivity to the dangers of bureaucracy while at the same time he recognized the merits of bureaucracy *in ideal circumstances*. He emphasized very strongly the dangers of bureaucracy even so far as to warn that massive, uncontrollable bureaucracy could very well be the greatest threat to *both* communism and free enterprise capitalism.[11]

We have thus far considered three men of ideas, men who represent many others as well and a prodigious field of effort in their time. Each pointed to the need for the principles and the theories that, by 1900, were generally regarded as essential if the administration of our growing organizations was to become more rational and more effective. The American, Taylor, emphasized the principles that viewed administration as management—the coordination of many small tasks so as to accomplish the overall job as efficiently as possible. Efficiency was interpreted to mean the cheapest net dollar cost to produce the finished article. Taylor assumed that labor was a commodity to be bought and sold as one buys oil or electricity, and that by "scientific management" the manager could reduce to a minimum the amount of labor that must be purchased. The Frenchman, Fayol, emphasized broader preparation of administrators so that they would be better prepared to perform their unique functions in the organization. He felt that the tasks administrators perform are, presumably, different from the things that engineers perform, but equally important.

Germany's Max Weber held that bureaucracy is a theory of organization especially suited to the needs of large and complex enterprises which performed services for large numbers of clients. For Weber, the bureaucratic concept was an attempt to minimize the frustrations and irrationality of large organizations in which the relationships of workers were on a highly personal basis.

The Era of Scientific Management, *1910–1935*

These three men—Taylor, Fayol, and Weber—were giants in the preWorld War I years who led the way in the early efforts to master the

---

[10] Richard H. Hall, "The Concept of Bureaucracy: An Empirical Assessment," *The American Journal of Sociology*, LXIX, No. 1 (July, 1963), 33.

[11] J. P. Mayer, *Max Weber and German Politics* (London: Faber and Faber, 1943), p. 128.

problems of managing modern organizations. There is no precise and universally agreed upon beginning or end point to the era; however, the period of 1910–1935 can generally be thought of as the era of scientific management. As the study of the problems of organization, management, and administration became established more and more firmly in the universities—just as Wilson and Fayol had predicted—these "principles" received increased attention and challenge from scholars and professors. Long before the era of scientific management came to its generally acknowledged end in the mid-1930's, the "new beginnings" existed for those who were attentive. Thus, students of administration were already at work in the 1920's. Some found the concepts then available inadequate to deal with such significant problems as the conflict arising from the demands of the organization, on the one hand, and the need of individuals to obtain a reasonable sense of satisfaction and reward from their participation, on the other.

Luther Gulick and Lyndall Urwick stand out among the many scholars who attempted to synthesize what is now known as the "classical" formulation of principles which would be useful in developing good, functional organizations. Central to the work of these two men was the idea that elements of the organization could be grouped and related according to function, geographic location, or similar criteria. They emphasized the drawing up of formal charts of organizations, showing the precise ways which various offices and divisions were related. Gulick and Urwick published a widely acclaimed book in 1937 [12] and were still highly influential after World War II.[13] Many school administrators are familiar with some of the organizational concepts that were popularized by them: (1) line and staff, (2) span of control, (3) unity of command, and (4) delegation of responsibility.

The search for sound principles for the study and teaching of administration was making progress. In our quest for historical perspectives we would do well to remember that many people now actively engaged in school administration learned these and similar concepts in years past as *the* fundamentals of school administration.

The Human Relations Movement, 1935–1950

In time, as the principles of scientific management were applied to industry with greater care, a need to be more precise about the effect of human factors on production efficiency was felt. The Western Electric

---

[12] Luther Gulick and L. Urwick, eds., *Papers on the Science of Administration* (New York: Institute of Public Administration, Columbia University, 1937).
[13] Luther Gulick, *Administrative Reflection on World War II* (University, Ala.: University of Alabama Press, 1948).

Company was one of the more enlightened industrial employers of the time and, in routine fashion, cooperated with the National Research Council in a relatively simple experiment designed to determine the optimum level of illumination in a shop for maximum production efficiency. Western Electric's Hawthorne plant in Chicago was selected for the experiment, and before the experiments were over, an impressive team of researchers was involved; of its members, Elton Mayo is probably the best known to educators. The original experiment was very well designed and executed, and it revealed that there was no direct, simple relationship between the illumination level and the production output of the workers. Since one of Taylor's "principles" stated that there *was* a relationship, this study raised more questions than it answered. The researchers identified six questions that they wanted to explore:

1. Do employees actually become tired?
2. Are pauses for rest desirable?
3. Is a shorter working day desirable?
4. What is the attitude of employees toward their work and toward the company?
5. What is the effect of changing the type of working equipment?
6. Why does production decrease in the afternoon?

These were rather simple, straightforward questions, but it is obvious that the answers to a number of them are psychological in nature, rather than physical. In the 1920's, these questions triggered one of the most far-reaching series of experiments in the history of administration which became known as the Western Electric studies and which led to discoveries that are not yet fully understood. However unexpected it may have been, one major finding of these studies was the realization that *human* variability is an important determinant of productivity. Thus, in the 1920's, the human relations movement was born.[14]

New concepts were now available to the administrator to use in approaching his work. Among them were (1) morale, (2) group dynamics, (3) democratic supervision, and (4) personnel relations. The human relations movement emphasized the human and interpersonal factors for administering the affairs of organizations. Supervisors in particular drew heavily on human relations concepts, placing stress on such notions as "democratic" procedures, "involvement," motivational techniques, and the sociometry of leadership.

---

[14] These studies, often called the Western Electric studies, may be known to the reader for another reason: they led also to identification of the so-called "Hawthorne Effect," which became important in improving techniques of behavioral research. These studies are summarized in Fritz J. Roethlisberger and William J. Dickson, *Management and the Worker* (Cambridge, Mass.: Harvard University Press, 1939).

The "New" Administration Emerges

Chester Barnard was, for many, a "master weaver" who was able to create a complete and integrated fabric out of what had seemed to be merely tangled threads in the literature on administration. Barnard was a successful corporation executive in New Jersey whose landmark book, *The Functions of the Executive*, appeared in 1938.[15] In this book, Barnard drew on and integrated concepts from many schools of thought that had appeared in the fifty years since Wilson's essay, as well as introducing some of his own ideas. He thus ushered in an era of understanding of administration that we now consider both "modern" and "new" by anticipating many presentday views of administration and organization. Although Barnard never claimed to be a scholar, his work did much to inspire students of administration to greater efforts to create a discipline of administration based on scientific inquiry.

During the 1940's, behavioral scientists were attracted in increasing numbers to this growing field, for it challenged their skills and knowledge. Psychologists, sociologists, and political scientists, as well as other behavioral scientists, could draw upon the following invaluable aids to scholarship:

1. *Specialized knowledge* of human behavior that had been acquired over the years in their disciplines
2. *Research methods* for studying human behavior
3. *Theoretical concepts* which gave them keen insights as to what to look for in organizational behavior

For example, the 1945 publication by Herbert A. Simon, a university professor with a strong background in political science, psychology, and business administration, of his book, *Administrative Behavior*, is a good example of how scholars began to advance knowledge in the field.[16] As Etzioni says of this book, it "opened a whole new vista of administrative theory," [17] and in that postwar era many new vistas were to be opened by behavioral scientists through their studies of human behavior in organizations. Whatever is "new" in the new administration is best viewed as a combination of the "classical" concepts of those who

---

[15] Chester I. Barnard, *The Functions of the Executive* (Cambridge, Mass.: Harvard University Press, 1938).

[16] Herbert A. Simon, *Administrative Behavior* (New York: The Macmillan Company, 1945).

[17] Amitai Etzioni, *Modern Organizations* (Englewood Cliffs, N. J.: Prentice-Hall, Inc., © 1964), p. 30.

had emphasized the *structure* of organizations and the *human relations* concepts which had received such strong emphasis in the 1940's. The "new" is behavioral in viewpoint—looking upon administration as very much involved in the behavior of people in organizational settings.

This viewpoint goes far beyond advocating pat, prescriptive teaching of "how to succeed in administration"—by applying "recipes." It gives promise of equipping administrators to understand their organizational environment in greater depth than previously. If this promise is kept, the "new" administration would appear to be better adapted to a world which is changing with bewildering speed, so fast, in fact, that we cannot reasonably forecast the problems and the circumstances that students now beginning their study of educational administration will face at the height of their careers.

To understand some of whatever it is that is being described as "new" in educational administration, let us take a look at four beliefs to which the adherents of the "new" would tend to subscribe:

1. *Administration is comprised of specialized knowledge, skills, and understandings which are different from the activities being administered* They can be identified and studied *as administration*, separate from the technical aspects of the operations being administered. This means that educational administration, for example, has much in common with business administration, public administration, hospital administration, and so forth. This concept becomes evident when we ask the question, "Do educational administrators differ significantly from administrators in business or government?" We must ask why we need educational administration—what is so unique about it that sets it apart from other forms of administration? Finally, of course, this value-belief makes us wonder whether long years of teaching help to equip one for the school administrator role or whether they handicap one instead. It is possible, and today many would say probable, that short teaching experience plus considerable study in the behavioral sciences, as well as administration, would be a better preparation for educational administrators.

2. *The practice of administration, in the "new" sense, is based on a realistic view of organizations as they actually exist.* We know that at the present time there is no general theory of administration by which we can model an "ideal" organization or administrative system. In an effort to sensitize the administrator to the realities of his organizational environment, therefore, the concepts and principles of a *number* of *theories* are explored as ways of understanding the behavioral aspects of administration. Theory, as used in this sense, is not some pet prejudice or bias; rather, it is a scientific attempt to explain phenomena of human behavior in complex organizations which are not fully understood yet.

3. *The scientific foundations of the "new administration" are in the*

behavioral sciences. In an effort to understand the true nature of the problems of administering educational organizations, the insights of disciplines such as psychology, sociology, anthropology, and political science are being explored. In addition to the basic viewpoints of these disciplines, and the knowledge content that they now represent, their research methods, that is, their ways of looking at reality, are being used increasingly. Developments in these disciplines have been very rapid in the last 25 years.

4. *Change is inevitable in educational administration, and innovation is urgently needed.* Observers of the educational scene have commented frequently on the tendency of schools to remain basically the same; yet it is obvious to all that fresh new breakthroughs are needed. School administrators are constantly heading into the unknown; who, for example, could have predicted in 1945 that the concept of the "neighborhood school" would ever seriously be challenged in this country? Who can predict what demands and expectations principals will face ten years from now? Change requires more adaptable, skillful administrators with a grasp of basic principles and a sensitivity to reality, rather than a determination to fight for traditional practices. The need for change also requires more precise understanding of the nature of change in organizations and how to bring it about.

To clarify further, let us ask what are some of the notions or concepts that are being dealt with. Let us consider a few of the many which are currently being studied:

THE CONCEPT OF REFERENCE GROUPS

In the school organization, important reference groups are: (1) pupils, (2) teachers, (3) parents, and (4) central office personnel. How they relate, interact, perceive, affect, and communicate with one another *as groups* is important for an administrator to understand.

THE CONCEPT OF LEADERSHIP

This involves the balance between the leader's need to maintain the organization and his need to give it new goals or new ways of achieving its present goals.

THE CONCEPT OF THE ADMINISTRATOR AS A MEDIATOR

We now recognize that any organization must put emphasis on *its* demands and—simultaneously—on the needs of the human beings in the organization. Ordinarily, one would assume that dual emphasis would cause some measure of conflict in every organization—and it does. But how much conflict is acceptable? And how can the administrator—a principal, say—effectively mediate this conflict between man and the organization?

THE CONCEPT OF ROLE

We all act out roles in life; for a school principal, one important role is that of *principal*. It is reasonable to assume that he behaves as *he* thinks principals ought to behave. To what extent does he play the role to meet the expectations that he thinks teachers have of principals? Does he modify the way he handles his role to meet his perception of what the superintendent of schools is looking for in a principal? Does he find himself in conflict because he must play different roles for different audiences?

Three Eras

It is not unreasonable to suggest that through an evolutionary process administration has passed through three differentiable eras. First, the scientific management era of Taylor and his disciples formulated rigid, technologically grounded principles for organizational management. The primary goal was increased output by means of increased efficiency, and thus the organization members were perceived as "primarily passive instruments, capable of performing work and accepting directions, but not initiating action or exerting influence in any significant way." [18]

Second, the human relations era modified Taylor's position severely by directing attention to the psychological and social aspects of organization. Whereas Taylor had emphasized the coordination of physical processes and the subsequent adjustment of human workers to these processes, the human relations advocates perceived the organization as an organic social system in which the human and social elements must be coordinated into a functioning whole. The Western Electric studies, conducted by Mayo, Roethlisberger, and others, led the experimenters to conclude that changes in the physical environment do not necessarily act as an antecedent to changes in output, but that productivity is more likely to be increased when greater emphasis is placed upon such variables as worker participation, satisfaction, cooperation, and the morale and cohesiveness of the group.

The principle of the Hegelian dialectic could be applied to adminis-

---

[18] James G. March and Herbert A. Simon, *Organizations* (New York: John Wiley & Sons, Inc., 1958), p. 6.

tration in order to illustrate how we have arrived at the present and third era of administrative theory. The Hegelian thesis which was originally believed was exemplified by the authoritarianism of Taylor; however, with the passage of time, the opposite viewpoint (its antithesis) came into vogue as Mayo's experiments led to an accentuation of morale or organizational humanization. The present era in which administrative theory is stressed is an outgrowth (the synthesis) which incorporates features of the work of Taylor and Mayo plus many newer behavioral insights not available to either man. The goal of present administrative theory is the development of conceptual frameworks through which we may systemize and integrate our knowledge of the various types of administration.[19]

One of the goals of the "new" administrative theory is to adapt models from other disciplines which are applicable to educational administration, as well as to business, hospital, or public administration.

The reader will find that to a surprising extent Barnard anticipated many of the currently accepted theories and that much of what is presently known or theorized about administration has been contributed by workers in many fields, especially the behavioral sciences. Progress has depended upon a constant dialogue involving researchers, theorists, and practitioners as they continue to raise questions, seek answers, and test theories.

Educational Administration Stirs

Educational administration was affected very little by the evolution of administration as a field of study until the middle of this century, which was largely due to the fact that the teaching of educational administration was sequestered from the mainstream of scholarly thought and research in which the revolution was occurring. Schools of education in even the most prestigious universities tended to have almost no contact with the business schools and the behavioral science departments on their own campuses. Traditionally, educational administration has been taught by former superintendents of schools whose knowledge of their subject

---

[19] A somewhat similar approach to the history of administration is taken by Bennis in his discussion of the phases through which organizational leadership has passed. He argues that scientific management consisted of "organizations without people" and describes the present era as the period of the "Revisionists"—in which attempts are being made to reconcile the conflict between traditional and modern organizational theory. For a discussion of this point, see Warren G. Bennis, "Leadership Theory and Administrative Behavior," *Administrative Science Quarterly*, IV, No. 3 (December, 1959), 259–301. See also Warren G. Bennis, *Changing Organizations* (New York: McGraw-Hill Book Company, 1966), Chap. 4.

came largely from years of hard-earned experience in the "front lines."
Courses in educational administration tended to be focused on practical,
"how-to-do-it" problems, drawing on the past experience of practicing
administrators. Emphasis was typically given to sharing the techniques
of these administrators for solving problems that had been tried in school
districts such as the ones that the students were familiar with.

Research in educational administration during the first half of this
century consisted principally of status studies of current problems or the
gathering of opinion. With unusual exceptions, little research in educational administration dealt with testing of theoretical propositions and
virtually none of it involved the insights and research methods that had
been developed by behavioral scientists. As Van Miller has observed,

> A lot of the study of administration has been a matter of looking back-
> ward or sideways at what was done or what is being done. It is striking
> to contemplate how much administrative experience has been exchanged
> and how little it has been studied scientifically. The current excitement
> arises from the fact that within recent years educational administration
> has become a field of study and of development as well as a vocation.[20]

The year 1950 may well be the turning point in the development of
educational administration in our time. When a history of the period is
written, it will reveal—as history often does—that a number of seemingly unconnected, apparently disparate, events were drawn into a fortuitous confluence that changed the course of events.

NATIONAL CONFERENCE OF PROFESSORS OF
EDUCATIONAL ADMINISTRATION (NCPEA)

The rumblings of change surely include the formation and development of the National Conference of Professors of Educational Administration. This group had its beginning at the February 1947 meeting of
the American Association of School Administrators, when some professors
met for a discussion of common problems. They planned a ten-day conference on leadership for education to be held in August of that year.
This was a fresh, new topic for professors of educational administration
in 1947, and the session that summer consisted of meetings by working
committees which produced a report entitled *Educational Leaders: Their
Function and Preparation*. NCPEA has been characterized by a lack of
formal organizational "make-work," by emphasis on productive work-

---

[20] Van Miller, *The Public Administration of American School Systems* (New
York: The Macmillan Company, © 1965), pp. 544-45.

sessions, and by the opportunities it offers for professors of educational administration to increase communication with colleagues in other institutions. In this connection, the involving of professors from other fields, such as economics, psychology, and sociology, as well as individuals from business, industry, and public administration, stimulated the interdisciplinary interests of professors of educational administration. For the first time these professors were opening up communication with colleagues who had access to knowledge and research methods being used in many fields. Each year since its inception, NCPEA has followed the pattern of a planning session in February leading up to a week-long conference in August. The conferences have been chiefly work-sessions in which the professors explored new ways of meeting the problem of developing better ways of preparing educational administrators in university programs.[21]

AMERICAN ASSOCIATION OF SCHOOL
ADMINISTRATORS (AASA)

This group chiefly represents the professional association of school superintendents. It has not encouraged school principals to join its ranks, and school principals do have their own national associations affiliated with the National Education Association. However, since, in 1947, many professors of educational administration had been drawn from the ranks of the superintendency, there was a natural inclination for them—and the NCPEA—to cast their lot with the AASA.

In 1946 and again in 1947, the AASA heard reports from its planning committee which dealt with the development of long-range plans for AASA. The planning committee reports did not propose a very bold or original plan, but they did urge AASA to concern itself with "professionalization" of the school superintendency. Specifically it was suggested that AASA (1) should encourage the development of better preparation programs in the universities, (2) should encourage school boards to use more adequate standards in selecting their school superintendents, and (3) generally, should participate more actively in the professional affairs of education. Although it is clear that AASA was not, at that time, entertaining any clear vision of spearheading a major innovation in school administration, it is equally clear that the group was in a mood to participate in changes.

In recounting this brief history, we must not overlook the advances

---

[21] Readers interested in the historical account of the first decade of NCPEA should see W. R. Flesher and A. L. Knoblauch, *A Decade of Development in Educational Leadership* (New York: NCPEA, Teachers College Press, 1958).

which have taken place since the post-World War II beginnings. Some nineteen years later, in 1968, the AASA announced and inaugurated its Academy for School Executives, which was to be a "war college" approach to the in-service education of practicing school administrators— especially superintendents, of course. The Academy has offered intensive "practical" in-service seminars and workshops on a regional basis especially designed to bring superintendents of schools into contact with new insights for meeting demands which they confront on the job. Many of the Academy leaders are professors and practitioners who were in the forefront of the early "new movement" in the 1940's and they have brought the interdisciplinary approach—with reliance on the behavioral sciences—to this significant effort.

The fact that school superintendents, elementary school principals, and secondary school principals belonged to three different associations in the 1940's had an interesting and long-range effect on events to follow. There was no single voice for educational administrators, and those who were to be the leaders in the events that were set in motion in 1947 —the professors—had closer ties with the superintendents than with the principals' groups.

THE KELLOGG FOUNDATION

For more than 25 years prior to 1947, the Kellogg Foundation had been encouraging activities to "improve the health, happiness and well-being of children and youth, without discrimination as to race, creed, or geographical distribution." The experience of the Kellogg-sponsored community health project centered on the improvement of the children's schools, and after many years indicated that community improvement projects of this kind were frequently hampered by the limited knowledge and skills of school administrators, particularly superintendents. "Too often," as Hollis A. Moore has stated it, "this leadership was faulty, un-imaginative, and grossly out of tune with the hopes and desires of a community. Many school administrators showed a lack of knowledge about community processes and the role of the school in the improvement of everyday living." [22] This had been observed and commented on by Kellogg Foundation advisers.[23] Thus, by 1946 the Foundation was seriously interested in in-service efforts to improve the leadership effective-

---

22 Hollis A. Moore, Jr., "The Ferment in School Administration," in Daniel E. Griffiths, ed., *Behavioral Science and Educational Administration*, The Sixty-third Yearbook of the National Society for the Study of Education, Part II (Chicago: The University of Chicago Press, 1964), p. 16.

23 Hollis A. Moore, Jr., *Studies in School Administration: A Report on the CPEA* (Washington, D. C.: American Association of School Administrators, 1957), p. 1.

ness of school superintendents as a way to enhance the attainment of their own objectives.

THE COOPERATIVE PROGRAM IN EDUCATIONAL
ADMINISTRATION (CPEA)

The stage was set. The AASA, The National Association of County and Rural Area Superintendents, and the Council of Chief State School officers—along with Kellogg Foundation financing—sponsored a nation-wide series of five exploratory conferences in different regions of the country to discuss the possibility of a major effort to improve educational administration—by which was meant the superintendency. The result was the development of a large-scale innovative program which has led us into the present "revolution" in educational administration. This program was the Cooperative Program in Educational Administration (CPEA) which was well financed by the Kellogg Foundation.

The CPEA was launched in 1950 with the establishment of the first Project Centers. By the summer of 1951, these regional centers had been created in eight different universities (see Figure 1–1).

The establishment of CPEA was the principal action that began a new era in educational administration; some call this era an era of "ferment,"

FIGURE 1–1. Cooperative program in educational administration project centers.

some call it simply "new," and a few think it deserves the appellation "revolution"—but all agree that it has triggered major changes that will be long lasting. The story cannot be recounted here in a few words, so we will here present only a few of the more important results of the 1950 breakthrough.

Each CPEA center operated its particular phase of the project independently, although there was considerable exchange of information and ideas. The general purposes of all eight centers have been stated as follows:

1. Improvement of the preparation programs for preservice training of potential administrators and the in-service training of administrators already in the field
2. Development of greater sensitivity to large social problems through an interdisciplinary approach involving most of the social sciences
3. Dissemination of research findings to practicing administrators
4. Discovery of new knowledge about education and about administration
5. Development of continuing patterns of cooperation and communication among various universities and colleges within a region and between these institutions and other organizations and agencies working in the field of educational administration [24]

Initially, the focus was on the improvement of university programs of training. Flexible time allotments for class periods were explored, new teaching techniques were developed, and new teaching "tools" were created. Some centers stressed interdisciplinary seminars and studies; others focused on the internship as part of the training program; still others concentrated on improving the content and the quality of teaching of administration courses.

Research developed rapidly at each of the CPEA centers. Again, the general goals of the various centers were similar, but the focus of individual research efforts was far from identical. Studies at various CPEA centers ranged from administrative behavior to school-board-member behavior, from role perception to decision making, from community power structures to problems of integration. Each center has produced monographs, books, and a wide variety of publications to disseminate its research findings. Each has exerted leadership, especially in its own region, in communicating to other institutions. Nationally, the cooperative group that was set up to foster this interuniversity communication was the University Council for Educational Administration; membership in it is granted by a vote of member universities and is restricted to institu-

---

[24] *Toward Improved School Administration: A Decade of Professional Effort to Heighten Administrative Understanding and Skills* (Battle Creek, Mich.: W. K. Kellogg Foundation, 1961), p. 13.

tions which have approved educational administration programs which lead to the doctorate. Criteria for membership include depth and breadth of program, research capabilities of staff, and quality of student dissertations.

Because the United States began to step-up its interest in educational research in the late 1950's, the CPEA centers and the UCEA-affiliated institutions were in a strong position to take advantage of the opportunity to expand the frontiers of knowledge in administration. A core of research-oriented scholars had been created, research interests had been whetted, and sophisticated research techniques were being used with increasing frequency. Thus, opportunities to multiply and further the research work that had been stimulated in the 1950's were quickly made available and then exploited. One major Federally assisted project through which considerable research in administration has been stimulated is the large Research and Development Center at the University of Oregon.

In addition, a number of smaller cooperative and regional programs have been created, many of which originated in the earlier "ferment" already discussed. In New York State, for example, there was only one CPEA center: Teachers College of Columbia University. However, as part of a larger project assisted by the Ford Foundation, the programs in educational administration at Cornell University, Syracuse University, the University of Rochester, and the University of Buffalo have developed close liaison and some cooperative effort aimed at improving the training of administrators. At a state level, the Council for Administrative Leadership (CAL) is composed of representation from many professional associations including principals, superintendents, and professors. CAL sponsors administrative research, publishes research findings, and serves as an agency for communication for all groups interested in developing administrative leaders in education. CADEA, the Committee for the Advancement and Development of Educational Administration, is another state-wide group which is composed of professors from all institutions of higher learning in New York State which have an interest in educational administration. It is an informally structured group, and its gatherings serve primarily as opportunities for professors to communicate with one another about developments in their field. Within each state and region, groups similar to those in New York are providing for the communication of problems, ideas, and knowledge that are the foundation of scholarly work in every field of scientific endeavor.

Summary

Much has happened in administration since the publication of Wilson's essay in 1887. For many years, and certainly until the post-World War II era, educational administration was largely isolated from the increasing sophistication that had been developing in such areas as business, public affairs, and the military. By 1950, however, the groundwork had been laid that permitted the Cooperative Program in Educational Administration to become a major breakthrough in educational administration. A significant part of that breakthrough was the stimulation of interdisciplinary research in administrative problems. Aided by the fortuitous increase in Federal interest, research was expanded during the 1950's and 1960's, increasing in quantity, quality, and breadth as new insights were continually discovered. By the mid 1960's, it seemed probable that education—far from being outside the mainstream of discovery in administration—was taking the lead in making new discoveries about administration through research. It is the purpose of this book, in the following chapters, to discuss selected aspects of this research, especially as they relate to school administrators.

❧ 2 ❧

about theory
and research

There is nothing impractical about good theory . . . . Action divorced from theory is the random scurrying of a rat in a new maze. Good theory is the power to find the way to the goal with a minimum of lost motion and electric shock.
—*Paul R. Mort and Donald H. Ross* [1]

In an era characterized by extraordinary faith in research and what it can contribute to the solution of problems, school administrators remain skeptical about the role of theory and research in their own profession. Although it is generally acknowledged in our society that systematic study can provide guidelines to the solutions of great problems such as the pollution of our environment, the overpopulation of our planet, the diseases which afflict mankind, and predicting the vagaries of the stock market, the school administrator tends to be wary of research in his own fields: education and administration. There are good reasons for wariness, some of which we will examine briefly. However, in this chapter we will stress (1) that administrators have, for a good many years, used theoretical formulations as bases for action, and (2) that the role and function of the scholar-researcher in the field of educational administration is properly seen as useful and productive, from the practical point of view, rather than meaningless and unrelated to the hard realities of life. Indeed,

---

[1] Paul R. Mort and Donald H. Ross, *Principles of School Administration* (New York: McGraw-Hill Book Company, 1957), p. 4.

it is difficult to envision how—without active researchers building an expanding body of theory and substantive knowledge—we can legitimately hope to master the increasingly complex problems of administering school organizations.

Of What Use Is Theory?

School administrators generally see themselves as people of action—the "doers"—while viewing theorists as "ivory-tower" scholars who are unaware of the hard facts of life. Not uncommonly, school principals and other administrators speak of being "on the firing line" and express the need for answers to real problems, not "nice" theories. The administrator tends to see himself as a pragmatist and feels the need to *decide* and to *act* in a world that demands *practical* responses to insistent demands. By comparison, he may be inclined to view the researcher as a dilletante who considers hypothetical niceties and need not face the consequences of his idealistic view of reality. Let us examine this notion, even though it has been somewhat oversimplified here.

We can begin by asking a simple question: What is it that motivates people to join an organization, stay in it, and work toward that organization's goals? Obviously, if we can obtain the answer to that question, we will have the solution to some serious organizational problems, including high teacher turnover and low motivation for better professional performance.

In order to understand that aspect of organizational behavior which deals with motivation we must turn to theory for insight and understanding. That such theory is not necessarily esoteric is evident when one examines McGregor's *Theory X* and *Theory Y* [2]—theories which attempt to explain certain aspects of the nature of man.

Theory X postulates three basic propositions:

1. The average human being has an inherent dislike for work and will avoid it if he can.
2. Because of this characteristic, most people must be coerced, controlled, directed, and threatened with punishment so that they will work toward the organization's goals.
3. The average human being prefers to be directed, prefers security, and avoids responsibility.

---

[2] This discussion of Theory X and Theory Y is adapted from Douglas M. McGregor, *The Human Side of Enterprise* (New York: McGraw-Hill Book Company, 1960), pp. 33–57.

Administrators who accept this theory, this attempt to explain the nature of man, will, of course, utilize its essential ideas in planning their policy making, in formulating their decisions, and in carrying out other facets of their administrative behavior.

Theory Y embraces some very different ideas:

1. Physical work and mental work are as natural as play, if they are satisfying.
2. Man will exercise self-direction and self-control toward an organization's goals if he is committed to them.
3. Commitment is a function of rewards. The best rewards are satisfaction of ego and self-actualization.
4. The average person can learn to accept and seek responsibility. Avoidance of it and emphasis on security are learned and are not inherent characteristics.
5. Creativity, ingenuity, and imagination are widespread among people and do not occur only in a select few.

One would expect that administrators who favor the explanation that *Theory Y* offers will significantly differ from advocates of *Theory X* in their administrative behavior. And both these theories are not presented here as something for the reader to accept or reject as mere "common sense"; they are merely proferred as a classically simple illustration of how theory is actually used by practitioners of educational administration in viewing the world—a guide to rational decisions and actions "on the firing line." Theory is as essential to administrative practice as it is to scholarship and research.

Three Recent Stages in Theory Development

The practical utilization of theory by school administrators is nothing new. Whether or not they are fully aware of it, school administrators have, over the years, been guided in their professional behavior largely by theoretical notions. For the most part, administrators would have scoffed heartily at the idea that they were being guided by such "ivory-tower stuff" as theory, and yet these very same administrators would be likely to assert firmly that they knew how to exercise leadership in the schools and how to get things done. However, the fundamental view that an administrator has of his organization and how it operates is, essentially, an expression of theory. A principal who expounds on "democratic administration" or a superintendent who insists that his subordinates "go through channels" to get things done are really trying to apply theoretical concepts to the practical problems of running organizations.

Raymond Callahan, in his highly readable book, *Education and the Cult of Efficiency*,[3] has dramatically documented one era of educational administration in this century: the period from about 1900 to 1930 when "business was king" in our culture. In his description of that era, Callahan makes it clear that the values then held by school administrators tended to shape their practice of administration. The era he describes coincides with the so-called era of scientific management, which was mentioned in Chapter 1 of this volume. The major social value of the period Callahan describes, in terms of administering and managing organizations, was *efficiency*, that is, achieving the lowest per-unit cost for operation. Callahan stresses the effect of the dynamic response of educators to criticism; in fact, he complains that many "Educators and especially the leaders in administration . . . joined the loudest critics, jumped on the various bandwagons and outdid themselves in bowing to the dominant pressures. Others capitulated too easily." [4]

This may well have been true, but the era described was—we must remember—also an era of great change, exploding knowledge, and technological transformation. If school superintendents began to see themselves as "executives" whose job it was to "manage" school "plants" in a manner similar to efficient and productive factories, they were interpreting their educational organizations in terms of the prevailing theoretical notions. Frederick Taylor's adherents, seeking to bolster their "principles of scientific management," had evidence that their principles and their techniques *did* work; there was reason to conclude that their concepts of human beings and their organizational behavior were correct. Thus, we can conclude that then, as now, school administrators were dealing with a growing body of insight and knowledge regarding organizational behavior, but that it was—and still is—incomplete. *Much of what we accept as "facts" of organizational life—the basic concepts on which we base our administrative behavior—is largely dependent on theoretical notions of reality.*

Taylorism, or "scientific management," postulated that the motivating drive that caused people to work in organizations was the notion of "economic man," that is, money is the motivator and the wise manager will manipulate pay to gain the maximum amount of incentive from it. Close and detailed supervision of work was seen to be essential to assure that each prescribed step of a plan was followed accurately. An inflexible hierarchy of command, the "line and staff" concept, was posited to be

---

[3] Raymond Callahan, *Education and the Cult of Efficiency* (Chicago: The University of Chicago Press, 1962).
[4] *Ibid.*, p. 259.

essential to the proper ordering and control of operations. These perceptions are representative of the perceptions that comprised what is today referred to as "classical theory" in administration. In many cases, these dicta were asserted firmly as "truth" or "fact" or "knowledge" when, in reality, much of classical theory was speculative and philosophical, with little systematic provision made for testing beliefs. Nonetheless, in schools the concept of "line and staff" still represents for many administrators something that is absolutely essential to the proper functioning of the school. Many would argue, too, that close systematic supervision of instruction is instrumental in improving learning in the school. Our purpose here is not to support one position or the other, but to emphasize that (1) if we see these ideas as true, they give direction to the decisions we make and the actions we take, and (2) that these are essentially theoretical ideas or models which we take to represent what is, in fact, true in a school, and, therefore, (3) these ideas illustrate the dependence of administrative practice on the existence of viable and coherent theory.

In the late 1920's, as Black Friday and the Great Depression approached, Elton Mayo's systematic researches were begun—and showed the existence of an entirely different panorama of how people function in organizations. It was discovered that people do not work *only* for the money they earn, although that money is important, but they feel keen satisfaction in belonging to a group and adhering to its standards and expectations; thus, the concept of *morale* was born. Group dynamics was developed and largely accepted as a fact of organizational life; the hierarchical structure and the supervision provided by management were no longer viewed as the primary determinants of production and efficiency. The concept of group morale, it was found, has much to offer administrators who wish to understand how to guide organizations more effectively. Although the term "human engineering"—a term that implies that management manipulates the forces that affect workers as people—is still heard far too often, a new emphasis on participation in management emerged. "Group dynamics" became the watchword of the day, with its emphasis on "group-ness," participative supervision, and the need for personnel relations.

Managers and administrators in industry, business, the military—all kinds of organizations, including schools—were admonished to pay attention to "the human side of the enterprise." In schools, particularly, this attention took the form of "democratic supervision" and, to some extent, "democratic administration." It is an interesting fact that the human relations movement had far more impact on supervision and elementary school administration than it did on educational administration in general. Supervisors, who were generally viewed in classical theory as "staff" people, found group dynamics highly useful in their relations to teachers, even though many administrators were able to cling to their notions of hierarchy and line-and-staff relationships (see Figure 2–1). In general, however, the human relations movement provided a way of looking at

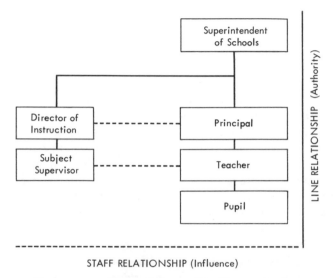

FIGURE 2–1.   Typical line-and-staff organization.

organizational problems which earlier theory had simply not included. If we look upon the administration of schools during the 1930's and 1940's as opposed to the administration of the 1920's, it is evident that school administrators are very much affected in their practice by theory (see Figure 2–2). Whereas at one time schools were looked upon as

Approximate Time-Period	Labels Applied to the Theory	Representative Concepts
1900 – 1930	Classical Theory	Line and staff Span of control Unity of command
1930 – 1950	Human Relations Theory	Morale Group dynamics Participative supervision
1950 – 1970	Behavioral Theory	Role Reference groups Leader behavior

FIGURE 2–2.   The growth of administrative theory, 1900–1970.

production facilities in which students are raw materials to be processed by workers (i.e., teachers) at the lowest per-unit cost, later—in the human relations era—emphasis was placed on the "pay-off" of personnel policies that recognized morale problems and the wisdom of involving a wide spectrum of the staff in decision making. And, again, we must emphasize that administrators do utilize *theory*.

The shift from the classical theory of organizational behavior to the human relations approach represented a breakthrough of "new" knowledge, new insight, new understanding—in short, new theory. Administrators could not remain aloof from what a few professors said they had discovered from their experiments in the Hawthorne plant of the Western Electric Company. The very substance of administration was basically altered as the insights stemming from this significant scientific breakthrough were enlarged upon and communicated in useful form to professional administrators of business, industry, and the military—a host of organizations, including schools.

Note that what has been described above as the "classical" theory of organization is also sometimes labeled in the literature as "structuralist" theory for obvious reasons: the emphasis on the design and the reinforcement of the framework that was perceived as the structure of a rationally developed organization. In a sense, one can view the human relations approach as antistructuralist: its focus was on the work-group and the particular needs of group members that had to be met in order to make the work-group maximally effective. The "new" era, in which we now find ourselves, and which this book explores, is committed to neither of these views, but attempts, instead, to view organizations as they "really" are and posits that there *is* structure to the organization, on the one hand, and there *is* human involvement—both group and individual—in the structure, on the other hand. Just as classical theory included a theory of motivation, namely, the simplistic notion of "economic man," and group dynamics looked upon motivation as a function of group membership, behavioral theory has an explanation about why people join organizations, stay in them, and seek to attain their goals. Let us now look at this theoretical notion in order to clarify just how theory is useful in the practical business of understanding, predicting, and channeling organizational behavior more effectively.

Behavioral Theories of Motivation

Much of contemporary organizational theory is based on theories of human motivation which are quite different from McGregor's "Theory X." One of the many theories of motivation currently taken seriously by administrators in business, the military, and many other kinds of organizations is Maslow's.[5] Maslow has suggested that the driving force which causes people to join an organization, stay in it, and work toward its goal, is actually a *hierarchy of needs.* When the lowest order of needs in the hierarchy is satisfied, a higher-order need appears, and, since it has the greater potency at the time, this higher-order need causes the individual to attempt to satisfy it.

The lowest order of human needs consists of the basic physiological necessities such as food, water, shelter, and the like. In less complex societies of the past it was possible for one to meet these needs individually or as a participant in relatively primitive organizations. The nomadic hunter or the peasant in a simple agrarian society spent much of his time and energy providing these necessities for himself. In our modern technologically oriented society, however, it is not possible for many of us to dig a well for water or hunt for game when we are hungry. Rather, we must earn money to purchase necessities by taking part in commonplace activities such as paying the rent, purchasing food at the grocery store, and paying taxes. In modern society, the basic drives of human existence cause us to become enmeshed in organizational life— we become participants in the organization that employs us as well as the myriad government agencies and private companies which provide essential goods and services on which we depend. Thus, at the simplest level of human need we are motivated to join organizations, remain in them, and contribute to their objectives.

However, because of the nature of man, once these needs are adequately met a new level of need that is one step higher in the hierarchy of needs automatically appears: the need for safety or security. This need, according to Maslow, now has the greater potency and the individual will seek to satisfy it. Security can, of course, mean many things to different people in different circumstances. For some, it means earning a high income to assure freedom from want in case of sickness or the onset of old age. Thus, many people are motivated to work harder to seek "success," which frequently is measured in terms of income. Or security can be interpreted in terms of "job security," which is so important, for example, to many civil service employees and school teachers. To them, the assurance of life tenure and a guaranteed pension may be strong motivating factors in their participation in employing organizations. Street gangs, which often have a well-developed organizational structure, are commonly joined for the safety they offer to their members in a threatening environment. Often a gang or coalition of gangs will "take

---

[5] A. H. Maslow, *Motivation and Personality* (New York: Harper & Row, Publishers, 1954).

over" a school and terrorize nonmembers into joining the gang or leaving the school. Many "dropouts" in urban high schools leave because they cannot find an organization that will meet their needs for safety rather than because they dislike the prospect of studying or learning.

New levels of need unfold as the needs below them are met. Once the need for safety is satisfied, the individual is free to try to meet his normal need for love and affiliation. Until the earlier needs are met, however— the basic physiological needs and the need for safety or security—the individual will be motivated by them more highly than by any psychological need. Thus, a man who is out of work and growing short on funds would probably find the promise of high pay a good reason for taking a job with a particular company. However, once the individual has enough income to get along reasonably well, he can begin to think in terms of his security. Moving up the hierarchy of needs, once the basic levels are assured the employee with a reasonably well-paying and secure job will begin to feel that having a sense of belonging and approval are important motivators in his organizational behavior. He will not only become aware of these needs, but will also tend to find situations in which they can be met; moreover, he will tend to behave in a way that is intended to produce the response in the organization that will best meet this need for love and affiliation.

Higher levels in the prepotent hierarchy of needs described by Maslow are the need for esteem, next, the need for knowledge and understanding, and, finally, the need to attain self-actualization. The latter is the highest order of need in the Maslow formulation and represents the need to develop into everything that one can become.[6] Thus, higher needs emerge in an orderly and predictable manner as lower needs are satisfied and only after they are satisfied (see Figure 2–3).[7]

Obviously, this sort of approach to understanding motivation is behavior-oriented and represents an attempt to explain human participation in an organization on a far more sophisticated and potentially useful level than McGregor's Theory X or the simple theory of "economic man." A number of scholars have speculated on and studied the problems of motivation,[8] and in so doing have provided richer and more prac-

---

[6] *Ibid.*, pp. 91–92.

[7] Terminology used in this figure was adapted from Maslow (*ibid.*) and Lyman W. Porter, "Job Attitudes in Management: I. Perceived Deficiencies in Need Fulfillment as a Function of Job Level," *Journal of Applied Psychology*, XLVI, No. 6 (December, 1962), 375–84.

[8] For an excellent brief discussion of representative literature in this area, see Richard C. Lonsdale, "Maintaining the Organization in Dynamic Equilibrium," in Daniel E. Griffiths, ed., *Behavioral Science and Educational Administration*, The Sixty-third Yearbook of the National Society for the Study of Education, Part II (Chicago: The University of Chicago Press, 1964), pp. 155–61.

Self–Actualization

↑

Autonomy

↑

Esteem

↑

Social Affiliation

↑

Security

↑

Physiological Requirements

FIGURE 2–3. Typical hierarchy of human needs related to motivation.

tically useful insights than have hitherto been available to the administrator concerned with organizational behavior in schools. Frederick Herzberg, writing some twelve years after Maslow, has presented an analysis of human motivation that has been finding attentive listeners in many large American corporations; his ideas are not in contradiction to Maslow's but are an enlargement, refinement, and extension of the kind of theorizing that Maslow and McGregor have engaged in. Herzberg states that there are two views of man, for "the human animal has two categories of needs." [9] One category deals with his animal needs: the need for safety, for food, for the avoidance of pain, and other basic drives. Added to those are the various fears that man has learned to attach to those needs and drives. There is another part of man's nature, though, and that is "man's compelling urge to realize his own potentiality by continuous psychological growth." [10]

By psychological growth Herzberg means processes such as maintaining individuality, being creative, being effective, and growing intellectually. These need-categories appear in different individuals in different "mixes," with some individuals being more highly motivated to meet "animal" needs and others finding psychological growth opportunities highly motivating. Herzberg goes on to describe as "hygiene factors" those rewards which the organization offers to meet the lower motivational needs of participants: rewards such as a pleasant working environment, pay incentives and pension plans, and job security. People whose greatest needs are satisfied by these rewards tend to get little

---

[9] Frederick Herzberg, *Work and the Nature of Man* (Cleveland: The World Publishing Company, 1966), p. 56.
[10] *Ibid.*

satisfaction from their work, to show little interest in how well they do their jobs, and to exhibit a chronic dissatisfaction with things such as salary, supervision, the status of their jobs, and their colleagues. However, people who are motivated by the satisfactions of their accomplishments on the job tend to be far less affected by "hygiene" factors and show an inclination to have positive feelings toward work and the work-situation and, in general, show a greater zest for involvement in the goals and tasks of the organization. Such people, Herzberg contends, respond better to true motivational factors (i.e., factors which foster psychological growth and self-actualization) than they do to so-called hygiene factors. From beginnings of this sort, Herzberg has developed and tested a *motivation-hygiene theory* which seeks to explain and predict what organizational policies and practices are necessary to attract and hold desirable participants, and—and this is equally important—which policies and practices seem to give promise of getting the maximum contribution from each participant. In short, we can use this theory or model of human motivation as a guide for developing effective practices in the administration of schools.

A number of leading American industrial and commercial organizations are making practical use of this kind of theory development. For a good many years it has generally been supposed that increases in wages would motivate workers to be productive, reliable employees, and much attention has been given to the problems of developing wage formulas and salary schedules, with their associated fringe benefit packages, which have been intended to achieve the necessary participation of employees at the lowest cost to the organization. It is well recognized, however, that wages alone are not sufficient inducement to do a good job; after a point, increases in wage packages do not solve the motivation problem adequately. A common complaint heard from business management is that wages continue to go up but productivity does not keep pace. The maturing of group dynamics in management has, of course, added to the range of available motivational inducements. Various schemes for enlarging participation in decision making have been tried, and a great deal of emphasis is placed on developing group morale. Air conditioning, background music, clubs, sports, travel, recreational activities, and consumer services ranging from haircuts on company time to discount car purchasing are representative of the many inducements offered by enlightened business and industrial organizations for keeping employees involved and motivated.

As wage packages become more expensive and the ability to add "extras" to the work situation seems near a practical limit, it has become apparent that neither of these motivational inducements is sufficient to provide the kinds of satisfactions many employees need. "Where does it all end?" a business administrator might well ask; "What more do they want?" No one really knows. But if we examine theory such as Maslow's prepotent hierarchy of needs, or Herzberg's motivation-hygiene theory we can find clues as to what else must be provided.

At this early stage it would seem that the traditional wages and working conditions package is no longer adequate; more provision for psychological growth through job satisfaction will probably be necessary in our affluent society. In fact, the need to apply this theoretical construct to education may well be evident before us now. An examination of Herzberg's theory, for example, makes one wonder how much of present-day unrest among teachers is due to our preoccupation with salary schedules and fringe benefits to the near-exclusion of making provision for teachers to achieve genuine satisfaction and self-actualization in their professional work. We may have been paying too much attention to hygiene factors and too little attention to motivational factors.

To sum up, we contend that theory—far from being removed from the practical task of administering schools—is, *and long has been*, a wellspring of administrative ideas, insights, and practices. The development of more adequate theory is essential to the development of better practice in the schools, for above all, theory is not merely the plaything of professors who are safely removed from the classrooms. To illustrate, we have selected one area of theory, *human motivation*, and have described selected stages in its historical development. These were (1) the theory of economic man, (2) Maslow's theory of a prepotent hierarchy of needs, and (3) Herzberg's motivation-hygiene theory. Administrators in the schools who presumably are intent on motivating the school's participants so as to obtain the best possible educational results will make decisions and implement them in terms of *their* concepts of what "will work"—whether these concepts have originated in intuition, folklore, or careful theory development. We thus feel that in this day of rapid change and emergence of new insights and new knowledge, school administrators will find it helpful to keep abreast of newly developing organizational theory.

What Theory Is—and Is Not

There is, of course, an extensive body of literature dealing with theory —its definition, its limitations, its implications, and its utility. Our discussion need not dwell on the philosophy which is so often the cause of delicate and seemingly endless discussions in academe. Rather than present a definition of theory, which must be defended against all comers, a number of scholars describe theory in terms of *characteristics* and what theory *seeks to do*.

For our purposes we will consider theory to be a thought process, a way of thinking about reality to better understand that reality and to describe it more accurately. One way of conceptualizing theory is to think of it as model-building: a sound theory is a *model* of reality. As is the case with models, theory is a *representation* of reality, but it should not be confused with reality itself. A popular notion about theory is that it deals with some kind of ideal state, some condition which ought to be. Modern behavioral science theorists do not share this notion but, instead, insist that theory helps to explain what *is* and not what ought to be. Occasionally, we hear someone say, *"That's a nice theory, but that isn't the way things are in the schools."* To the extent that the statement is actually true, the theory involved may well be considered lacking in usefulness, for it presents us with a model that is inaccurate. Theory which offers us an accurate representation of reality, no matter how small that slice of reality is, can serve some very useful functions:

1. *It can help to organize our knowledge into a systematic, orderly body.* In the case of educational administration, this body of knowledge appears at the present time to have many gaps—which leads to a second important use of theory:
2. *It can provide a guide to researchers.* By establishing the limits of our knowledge and pointing to the gaps in this knowledge, theory can assist the researcher in formulating problems for the study of unknown areas.

It is that knowledge which falls within the present limits of what we know, as differentiated from folklore and personal prescriptions, which provides the foundation for the emerging discipline that we call educational administration. One of the dominant characteristics of the "new" administration has been the conscious effort to expand the domain of knowledge of the discipline, to systematically reduce the gaps of ignorance through the building of hypothetico-deductive theory.

At the present stage of the genesis of administration as a discipline it would be too much "to expect a full-blown grand theory of educational administration." [11] Attempts of such dimensions as Parsons, Shils, and their colleagues have undertaken in order to move toward a general theory of action for the social sciences [12] must wait in educational admin-

---

[11] Roald F. Campbell, John E. Corbally, Jr., and John A. Ramseyer, *Introduction to Educational Administration*, 3rd ed. (Boston: Allyn & Bacon, Inc., 1966), p. 93.

[12] Talcott Parsons and Edward A. Shils, eds., *Toward a General Theory of Action* (Cambridge, Mass.: Harvard University Press, 1951).

istration until the knowledge domain of the discipline has been systematically expanded and thus more gaps filled in than is the case at the
present time.

Outside the field of education, approaches to such a general theory
seem to be much more advanced than in education; it is not yet clear,
however, which of these larger attempts will prove most fruitful and
most relevant, for either the field of administration in general or educational administration in particular. An example is the work of Herbert
Simon, who noted that the search for *principles* of administration, such
as Woodrow Wilson had called for, seemed to produce, "little more than
ambiguous and mutually contradictory proverbs," [13] which guided—or
misguided—the practice of administration. Simon called for a more fundamental approach that would take into consideration the conditions of the
situation in which administration occurs. That approach was, for Simon,
a *theory* which, in broadest outline, attempts to picture the organization
as a decision making device. In atttempting to reach the best decisions,
the organization deals with rational factors (largely facts) and irrational
factors (largely human values and limitations). Chris Argyris' name is
often associated with a theory of organizational behavior that focuses on
the assumptions that (1) the individual has a personality and goals, (2) the
organization has its own needs and goals, and (3) these two are incom-
patible in significant ways.[14] There have been other attempts to develop
global theories of administration than the work of these two distin-
guished scholars; but in this book we cannot deal exhaustively with such
a complex field. The reader who wishes to enlarge his knowledge of this
vital subject must turn to sources other than the present volume.[15] We
should, however, take note of a unique book dealing with administrative
theory, Chester Barnard's *The Functions of the Executive*.[16]

Barnard was, by any measure, a practical and successful business executive. *The Functions of the Executive* was published in 1938 when
Barnard was the President of the New Jersey Bell Telephone Company;
it is actually a compilation of lectures which its author had given the

---

[13] Herbert A. Simon, *Administrative Behavior* (New York: The Macmillan Company, © 1950), p. 240.

[14] Chris Argyris, *Personality and Organization* (New York: Harper & Row, Publishers, 1957). Argyris has written extensively on the incompatibility of man's basic
needs and the demands of formal organizations.

[15] Interested readers may wish to consult the following readings: Daniel E. Griffiths, "The Nature and Meaning of Theory," in Griffiths, ed., *op. cit.*; Daniel E.
Griffiths, *Administrative Theory* (New York: Appleton-Century-Crofts, 1959); and
Andrew W. Halpin, *Theory and Research in Administration* (New York: The Macmillan Company, 1966), esp. Chap. 1.

[16] Chester I. Barnard, *The Functions of the Executive* (Cambridge, Mass.: Harvard
University Press, 1938).

previous year. Barnard was an educated man, of course, but he was not an academician or a professional theorist; in fact, as he pointed out, his writing stemmed from 30 years of practical experience—*precisely the credential which behavioral scientists cannot bring to their observations.*[17] Barnard's work is that much more remarkable because of its enduring "lighthouse" effect, for it points the way for scholars and researchers. In 1959, Griffiths stressed that "most, if not all, of the present theories in the market place have their genesis in Barnard" [18]; a similar statement would be no exaggeration today. Thus, in a series of eight lectures given at Lowell Institute in 1937, Barnard introduced the theoretical underpinnings of administration which were to be considered "new" for well over 30 years.

Barnard's work dealt with the theory of formal organizations, including the theory of authority, the theory of decision making, and the theory of motivation. With regard to this last aspect of his work, Barnard's book —which was still in print and widely sold in the late 1960's—foreshadowed the development of a number of theories of administration, rather than a single global theory. This development of mid-range theories, and attempts to relate these theories to each other, is a stage which in time may lead to the development of an overall general theory. For the present, we have at our disposal a number of useful theories which can help administrators to better understand, predict, and control organizational behavior, among which are role theory, social systems theory, communications theory, bureaucratic theory, and compliance theory, although there are many other kinds.

Over the years, Daniel Griffiths has dealt with what he describes as "the theory problem" [19]: the scant enthusiasm with which practicing school administrators tend to embrace theory. One reason for this lack of enthusiasm is undoubtedly that there is considerable misunderstanding of what theory *is*. Perhaps, as Griffiths emphasizes, what theory *is* can be clarified by noting what theory *is not:* (1) it is not some sort of dream or idle speculation; (2) it is not a philosophy—which would deal with values (what *ought* to be), for "theory is . . . the best and most accurate mental picture of how an organism [actually] works" [20]; (3) theory is not a personal notion of how to get a job done; (4) neither is it "a synonym for *speculation, supposition*," [21] or some idealized notion of

---

[17] *Ibid.*, p. xii.
[18] Griffiths, *Administrative Theory, op. cit.*, p. 63.
[19] *Ibid.*, p. 1.
[20] Paul R. Mort and Donald H. Ross, *Principles of School Administration* (New York: McGraw-Hill Book Company, 1957), p. 4.
[21] Griffiths, "The Nature and Meaning of Theory," *op. cit.*, p. 96.

what ought to be; (5) nor is theory merely a respectable term mean-ing "impractical." This is not to say that the label *theory* has not been loosely applied in the above ways too many times for far too long in education courses. In fact, in an effort to emphasize the "practical" in our professional preparation programs for school administrators we have too often avoided theory, and thereby unwittingly stressed the impractical. "The most impractical education," Robert M. Hutchins has pointed out, "is the one that looks the most practical, and the one that is most practical in fact is the one that is commonly regarded as remote from reality, one dedicated to the comprehension of theory and prin-ciples." [22]

The Testing of Theory: Research

Sound theory, which is to say, theory that gives us an accurate picture or model of how the organization actually functions, is useful in that it enables us to better understand, predict, and ultimately control what is happening in the busy "confusion" of a school. A theory must be tested for soundness before we can trust it. We can test a theory by method-ically studying it either clinically or in the field. The methods of such study are set by widely recognized rules of procedure and evidence that comprise the domain of research. There can and should be a dynamic interplay between theory and research. As carefully derived data are accumulated, they can be compared with the theoretical model for "fit." In turn, the model can be revised so as to be more accurate. This process, carried out systematically and carefully over time and in enough repre-sentative situations yields insights which are dependable enough to be thought of as "knowledge."

An excellent illustration of the process of developing a theory and then verifying it through research is found in Frederick Herzberg's *Work and the Nature of Man*.[23] In an earlier publication, *Motivation to Work*,[24] published in 1959, Herzberg and his colleagues reported a study of the job attitudes of some accountants and engineers. This work led them to formulate some hypotheses about motivation which were subsequently tested for their applicability in a number of research studies conducted with other employees by other researchers working independently; in fact, the original study was replicated nine times by independent researchers on various population groups who thus corroborated the

---

[22] *Education U.S.A.* (April 15, 1968), 182.
[23] Herzberg, *op. cit.*
[24] Frederick Herzberg *et al.*, *The Motivation to Work* (New York: John Wiley & Sons, Inc., 1959).

concepts that emerged from the original study. This corroboration increased the reliability of the original work and made possible the broadening of the original hypotheses into a full-blown theory: the motivation-hygiene theory.

However, we must note in regard to Herzberg's research, which has been mentioned here for illustrative purposes, that behavioral science research continues to be plagued by a lack of certitude. Although many studies support the motivation-hygiene theory, there are others which seem to refute it. The problem is apparently one of research technique and is due in part to the present youthfulness of the behavioral sciences. Research which depends on interviews for obtaining data tends to support the Herzberg theory, and studies which employ so-called objective techniques tend not to support this theory. Therefore, although there are those who may disdain behavioral science research as meaningless, others —who may be quite willing to acknowledge the difficulties of building a young science—point out that the "hard" sciences have endured many such controversial problems in their long search for respectability and reliability. Indeed, such inconsistencies exist today in many areas of the physical sciences and must be accepted as part of the process of expanding empirical knowledge in an orderly way—the process of scientific inquiry.

Not all research on organizational behavior in schools is based on theory, of course. Not all of it should be. There is plenty of room in the research world for the shrewd observer who says, "I've seen this event occur under these conditions time after time. Can I expect that it will *always* occur thus?" Or, similarly he could ask, "What are the variables in the situation that are involved in the occurrence of the event?" There is also room in the research world for the one who asks the naive kind of question which nobody has yet thought to ask. There is nothing wrong in a researcher asking, "I wonder what would happen in the situation if I applied Intervention X (referring to any variable that he wanted to use)?" However, the development of a body of knowledge adequate as a basis for the professional practice of administration generally requires a more systematic approach than this.

Of the many deserved criticisms of the "state of the art" of research in educational administration, one of the most revealing is that much of it has been "naked empiricism," that is, too many attempts at research have been "one-shot" affairs with limited relationship to the existing domain of knowledge through the use of theoretical concepts. Although one cannot demand that all research be theory-oriented, we can and should be concerned with the building of an orderly, comprehensive discipline; this requires the testing of theory and the relating of theories to each other.

Even the shrewd observer or the curious but naive observer has an obligation as a researcher to study the existing literature for knowledge, theories, and concepts that will provide leads to answers to his questions. To be ignorant of what has preceded the present state of administrative theory is no virtue. In some cases the observer will find in the recorded research literature clues or insights that will foreshadow the results of his research. The expectation thus aroused in the researcher is referred to as *direction* in the research. The stronger and more adequately this direction is supported by theory and the concepts derived from previous studies, the more significant the research is likely to be for the knowledge domain of the discipline. This is because such research represents a somewhat orderly progression in which we build outward from the known domain of the discipline by utilizing rational hypotheses to express—after taking into consideration what is presently "known" or accepted—whatever we would *expect* to be true in the new situation under observation. Such an approach is significantly different from the near-endless collection of status studies which once were considered to be research in educational administration; it is referred to as hypothetico-deductive research and its increasing use has been a hallmark of the "new" educational administration. Many hypothetico-deductive studies have dealt with organizational behavior in schools.

Language of Theory Development

In a discussion of theory one almost inevitably becomes entangled in the problem of using words or terms to label meaningfully the components involved. We will describe some of the terms that are more commonly used in discussing theory and its related research in organizational behavior. These terms will be used consistently throughout this book and may also be helpful to the reader when he turns to other literature or discusses organizational behavior with his collegeagues.

A systematic hierarchy of notions which is generally known to those who are interested in theoretical aspects of organizations is shown in Figure 2–4. Perhaps it would be helpful to take a brief look at some of the more commonly used terms to see how they can be used in research in organizational theory. In so doing, we will note the strong tendency to draw mental parallels between the use of the terms in the physical sciences and their use in the behavioral sciences. This is useful insofar as it is applicable, for we know that in applying behavioral science methods to administrative and organizational theory there is an obvious need to develop a disciplined precision for such terms—and in this the physical sciences have set a good example.

FIGURE 2–4. Hierarchy of
terms useful in dealing with
theory.

FACTS

It is obvious, of course, that all theory begins with facts: things we observe, directly or indirectly, quantify, and report. The history of the physical sciences includes many years of effort to develop techniques for the accurate gathering and reporting of factual information. At the present time, in dealing with organizational behavior one has to proceed with great care when dealing with events described as "facts." This is partly due to the relative immaturity of the behavioral sciences: techniques and instruments must still be developed and refined. However, we must also be careful because of the nature of the situation we are dealing with.

Our perception of what is a "fact" or what is "true" about the behavior of others is very much affected by what we bring to the situation— our own expectations, biases, beliefs. An illustration, perhaps, is the difficulty that white middle-class Americans have in describing—in a factual way—the behavior of black disadvantaged Americans. In observing the behavior of people in organizations, each situation is always changing and can rarely be precisely replicated. The very presence of an observer in the group can alter the behavior of the individuals in the group.

In dealing with theory and research in organizational environments, then, we are dealing with a highly dynamic, responsive milieu. When we focus on behavior in such environments, our natural inclination is to label our own perceptions or value judgments as "facts"—an inviting trap. For example, a principal may be too deeply involved in his school organization to be an accurate reporter of significant behavioral phenomena in his school. However, observations reported by objective, unobtrusive "outside" observers will probably be more accurate for understanding what is "really" occurring. But it must be borne in mind that the only "fact" in such a situation is the *observer's report*. Even as we remain aware of the phenomenon of selective perception, we can treat the *report* as a fact, at the same time keeping an open mind as to how nearly the report is factual. For example, a panel of experts could be used to judge the atmosphere or climate of a school. This would be useful if we treated their *judgment* as a fact. However, until we could know more accurately what behaviors in the school the judgment was based on, it would be difficult to proceed with any amelioration of problems.

Essentially, we are able to use two classes of measures in assessing what is—in "fact"—occurring behaviorally in an organization: *observed behavior* and some *product of behavior*. As a simple illustration, we could assert that "classes are interrupted too often by announcements on the public address system." Whether this is a "fact" is a matter of judgment. However, an observer could be assigned to record how frequently interruptions actually occur; such a record gives us some "hard data" which must be accepted as factual. We could make similar observations in two schools and analyze the similarities and differences between them. We could record such information over a period of time to get base data and then introduce controlled variables to see what, if any, effect the variables might have on the number of interruptions per class. Similarly, we can observe faculty conferences and record the frequency and type of participation of those present. Frequency of attendance at meetings, lateness in arriving at school in the morning, and referrals to guidance are all typical kinds of evidence which can be derived from *observed behavior* and quantified clearly enough to be regarded as factual in the building of theory. *Behavioral products* which provide us with factual data can range from test results and scores on performance scales to wear-and-tear of the physical plant and the incidence of graffiti on the walls. The trend in recent years has been for researchers and theorists in organizational behavior to emulate the "hard" sciences—that is, the physical sciences— by working with measurable "hard" data which describe behavior, rather than accepting folk wisdom (which "everybody knows") as a basis for theorizing.

CONCEPTS

When we attempt to describe examples of organizational behavior, we must use terms that are reasonably precise and descriptive. Such terms —with their delimited and universally understood meanings—are called *concepts*. Griffiths describes a concept simply as "a term to which a particular meaning has been attached," [25] a somewhat oversimplified description, but one which does emphasize the need in administration for clearly

---

[25] Griffiths, *Administrative Theory, op. cit.,* p. 38.

defined labels to specify precise ideas. To describe a complex example of organizational behavior we must use concepts in sets to relate them to each other. Careful development and use of concepts increases the clarity and ease in communicating about, say, organizational behavior, which does not have the "hard" characteristics of the physical sciences. Careless use of the labels used to identify concepts can, of course, create confusion and uncertainty as to what is meant. Therefore, concepts such as *leadership* or *role* become useful in theory development as attempts are made to relate two or more together: what seems to go with what? Concepts, we must remember, are ideas with which we deal and as such we need not "prove" them. They are useful so long as they describe accurately what we mean.

HYPOTHESIS

An hypothesis is something that is assumed, or taken for granted—without being accepted as true—for the purpose of testing the assumption. The scientist, whether he deals in the behavioral or the physical realm, is not content to collect facts or identify concepts, for his goal is to link together the things which seem to be related to each other. His guide is an hypothesis which states the relationships that he expects to find, that is, under one set of circumstances certain facts should hold true. We must be able to test the hypothesis. Kerlinger states it thus:

> There are two criteria for "good" hypotheses and hypothesis statements . . . . One, hypotheses are statements about the relations between variables. Two, hypotheses carry clear implications for testing the stated relations. . . . A statement that lacks either or both of these characteristics is no hypothesis in the scientific sense of the word.[26]

THEORY

A theory is the systematic relating of a set of general hypotheses or assumptions; the hypotheses on which a theory is based must be so well verified as to have gained rather general acceptance as being *true*. The assumptions should thus reflect actual human experience or observation. A theory, itself, gives rise to hypotheses which can be tested; this process, in turn, serves to strengthen or cast doubt on the theory. In time, with repeated hypothesizing and testing, a theory can lead to empirical laws or general principles. This is the next stage, however, and theory does not have that certitude nor can it be empirically "proven."

---

[26] Fred N. Kerlinger, *Foundations of Behavioral Research* (New York: Holt, Rinehart & Winston, Inc., 1964), p. 20.

However, theory can be developed in a number of ways: (1) by compiling reported observations of practitioners, (2) by synthesizing status or survey types of research, (3) by adapting constructs from other disciplines, or (4) by utilizing the logical processes of deductive reasoning. Chester Barnard's *The Functions of the Executive* [27] is a brilliant, unusual example of a practitioner who established theory by reporting his observations. Paul Mort's many survey studies, in contrast, which were conducted by him, his colleagues, and his students over many years at Columbia Teachers College, provided the essential findings necessary for arriving at a theory of educational administration by the processes of logical deduction. At the Midwest Administration Center of the University of Chicago, however, considerable attention has been given to the possibilities of adapting theories from the behavioral sciences and other disciplines to the needs of educational administration.

Summary

In this chapter the role and function of theory have been described in historical context. The nature of theory and its relation to practice was illustrated by a description of three theories of motivation that have been popular in this century and which have had significant impact on schools as organizations: (1) the theory of economic man, (2) Maslow's theory of motivation, and (3) Herzberg's motivation-hygiene theory. Brief attention was given to the relationship of research to theory, and some of the key terms used in dealing with theory were discussed.

In the next few chapters we will deal with some of the important theories and concepts of organizational behavior in schools.

----

[27] Barnard, *op. cit.*

3

complex organizations and bureaucracies

Our society is an organizational society. We are born in organizations, and most of us spend much of our lives working for organizations. We spend much of our leisure time paying, playing, and praying in organizations. Most of us will die in an organization, and when the time comes for burial, the largest organization of all—the state—must grant official permission.

—*Amitai Etzioni* [1]

The school administrator's interest in organizations is greater than that of the well-informed citizen who is concerned about the impact of the growth of organizational life on the individual and on society. The administrator devotes his professional life to the strategies and techniques of planning, coordinating, and controlling the affairs of organizations. His professional environment *is* an organization, and, to a considerable extent, it is the setting in which he makes decisions, exercises leadership, and in general "behaves" as a school administrator. Obviously, the better equipped he is to understand and analyze his professional environment—the organization—the more effective he can be on the job. This is why school administrators are taking an increasingly intense interest in the insights that behavioral scientists have been developing about organizations in recent years.

---

[1] Amitai Etzioni, *Modern Organizations* (Englewood Cliffs, N. J.: Prentice-Hall, Inc., © 1964), p. 1.

A Modern Synthesis

Present day views of organizations generally represent some kind of synthesis of two earlier-held concepts: the *formal* organization and the *informal* organization. In this century we have passed through two recognizable periods in which sharply differing ideas of what organizations are like and how they should be administered have emerged. It seems clear that we are now in a third stage; a distinguishing characteristic of the present era is that rather than being an outright rejection of all that preceded it, this era represents a blend or *synthesis* of important earlier understandings and new knowledge and understanding. The three periods, which were described briefly in Chapter 1, are:

1. The era of *scientific management,* which gave rise to the so-called *classical theory of administration,* about 1910–1935
2. The *human relations* era, about 1935–1950
3. The era of the *behavioral approach,* about 1950 to the present

At this point we shall present some of the essential characteristics of the earlier ideas and then devote the major portion of this chapter to contemporary thought.

What is now called the classical theory of administration [2] emerged in the first quarter of the present century. The major theorist of the period was Frederick W. Taylor,[3] who adopted the more appropriate term, *scientific management,* for his approach to the problems of creating better organizations during a court battle in 1910.[4] Essentially, "Taylorism," "the task system," or "scientific management"—all of which are now referred to as classical theory—was structured around two fundamental ideas: *motivation,* the explanation of why a person participates in an organization, and *organization,* specifically, techniques of dividing up specialized tasks and the various levels of authority.

In the classical view, motivation is a fairly simple concept, essentially, that of "economic man"; that is, people work for an organization—and continue to work for it—because they need money—they must earn enough money to meet basic physiological needs and/or they want a little more than that, a profit. Applying this concept or "principle" presented many problems in terms of specific techniques. To keep motivation high, of course, there must not be a surfeit of money offered to the

---

[2] *Ibid.,* p. 20.

[3] For an excellent short account of Taylor's work, see Raymond Callahan, "Reform-Conscious America Discovers the Efficiency Expert," in *Education and the Cult of Efficiency* (Chicago: The University of Chicago Press, 1962), Chap. 2.

[4] *Ibid.,* p. 19.

worker, but the minimum reward to keep him at his job. Payment by piece-work was a favorite technique, and so was the bonus. Pay periods were kept short—the longest was once a week, and paying daily was even better, because the worker's motivation could be reinforced frequently.

In dealing with organization, classical theorists emphasize division of labor, breaking down the total job into its specialized steps and processes [5] whereby each worker becomes highly skilled in his special task. The organization is structured according to a plan that organizes all the small, specialized steps into a pattern, thus assuring that the total task of the organization will be accomplished. In the classical view, not only is the detailed plan vital, but strong central control and careful supervision at every step are essential to keep things coordinated. When diagrammed, this type of organization takes on a pyramidal form with a strong executive in control at the top and subordinate executives in successive lower layers of the organization, none of whom has more people under his direct authority than he can personally supervise. The aspects of organization stressed by classical theory—specialization of work, span of control, the pyramid of control, and the clearly segmented divisions—have come to connote what is today known as *formal organization*.

For a good many years this was the dominant concept in administrative thinking. Its imprint is familiar to us all; most readers can point to examples of the classical approach in action in business, industry, the military, and in schools. In the case of schools, the *organizational* aspects of classical theory appear to be most in evidence. The *motivational* ideas, however, seem to have had less impact on the schools because of the absence of factory-type pay schemes, although the concept of money as the chief motivation for teaching is not new to the profession. It is obvious, of course, that when we think of organizations in terms of classical theory, we emphasize concepts such as authority, a clear-cut hierarchy with centralized control, a definite division of functions and responsibilities, and orderly channels of communication.

The human relations concepts of organization stem from four discoveries that are generally credited to Elton Mayo and his associates:

1. *The "output" of a worker—hence, the output of the organization— is determined more by his social capacity than his physical capacity.*
2. *Money is only one motivation for working in an organization;* there are other, and perhaps more important, rewards that the worker seeks.
3. *Highly specialized division of labor is not the most likely way of maximizing efficiency of an organization.*

---

[5] This theory is comprehensively described in Luther Gulick and L. Urwick, eds., *Papers on the Science of Administration* (New York: Institute of Public Administration, Columbia University, 1937).

4. *Individual workers react to the organization—its hierarchy, its rules, and its reward-system*—not as individuals, *but as members of groups.*

These discoveries, which emerged during a series of experiments conducted between 1927 and 1932, have been confirmed many times since. It is interesting to observe that their appearance was contrary to what the researchers had expected to find; in fact, this is a good example of serendipity in research. These discoveries led, as we have said, to the human relations movement with its emphasis on group-ness. Actually, in school work the human relations movement seems to have had more impact on supervisors than it did on administrators. This is in part due to the fact that administrators are in line positions where they are responsible for exercising power and authority over their subordinates. Supervisors, very generally, are in staff positions for which influence is often dependent upon expertise and the informal position of these supervisors in the work-groups of the faculty.

Be that as it may, the emergence of democratic administration was rooted in human relations concepts, which has been a confusing idea to many school administrators—and to many teachers as well. At times, administrators wishing to do the "right" thing (i.e., be democratic administrators) would often attempt to decrease the visibility of their power in an honest desire to be democratic, not authoritarian. Yet the power was still there, although perhaps momentarily hidden, but it would appear and vanish unpredictably and rapidly. In many situations teachers felt that their positions were not "democratic" at all, but that they were being maneuvered into agreeing to decisions which generally had been arrived at previously. This feeling of being manipulated by a clever administrator who knew clearly where he was heading has probably contributed to the cynicism and suspicion among teachers that are commonly encountered in our schools. The notion of democratic administration has proven to be a difficult one to accept in conjunction with the realities of organizational life in schools. This notion is not discussed very much today because there are newer insights available, newer concepts that are proving to be more workable and more useful. Let us now look at some of these newer concepts about organization which comprise the synthesis of classical, human relations, and the more current behavioral theories.

The School: A Complex Organization

A *complex organization* has two specific characteristics: the formal structure of the organization and the informal structure.

First, and most important, the complex organization has a "fabric of roles" [6] that comprises its formal structure. These roles are occupied by the individuals who "behave" in accordance with established prescriptions for their roles. In such an organization, the structure of roles remains constant even though there will be personnel changes because of retirement, transfer, or other causes. If a member of the organization is replaced, the newly recruited member is expected to step into the vacated role and—essentially—to carry out the same working relationships as his predecessor. This constant structure of roles, of course, distinguishes the complex organization from smaller and simpler groups in which the structure of roles may be less defined and not as well ordered. The fact that a school is a complex organization in this sense renders some of its problems much like those of a military unit, an industrial organization, or a government agency.

Second, the complex organization has another characteristic which usually becomes obvious when we look at its organization chart. Typically, the school's organization chart specifies the formal roles that have been assigned to it. But the organization chart also describes the authority of one role over another and it delineates the boundaries of administrative units. However, the organization chart is rarely used by a seasoned administrator as more than the mere essence of a description of the organization, because there is an informal group structure in every formal organization. The organizational chart describes the *formal organization* but omits the *informal organization*. And the complex organization is comprised of two or more informal organizations.

There has been a great deal of research on informal organizations, how they function, and how they relate to formal organizations; the published literature is extensive. One of the best-known studies was done by Roethlisberger and Dickson as a part of the famed Hawthorne plant studies.[7] Other well-known studies of informal organizations have been done in a union,[8] in the military,[9] and in housing developments.[10] Iannacconne [11] has, perhaps, contributed the best-known work on informal organizations in schools.

---

[6] The concept of a "fabric of roles" is widely discussed in the literature. For example, see Robert S. Weiss and Eugene Jacobson, "A Method for the Analysis of the Structure of Complex Organizations," *American Sociological Review*, XX, No. 6 (December, 1955), 661–68.

[7] F. J. Roethlisberger and William J. Dickson, *Management and the Worker* (Cambridge, Mass.: Harvard University Press, 1942).

[8] Martin S. Lipset, Martin A. Trow, and James S. Coleman, *Union Democracy* (New York: The Free Press, 1956).

[9] Samuel A. Stouffer *et al.*, *Studies in Social Psychology in World War II* (Princeton, N. J.: Princeton University Press, 1949), 4 vols.

[10] Leon Festinger, Stanley Schachter, and Kurt Back, *Social Pressures in Informal Groups* (New York: Harper & Row, Publishers, 1950).

[11] Daniel E. Griffiths *et al.*, *Organizing Schools for Effective Education* (Danville, Ill.: The Interstate Printers and Publishers, Inc., 1962), p. 240.

Although the formal organization can pattern, in an orderly way, the *roles* under its jurisdiction such as the *teacher role* and the *principal role*, we must remember that these roles are filled by people who have their own unique personalities and social needs. In the final analysis, in order to get the organization's work done the people in the various roles (i.e., the *role incumbents*) must meet face-to-face and interact: they must communicate, make decisions, plan, and so forth. This requires interaction between *people*, not just interaction between *roles*. Thus, in the school a teacher is much more than the job description would indicate, much more, surely, than the table of organization would indicate. He is a *person* and he seeks friendship groups; and he has a need for a *primary group* affiliation with people, in addition to his professional affiliation with the formal organization.

Administrators commonly observe some of the behavioral evidence that such informal groups exist when they note the presence of "kaffee-klatsches," lunch groups, bowling teams, "old-timers," and so forth. Personal characteristics including age, sex, and marital status appear to affect which members are included in a primary informal group. To a large extent, too, the school's informal organizations will be work-oriented: teachers of the same grade level or in the same department, or those whose work-places are close together tend to belong to the same primary groups.

There is abundant evidence that (1) informal organization is essential to the functioning and administration of an organization and (2) the primary groups of the informal organization have great power. First, it is impossible to conceive of a school organization so well-structured and so thoroughly planned as to eliminate the human factor. But, more important, it is almost as impossible to conceive of a school organization today that does not recognize the need of its personnel to develop primary-group affiliations that will reward them with universally sought social and psychological satisfactions. The power of the informal organization is of great practical concern to the administrator, of course, because he is always interested in getting things done. It is the informal primary group, to a very large extent, which sets behavioral "norms" for those who occupy teacher roles. Administrators may make the error of viewing compliance as a matter of their own official authority versus an individual teacher, but in reality, the teacher may have the support of one or more primary groups in facing the principal's authority. When this is the case, the administrator finds that, as a practical matter, his authority is somewhat different than appears on the organizational chart. When the administrator insists on wielding his legal power and authority over a teacher, regardless of the group power that may support the teacher, the result may be a shift in the primary-group's norms, for unless the informal organization is dealt with realistically, it can react in a variety of ways such as lowering work norms and reducing cooperation with the legal authority of the administrative hierarchy.

Iannacconne [12] has given us a useful picture of the complexities of the school's power structure which involves the legal power and authority of the formal organization and the extralegal power of the informal organizations. He points out that informal primary groups are linked together in two chief ways: (1) when a teacher is a member of two primary groups, the linkage between the groups through him is referred to as *articulation* (see Figure 3–1), and (2) when two teachers, each of

FIGURE 3–1. Illustration of articulation between two primary groups in informal organization.

whom is a member of a different primary group, regularly interact, they provide a linkage between their two primary groups that is called a *bridge* (see Figure 3–2). Dealing with teachers in these categories allows the principal to extend his influence more widely through the primary groups of the informal organization. In the case of conflict, of course, such linking of teachers could marshal rather widespread opposition to the principal.

---

[12] Laurence Iannacconne, "An Approach to the Informal Organization of the School," in Daniel E. Griffiths, ed., *Behavioral Science and Educational Administration*, The Sixty-third Yearbook of the National Society for the Study of Education, Part II (Chicago: The University of Chicago Press, 1964), p. 234.

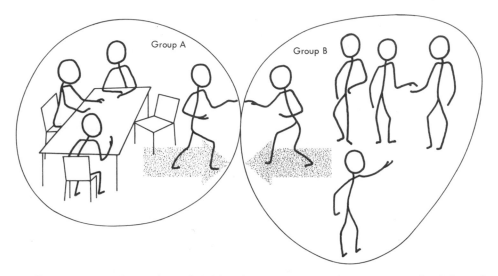

FIGURE 3–2. Illustration of bridge between two primary groups in informal organization.

The School: A Social System

Since the late 1950's, the use of social systems theory as a way of understanding school organizations has been increasing, for this concept provides for two types of systems: *open* and *closed*. A closed system is independent of its environment and, therefore, does not describe schools as organizations. However, a school may be described as an open system when it is characterized by an input-output relationship with its environment, thus differentiating it from a closed system. In addition to an input-output relationship with its environment, open systems have other distinguishing characteristics, some of which have been described by Griffiths as follows:

1. Open systems tend to maintain themselves in *steady states*. A steady state is characterized by a constant ratio being maintained among the components of the system. A burning candle is often used as an example of a steady state. Upon being lighted the flame is small, but it rapidly grows to its normal size and maintains the size as long as the candle and its environment exist.
2. Open systems are *self-regulating*. In the illustration above, a sudden draft will cause the flame to flicker, but with the cessation of the draft the flame regains its normal characteristics.
3. Open systems display *equifinality;* that is, identical results can be ob-

tained from different initial conditions. Hearn points out that equi-finality in human beings (they are open systems) is illustrated by the case of two babies, one born prematurely, the other full-term. While at birth they may look very different and may be in different stages of development, within a few months the differences will have disappeared. . . .

4. Open systems maintain their steady states, in part, through the *dynamic interplay of subsystems operating as functional processes*. This means that the various parts of the system function without persistent conflicts that can be neither resolved nor regulated.

5. Open systems maintain their steady states, in part, through *feedback* processes. In general, feedback refers to that portion of the output which is fed back to the input and affects succeeding outputs. . . .[13]

Thus, we have a picture of an open social system, a school which exists in a larger environment which is social *and* physical and interacts with this environment as well. It responds to inputs of energy and stimuli from its environment and it affects its environment with its out-put. Environment, as we are using the term, includes the school's own subsystems, as well as its various suprasystems—including the community. The use of systems theory can lead to a search for more precise delineation of the boundaries which mark the limits of the organization. Principals and teachers, for example, are often concerned with maintaining their legitimate authority and defending their place in the school situation when parental interest is interpreted as a challenge. This frequently leads to attempts to define the boundaries of the school organization in relationship to the environment.

Systems theory is also useful in analyzing the factors which influence the behavior of individuals in organizations. Getzels and Guba,[14] for example, describe the organization as a social system which features a hierarchical role-structure. For each role in the structure—principal, teacher, or custodian—there are certain behavioral expectations. Everyone in the social system (including the role incumbent) is an observer of others and thus has certain *perceptions* and *expectations* of how those in other roles will behave. For example, no one in the system—teacher, parent, superintendent, custodian, or any other referent—has the same expectation of the role of the principal as any other member of the system.

However, overall there *is* an institutional role expectation for the principal: things he must do, decisions he must make, ceremonies he must

---

[13] Daniel E. Griffiths, "The Nature and Meaning of Theory," in Griffiths, ed., *ibid.*, pp. 116–17.

[14] Jacob W. Getzels and Egon G. Guba, "Social Behavior and the Administrative Process," *School Review*, LXV (Winter, 1957), 423–41.

perform. But the role incumbent—the person who happens to occupy the organization's role of principal at the moment—is a person with all the distinctive personality characteristics and needs of an individual. According to Getzels, there are thus two *dimensions* which are significant factors in producing organizational behavior: the *personal dimension* and the *organizational dimension*. The general model which is being so widely used in educational administration is generally referred to as the "Getzels-Guba model." It may be depicted as in Figure 3–3.

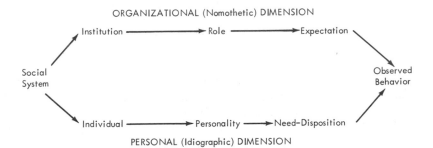

FIGURE 3–3. Model of the organization as a social system (the so-called "Getzels-Guba model"). From Jacob W. Getzels, "Administration as a Social Process," in Andrew W. Halpin, ed., *Administrative Theory in Education* (Chicago: Midwest Administration Center, University of Chicago, 1958), p. 156.

Viewed in this way, each behavioral act is seen as stemming simultaneously from the nomothetic and the idiographic dimensions. But how do these dimensions interact? What proportion of each dimension is present in organizational behavior? That depends, of course, on the individual and on the institutional role and is best expressed as a function of the interplay between the two dimensions. Getzels gives us this general equation to express it:

$$B = f \ (R \times P),$$

where B = observed behavior,
R = institutional role, and
P = personality of the role incumbent.[15]

The Getzels-Guba model has been used as the theoretical framework for a number of studies, for example, by Bridges in a study of the effect of the amount of experience that elementary school principals have on

15 Jacob W. Getzels, "Administration as a Social Process," in Andrew W. Halpin, ed., *Administrative Theory in Education* (Chicago: Midwest Administration Center, University of Chicago, 1958), p. 157.

teachers' perceptions of their organizational behavior.[16] Discomfiting though the following finding may be to principals, Bridges' data showed that the longer the principal has been in his bureaucratic role the more likely it is that teachers will fault him on the basis of perceived organizational behavior. We mention this interesting study to point out that it is possible to use the Getzels-Guba model, as Bridges did, to speculate as to the reasons for this surprising finding.

Systems theory is presently showing promise in evaluating organizations. Traditionally, organizations—including schools—have been evaluated in terms of the goals which have been set for them. The question thus arises: how well did the organization achieve its goals? As school administrators well know, this tends to make the evaluation of the organization negative in tone. Since it is, indeed, a rare organization that fully achieves all of its goals, evaluation tends to become either criticism for not doing better or a long discussion of the reasons for the lack of success. This type of evaluation is described as the *goal-model* of organizational evaluation and it assumes that success would be complete or nearly complete attainment of the organization's goals. In practical terms, organizations are usually evaluated on the basis of two dimensions: *performance* (profit, production rate, sales, etc.) and *human factors* (attitudes, morale, motivation, group cohesiveness, etc.).

Full effectiveness is never possible under the goal-model concept of evaluation, and the question of just how effective the organization *should* be is left unanswered. Etzioni declares flatly that "low effectiveness is a general characteristic of organizations" and goes on to describe goal-model evaluation of organizations as "analogous to an electrical engineer who would rate all light bulbs 'ineffective' since they convert only about 5 per cent of their electrical energy into light, the rest being 'wasted' on heat." [17] To continue the analogy, we can rate light bulbs by comparing the bulbs themselves to determine their *relative* efficiency. The *system model* for evaluating organizational effectiveness, rather than dealing directly with goals, is concerned with the operating relationships that must exist for the organization to function.

Systems criteria tend to focus on organizational conditions that must be present as a prior condition for effective operations. Likert has suggested multiple criteria for this purpose which would refer to areas such as loyalty and a sense of identification with the organization and its purposes, the adequacy and fluency of communication, the incidence

---

[16] Edwin M. Bridges, "Bureaucratic Role and Socialization: The Influence of Experience on the Elementary Principal," *Educational Administration Quarterly*, II (Spring, 1965), 19–28.

[17] Etzioni, *op. cit.*, pp. 16–17.

of teamwork, and the extent of confidence and trust among workers.[18] It is well known that there is no direct relationship between morale and organizational goal attainment, but it is probable that adequate attention must be paid to the basic social system needs of the organization as a prior condition of effectiveness. Selznick lists five such needs for the social system model:

1. The security of the organization as a whole in relation to social forces in its environment
2. The stability of the lines of authority and communication
3. The stability of informal relations within the organization
4. The continuity of policy and the sources of its determination
5. A homogeneity of outlook with respect to the meaning and role of the organization [19]

The School: A Bureaucracy

A bureaucracy is an administrative system that is adapted to the needs of large and complex organizations that deal with large numbers of clients. It also may be classed as a social invention [20] in much the same way as our entire industrial society may be classed as a social invention. Here we must mention the name of Max Weber, for Weber is frequently looked upon as the master theoretician of bureaucracy, and his thinking still has great impact on those who are interested in problems of administering large-scale organizations. Weber was a German sociologist whose scholarly career spanned the last few years of the nineteenth century and the early years of this century. Not surprisingly, he was keenly interested in the industrial organizations that were then developing rapidly into giants in his native Germany. He was particularly interested in the impact that these new huge organizations would have on life and society. As he viewed his contemporary scene, Weber saw three types of organizations in existence:

1. *Charismatic organizations,* in which there was a single leader to whom everyone owed loyalty and allegiance
2. *Traditional organizations,* such as the Junkers' officer corps or the empires of hereditary landowners in which the right to occupy man-

[18] Rensis Likert, "Measuring Organizational Performance," *Harvard Business Review,* XXXVI, No. 12 (March–April, 1958).

[19] Philip Selznick, "Foundations of the Theory of Organizations," *American Sociological Review,* XIII, No. 1 (February, 1948), 25–35.

[20] Robert Dubin, ed., *Human Relations in Administration,* 2nd ed. (Englewood Cliffs, N. J.: Prentice-Hall, Inc., © 1961), p. 140.

agerial positions was inherited and was handed down from generation to generation

3. *Bureaucracies*, in which the organizational structure is designed specifically to make maximum use of administrative specialists who possess a high level of expertise. Positions are created on a functional basis and office holders are recruited to fill them on the basis of their technical competence to do the work required in those positions.

In contrast to "one-man," or charismatic, organizations and those which are tradition-oriented, Weber saw the bureaucracy as a very desirable pattern because it was rational and unbiased, and it avoided the use of human emotion and favoritism as major factors in the making of administrative decisions.

In the burgeoning organizations that Weber saw developing around him in the early years of this century—industrial, military, and political—he found the elements of bureaucracy. It was Weber who, more than any other person, studied the bureaucracy of his time and attempted to identify the most desirable characteristics of the best bureaucratic organizations that then existed. Presthus' list of five characteristics of a bureaucracy is prominent in the vast body of literature on the subject:

1. Fixed and official jurisdictional areas, regularly ordered by rules, policies, regulations, and by-laws
2. Principles of hierarchy and levels of graded authority that ensure a firmly ordered system of super- and subordination in which those in higher offices supervise those in lower ones
3. Administration based upon written documents
4. Administration run by full-time, trained officials
5. Administration planned according to stable and comprehensive general policies [21]

These five characteristics describe the basic elements of an ideal bureaucracy. And strange as it may seem to us today, bureaucracy was once looked upon as a highly useful and desirable creation—because it was *efficient*, indeed, the most efficient form of organization yet invented. And it was efficient—at least compared to "one-man" and tradition-oriented organizations—because irrational emotional biases such as caste and class were eliminated from administrative decisions. Moreover, role incumbents (the bureaucrats) were highly trained experts in their specialties. In addition, bureaucracy was seen to be efficient because it was orderly, disciplined, and—being based upon clear, written policies—it

---

[21] Robert Presthus, *The Organizational Society* (New York: Alfred A. Knopf, Inc., 1962), p. 5.

was precise. In Weber's time, bureaucracy was an attempt to exercise rationality in the organizational affairs of men as the rise of a technological society overthrew the familiar traditional social structure that had seemed so rational and adequate until that time. In theory, the focus was on *role* in the bureaucratic organizational hierarchy rather than on the individual who filled the role. The hope was to replace a managerial "cult of personality" with a system of roles, institutionalized and reinforced by legal tradition, by the use of rationality and predictability in the administrative process, the elimination of unanticipated consequences, and emphasis on technical competence rather than the "iron whim" of managers.

It is an obvious understatement to say that bureaucracies have not universally achieved high levels of efficiency. Indeed, for one to be called a bureaucrat today is an affront; certainly the appellation does not carry the desirable connotation in our time that it held for Weber. School principals, like most Americans, tend to associate bureaucracy with red tape, delay, and inefficiency. In fact, Weber himself, the very man who developed the theory of bureaucracy, eventually came to fear it. He even later proposed that bureaucracy might eventually strangle capitalism and entrepreneurship. He, and others, has even proposed that the real enemy of capitalism and democracy is not communism, but bureaucracy. Indeed, just as we can ascribe much of the theoretical bases of bureaucracy to Max Weber, we can also trace the more recent antipathy toward omniscient bureaucracy to him:

> It is horrible to think that the world could one day be filled with nothing but those little cogs, little men clinging to little jobs and striving toward bigger ones. . . . This passion for bureaucracy is enough to drive one to despair . . . and the great question is therefore not how we can promote and hasten it, but what can we oppose to this machinery in order to keep a portion of mankind free from this parcelling-out of the soul from this supreme mastery of the bureaucratic way of life? [22]

Much of the vast literature on bureaucracy deals with *pathologies* in the organizational behavior of bureaucrats and bureaucracies.[23] To be

---

[22] Reinhard Bendix, *Max Weber: An Intellectual Portrait* (Garden City, N. Y.: Doubleday & Company, Inc., 1960), pp. 455–56.

[23] For a summary of the major literature on bureaucracy, see Peter M. Blau, *Bureaucracy in Modern Society* (New York: Random House, Inc., 1956). Of the many writings dealing specifically with bureaucratic pathologies, school administrators will find the following of particular interest: Frederick Dyer and John Dyer, *Bureaucracy vs. Creativity* (Coral Gables, Fla.: University of Miami Press, 1965); Harry Cohen, *The Demonics of Bureaucracy* (Ames, Ia.: The Iowa State University Press, 1965); and Marshal Dimock, *Administrative Vitality: The Conflict with Bureaucracy* (New York: Harper & Row, Publishers, 1959).

without bias or prejudice is desirable for an employee, but in extreme form it becomes a sort of Walter Mitty approach, and the employee turns into a ritualistic bureaucrat who overemphasizes impersonal rules to the point of driving clients to despair. Therefore, although there do exist ideal situations in bureaucracy, structuring these ideal situations in practice may be difficult indeed. The career orientation of bureaucrats may make them more interested in protecting that career than in dealing with clients. Rules sometimes become more important to bureaucrats than the problems they are supposed to solve, and we hear the charge, "red tape." Specialization can reach the point where we encounter ritualistic behavior, which leads to "the old run-around"; clients are shunted from desk to desk as bureaucrats haggle over which rule applies to the particular case, and argue over precedent and jurisdiction rather than solving the client's problem and settling the jurisdictional problem within the organization at a later time.

There have been many criticisms of bureaucracy. A typical catalog of the more serious faults would include the following:

1. Bureaucracy encourages overconformity, inducing "group think."
2. In time, bureaucracy modifies the very personality of bureaucrats such that they become the drab, colorless, routinized "organization men."
3. Innovative ideas wilt from the distortion and long delays which result from communications overloading as attempts are made to transmit ideas through the hierarchical layers of the organization.
4. Bureaucracy does not take into account the presence of informal organizations, including the primary groups to which role-incumbents belong.

How inevitable is the formation of bureaucracies? As our organizations increase in size and complexity, must we assume that bureaucracies will become increasingly large and unmanageable? In essence, the question is: What hope is there that a better pattern for large organizations will be invented? At the moment there are three recognizable and fairly clear-cut choices that we can consider.

The first can be simply stated: bureacracy *is*—and it is like death and taxes, for we must simply learn to live with it with as much grace as we can muster. This view holds that our present bureaucracies are so entrenched, so indispensable, and so immovable as to constitute an integral part of our way of life, now and in the future. The key to minimizing frustration is to learn how to live successfully with our bureaucracies, to learn how to adapt to them, to accept the price they extract (even in human and personality terms) for services rendered, and to make the most of them.

The second view is much more hopeful: we need bureaucracies in our modern world. With increasing populations and the growing complexities of life, we simply cannot dismantle our bureaucracies and hope to keep things running smoothly. When functioning properly, a bureaucracy gives us four advantages that become increasingly important with the passage of time:

1. *Bureaucracy is efficient.* It provides administrative services to large numbers of clients systematically and uniformly. The staff—consisting of trained specialists—proceeds with little lost time and motion.
2. *Bureaucracy is predictable.* Rules are written and explicit. The hierarchical status of roles, and their authority, is clear.
3. *Bureaucracy is impersonal.* Rules and procedures are applied on the basis of predetermined criteria, and hence, in an unbiased and fair way.
4. *Bureaucracy is fast.* Uniform rules are impartially applied to process thousands of cases quickly. Specialists collaborate on important problems to solve them without delay.

However, even though bureaucracy is often seen to be indispensable and unbeatable as an administrative system, it is unquestionably true that (1) all bureaucracies are not equally effective, and (2) a given bureaucracy varies in its "state of health" from time to time over the years.

Bureaucratic Dysfunctions

Blau described the dynamic aspects of bureaucracy,[24] illustrating that a bureaucracy is not a rigid and unyielding system, for bureaucrats do make changes and adaptations of rules to meet the need for flexibility to at least some extent. However, bureaucracies also develop *dysfunctions*, that is, they continue to operate, but the bureaucratic machinery turns out some kind of output that can best be described as unanticipated consequences. A bureaucratic unit may, for example, be so concerned with smooth functioning that padded statistical reports, inaccurate evaluations of effectiveness, and the stuffing of file cabinets with useless information may become more important than giving clients adequate service. Merton describes the effect of overtraining of specialists which renders the bureaucrat unable to see the effects of his own operations. Veblen uses the term "trained incapacity" in describing the rigid bureaucrat who cannot apply rules to actual cases, much less adapt these rules to the needs of clients. These and other dysfunctions can cause observable symptoms

---

[24] Peter M. Blau, *The Dynamics of Bureaucracy* (Chicago: The University of Chicago Press, 1955). The reader will also find of interest a later book which follows up some of Blau's observations in an organization a decade later: *cf.* Cohen, *op. cit.*

that may shed doubt on the effectiveness of bureaucracy. *Displacement of goals* is one common symptom, in which adherence to rules becomes an end in itself. Bureaucratic rules are originally conceived for facilitating services to the client, but in some organizations these rules eventually become the main concern of the bureaucracy to the detriment of service to the client. The symptom that is the reverse of goal displacement we call *debureaucratization.* In such a situation the goals and activities of the bureaucracy are subverted in favor of the goals and interests of outside groups. In extreme cases of debureaucratization, some of the functions and activities of the bureaucracy may even be taken over by the outside group. This is often accomplished by an outside group to which a bureaucrat belongs that puts pressure on the bureaucrat to perform tasks that are within the scope of the bureacracy but outside the scope of the organization. School administrators are usually members of community organizations, some of which may attempt to enlist his aid in circumventing some of the school districts' rules. It is possible, for example, that much of our civil rights anguish has been caused by debureaucratization, rather than the social and political policies of this country. In many cases, the cry for fair play could be more accurately directed toward the bureaucratic machinery of our public agencies and the debureaucratic behavior of role-incumbents than toward policy makers. Many students of organization believe that bureaucracy is essential to our increasingly urban and complex way of life, and that we must have faith that its serious aberrations can be eliminated, or at least acceptably controlled.

A third view of the role of bureaucracy in the future of our organizational culture is based, in part, on the premise that bureaucracy is not likely to be recorded in history as the final step in the development of administrative systems. This view is also based partly on observation of events which are now unfolding in contemporary organizations. Essentially, the view is that, in the perspective of history, bureaucracy as it is known today will prove to have been an important phase in the development of administrative systems. As the word "phase" suggests, however, the more accurate perspective in which to place present bureaucratic systems is that of a transitional answer to emerging needs. As organizational needs change, and as our organizational sophistication grows, bureaucracy, as we now think of it, may well prove to be neither inevitable nor eternal, although when we realize how well entrenched and seemingly invincible present bureaucracies are, and how we are enmeshed, if not engulfed, in them, such an outlook seems Pollyannish and requires further explanation.

Like all other organizations, the school exists primarily to attain a set of goals. In order to survive long enough to achieve these goals, the school organization must heed two imperatives:

1. *The internal system*, i.e., the organization's operations must be kept functioning and a balance of needs and satisfactions of participants, on the one hand, and of the organization, on the other, which Bennis calls "reciprocity," [25] must be maintained.
2. *The external system*, i.e., the organization must conform to pressures and changes of its environment; Bennis calls this "adaptability." [26]

But, as has been discussed above, highly bureaucratized organizations encounter serious problems in meeting both these imperatives.

Although the impersonal, unemotional nature of the bureaucratic system has advantages for the organization, it tends to be insufficient to meet the various personal and social needs of participants. Money alone has not proven to be sufficient reward for motivating individuals to continue participation in an organization in which they cannot find adequate primary-group relationships. The internal operating effectiveness of the bureaucracy can be threatened if the social needs of participants, including the need to be involved in decision making at appropriate levels, are not satisfied. The bureaucracy which is too demanding fails to meet the internal test of reciprocity. And externally the bureaucratic organization faces a world characterized by rapid, significant change, an increasingly educated society, and more mobile and career-oriented people. It is a world of technological changes and new pressures, and the organization cannot predict where the next significant breakthrough will emerge. It is reasonably clear to the school administrator, for example, that the next momentous change in his school will not be generated from within his organization—or even within his profession. Where will it come from? A new Sputnik, perhaps? More racial unrest? Another war? Vast new federal programs? Perhaps this change will emerge in the form of a vast new instructional technology arising from the entrance of the electronics and mass-media corporate giants into the textbook publishing field. Perhaps, but we simply do not know what new invention, what new discovery, what social pressures will determine the future forces of change to which the school organization must adapt if it is to survive.

We only know that significant change will come and that those organizations which can adequately adapt will be adjudged the most satisfactory. A glance at the current scene in the world of business organizations, the military, government, and other organizations, including the schools, confirms this view. For education, for example, the great crisis is in the cities, and it seems that the larger the city, the worse the crisis. Observers of city school systems point to large, rigid bureaucratic organizations

---

[25] Warren G. Bennis, *Changing Organizations* (New York: McGraw-Hill Book Company, 1966), p. 7.
[26] *Ibid.*

with their characteristic built-in capacity to resist change and to over-react when they do attempt to change. This is, of course, neither new nor novel.

The Peace Corps is a good example of an attempt to develop an organization specifically designed to be nonbureaucratic and to maintain a high level of internal reciprocity and external adaptability. Written rules were minimized, role-structure was made simple, specialization was de-emphasized, the hierarchy was limited, and the approach to problems remained highly personal and human. This was quite a different organization, as an organization, than the typical highly structured federal bureaucratic agencies. Many popular writers have commented on the exciting possibilities of this kind of organizational approach.[27] And this technique is not unique to the Peace Corps, for it has frequently been used in many other fields. Special military groups organized on this basis are often structured so as to develop new adaptive procedures in strange environments.[28] This technique is being used with growing frequency in business, which is finding it increasingly necessary to pay attention to internal and external organizational problems in a highly competitive world of explosive technological change.

Since the studies of the Sears Roebuck reorganization began to gain general attention in the 1950's,[29] for example, the trend in many business and industrial organizations has been toward organizations having fewer hierarchical layers between top management and the operating units. The profile of such an organization has a broad base and a relatively short distance to the top. This reflects a broader delegation of responsibilities and shortening of the channels of communication to the top decision making level. However, much more is involved in this concept than changing the profile of the organization chart. One aspect of this concept is *reciprocity*, the balance between meeting the needs of the formal and the informal organization, and another is *adaptability*, the ability of the organization to respond to pressures of change. This concept is thus basically human and concerns obtaining the maximum commitment and production from participants. In education we have traditionally developed organizations to facilitate close supervision of personnel in the lower ranks. Such organizations tend to be sharply pyramidal, with little dele-

---

[27] Popular literature is replete with examples, such as, C. Northcote Parkinson, *Parkinson's Law* (Boston: Houghton Mifflin, 1957), and William H. Whyte, Jr., *The Organization Man* (New York: Simon and Shuster, 1956).

[28] Janowitz points out that the military is generally thought of as bureaucratic, but that it actually shifts rapidly from bureaucratic to nonbureaucratic organizational forms as needs arise. See Morris Janowitz, *Sociology and the Military Establishment* (New York: The Russell Sage Foundation, 1959), pp. 15-39.

[29] William F. Whyte, "Human Relations Theory: A Progress Report," *Harvard Business Review*, XXXIV, No. 5 (September–October, 1956), 127.

gated responsibility and strong central control. But research on this kind
of supervision does not indicate favorable results are thus obtained. There
is increasing reason to believe that if it is important to the attainment of
organizational goals for the participant to develop initiative and assume
responsibility, close supervision may be the wrong method for attaining
such goals.[30]

Organizations structured according to the span of control concept are
sharply pyramidal, with one person controlling only those individuals
whom he can personally supervise. Upward communications in such organizations is difficult and control is strong; moreover, these organizations
tend to be highly bureaucratic, being slow to change and adapt. Participants in them find the emphasis for behavior to be largely nomothetic,
or organization centered. In the future other kinds of organizations will
undoubtedly be needed, staffed, and organized around a "climate of
beliefs" [31] with regard to effective human behavior in organizations which
will make them more responsive both to internal needs and external pressures. This climate of beliefs, or system of values, will include the following, as described by Bennis:

1. Full and free communication, regardless of rank and power
2. Reliance on consensus, rather than on the more customary forms of
   coercion or compromise, to resolve conflict
3. The idea that influence is based on technical competence and knowledge, rather than on the vagaries of personal whim or prerogatives of
   power
4. An atmosphere that permits and even encourages emotional expression, as well as task-oriented acts
5. A basically human bias, one which accepts the inevitability of conflict
   between the organization and the individual, but which is at the same
   time willing to consider such conflicts on rational grounds [32]

An organization committed to such a system of values is not likely to be
the sharply pyramidal bureaucratic structure found in many school districts today.

Summary

In this chapter we have discussed selected aspects of modern thinking
with regard to complex organizations and bureaucracies, paying particular

---

[30] *Ibid.*
[31] Bennis, *op. cit.*, pp. 18–19.
[32] Adapted from *ibid.*, p. 19.

attention to schools. The concepts of the *complex organization*, the *social system*, and the *bureaucracy* were emphasized. By the use of these concepts, the school administrator can view his organization in terms of fundamental principles which may be used as a guide to administrative action. One application, for example, might be in the designing of an organizational structure: Should the structure be sharply pyramidal or should it take some other profile—and for what purpose? Another application of these concepts would be to examine the school organization for pathological symptoms which can be corrected. The most important possible use of these organizational concepts for us now, however, is that they may be useful when we deal with matters such as *leadership, organizational climate, decision making,* and *change in an organizational setting* in the following chapters.

⚜ 4 ⚜

interpersonal relations
and organizational behavior

The urging of the times has aroused a sense of the need for change. In this mood, a respectable segment of organizational theorists are building their positions as activists who seek to change society through effects on interpersonal behavior . . . . When one . . . considers the extraordinary number of hours managers and leaders in various organizations spend in directing and guiding work in interpersonal settings, the widespread appeal of this area of study to practitioners is readily understandable.

—Abraham Zaleznik [1]

Probably everyone has, on occasion, had the experience of unfolding a map so that it is upside down. When this happens, one is immediately disoriented—even if the map is of one's home state—and, as soon as one sees what is wrong, one turns the map around so that it is "right side up." In the case of a map, of course, "right side up" means that north is at the top of the page. However, if one deliberately turns a map around and studies it a while, the same familiar territory begins to look "different" and one sees new relationships which had long been hidden by conventional ideas of how to view a map. Thus it is also with the way we tend to view organizations.

Faced with the following problem: *Illustrate the structure of a typical organization*, many school administrators would tend to produce an organizational chart somewhat similar to the one shown in Figure 4–1. This, of course, depicts a skeletal outline of a typical line-and-staff organization showing the hierarchical relationship of offices. Labeled so as to apply

---

[1] Abraham Zaleznik, "Interpersonal Relations in Organizations," in James G. March, ed., *Handbook of Organizations* (Skokie, Ill.: Rand McNally & Co., 1965), p. 574.

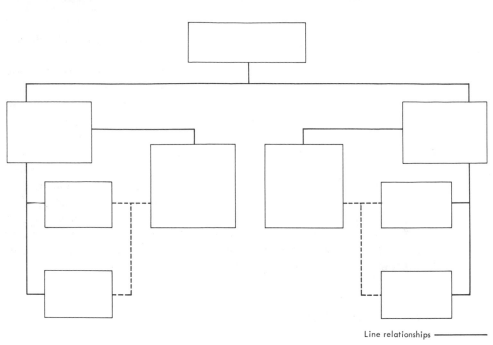

Line relationships ————————

Staff relationships — — — — — — — —

FIGURE 4–1. Typical line-and-staff organizational chart.

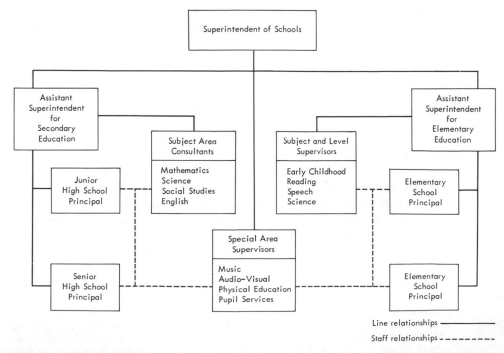

Line relationships ————————

Staff relationships — — — — — — — —

FIGURE 4–2. Typical application of line-and-staff pattern of organization to school district.

specifically to a school organization, the organization chart might look like the one shown in Figure 4–2. Needless to say, such charts have been—and still are—useful, practical ways of depicting organizations which will undoubtedly continue to be an important part of the planning and administration of organizations for a long time to come. But if we are to develop fresh insights into the problem of making our organizations more effective, we must provide ourselves with a fresh view of organizations on occasion.

One relatively fresh view of organizations is provided by role theory, a construct which is not necessarily tied to social systems theory, but which will here be presented against that background in order to suggest an interrelationship that is being found useful by an increasing number of students. After a brief description of some aspects of the social systems background, we shall turn to a consideration of role theory.

Social Systems Theory

Systems theory exists in both the physical and the behavioral sciences. "A *system*," Griffiths tells us, "may be simply defined as a complex of elements in mutual interaction." [2] As was discussed in the previous chapter, systems can be divided into two main classes: "open" systems, which interact with their environments, and "closed" systems, which do not interact with their environments. Social systems theory generally deals with so-called "open" systems because, as we shall see, a "closed" social system is difficult to envisage. In the physical realm, a burning candle has become a classic illustration of an open system: it affects its environment and is affected by it, yet it is self-regulating and retains its own identity. If a door is opened, the candle may flicker in the draft, but it will adjust to it and return to normal at the first opportunity—provided, of course, that the environmental change (the draft) was not so overwhelming as to destroy the system (i.e., extinguish the flame).

It is not so simple to describe *social* systems on even this superficial level. Griffiths speaks of the organization (the system) as existing in an environment (the suprasystem) and having within it a subsystem (the administrative apparatus of the organization). He diagrams it as in Figure 4–3. The boundaries of the various systems and subsystems are suggested in the figure by the tangential circles; however, we must bear in mind that these boundaries are permeable, permitting interaction between the

---

[2] Daniel E. Griffiths, "Administrative Theory and Change in Organizations," in Matthew B. Miles, ed., *Innovation in Education* (New York: Teachers College Press, 1964), p. 428. © 1964 by Teachers College, Columbia University. Reprinted by permission of the publisher.

systems and their environments. One application of this viewpoint can be illustrated by labeling the figure as in Figure 4-4. It then becomes obvious that factors which interfere with the interactive and adaptive relationships between the components of the interrelated parts of the system could pose a threat to the functioning of the whole. One form of interference would be a loss of permeability of one or more of the boundaries, thus tending to make the system "closed" and less sensitive to environmental change.

Where does the individual fit into all of this—where does he appear? Richard Lonsdale, a colleague of Griffiths', has expanded and modified the original model as in Figure 4-5. Here, again, an arbitrary relabeling of the diagram can specify—a little more clearly, at least—one way in which this view would apply to people working in schools: The individual person finds himself functioning in the organization not only as his indi-

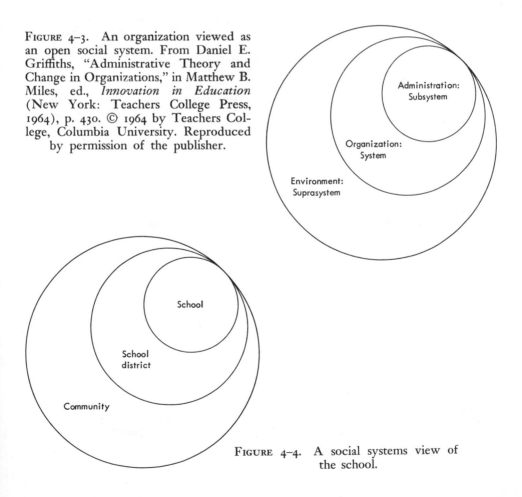

FIGURE 4-3. An organization viewed as an open social system. From Daniel E. Griffiths, "Administrative Theory and Change in Organizations," in Matthew B. Miles, ed., *Innovation in Education* (New York: Teachers College Press, 1964), p. 430. © 1964 by Teachers College, Columbia University. Reproduced by permission of the publisher.

Administration: Subsystem

Organization: System

Environment: Suprasystem

School

School district

Community

FIGURE 4-4. A social systems view of the school.

vidual self, but also as one who occupies a certain *role* within the social system in the organization. In the hypothetical case illustrated in Figure 4–6, the person occupies the role of "teacher" in the chemistry department of John F. Kennedy Senior High School, a situation possessing a number of useful implications for anyone interested in analyzing, predicting and perhaps controlling organizational behavior.

When we consider the individual person carrying out his unique role in an organization, we become concerned with the complex web of human involvement and its attendant behavior in organizational life. As the individual, with all his needs, drives, and talents, assumes his official role, he shapes that role to some extent, and he is also shaped by it. The dynamic interaction of people with varying psychological make-ups in the organizational setting is thus the domain of role theory.

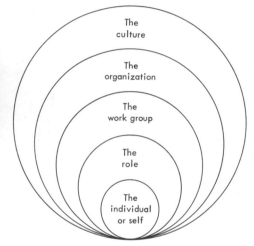

FIGURE 4–5. Levels of interaction of the individual and the organization. From Richard C. Lonsdale, "Maintaining the Organization in Dynamic Equilibrium," in Daniel E. Griffiths, ed., *Behavioral Science and Educational Administration,* The Sixty-third Yearbook of the National Society for the Study of Education, Part II (Chicago: The National Society for the Study of Education, 1964), p. 143.

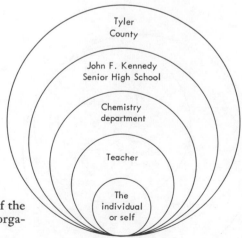

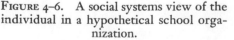

FIGURE 4–6. A social systems view of the individual in a hypothetical school organization.

Role Theory

How people perform their roles in organizations has attracted a great deal of scholarly attention in recent years. As we pointed out in Chapter 3, the interpersonal behavior exhibited by participants in complex organizations as they deal with one another in face-to-face encounters seems to be crucially important in determining the effectiveness in the organization. In attempting to analyze face-to-face interpersonal behavior of people in organizations, Erving Goffman, in *The Presentation of Self in Everyday Life*,[3] drew a useful analogy between "real life" situations and the unfolding of a play on the stage. People in organizations have definite roles to perform, and many interactive factors help to determine precisely what kind of "performance" each role will receive: Each "actor" must interpret his role, and this interpretation depends to some extent on the kind of person he is and what he brings to the role. But behavior in a role as part of an organization—no less than for an actor on the stage—will be influenced to some extent by dynamic interplay with other people: other actors and the audience. Role performances are also shaped by the expectations of the director and others attempting to control a situation. Presumably, each actor attempts, to some degree, to behave in conformity with these expectations—and the expectations of his colleagues and others in his referent groups as well. Goffman describes the actors in an organization as being on stage when they are formally carrying out their roles, but he points out that there is a different behavioral standard backstage. Those of us connected with schools, for example, know that a certain kind of behavior is exhibited by teachers in the presence of students and their parents which differs from their behavior in the teachers' cafeteria.

Role theory has been used extensively by observers and researchers in many kinds of organizations in efforts to better understand and predict organizational behavior. A vocabulary of generally understood terms is fairly well established in the literature. Some of the more commonly used terms are:

1. *Role.* The various offices or positions in an organization carry with them certain expectations of behavior held by both onlookers and by the person occupying the role. These expectations generally define role, with some additional expectation that the individual will exhibit some of his own idiosyncratic personality in his role behavior.

[3] Erving Goffman, *The Presentation of Self in Everyday Life* (Garden City, N. Y.: Doubleday & Company, Inc., Anchor Books, 1959). A later study by the same author in a similar vein is *Encounters* (Indianapolis: Bobbs-Merrill, 1961).

2. *Role description.* This refers to the actual behavior of an individual performing a role, or, more accurately, to a report stemming from one individual's perception of that behavior.
3. *Role prescription.* This is the relatively abstract idea of what the general norm in the culture is for the role. What kind of role behavior is expected of a teacher in this country, for example?
4. *Role expectation.* This refers to the expectation that one person has of the role behavior of another. Teachers, for example, expect certain behavior from a principal, and the principal has his own expectation of behavior for teachers. Thus, as teacher and principal interact in their roles in the school, they have complementary role expectations.
5. *Role perception.* This is used to describe the perception that one has of the role expectation that another person holds for him. In dealing with the P.-T.A. president, for example, the principal knows that he has some role expectation of him; his estimate of that expectation is role perception.

Because role theory is relatively well-developed, its language is rather specialized and there are numerous other descriptive labels—some well-established, some not. Naturally, a person plays more than one role in life; indeed, he may well play more than one in an organization. In the case of multiple roles, the term *manifest role* is used in referring to the obvious role that one is performing, but one also occupies *latent roles.* For example, in his classroom, the teacher's manifest role is "teacher"; but he may also be the building chairman for the teacher's union and that role—while he is teaching—is a latent role. A history teacher may also be an activist in a Black Power organization, and thus he holds a latent, as well as a manifest, role.

Role conflicts are commonly thought to be a source of less-than-satisfactory performances in interpersonal behavior in organizations. There are many sources of role conflict, all of which inhibit optimum performance by the role incumbent. An obvious role conflict is a situation in which two persons are unable to establish a satisfactory complementary, or reciprocal, role relationship, which can result from a wide variety of causes and—not infrequently—may involve a complex set of conflict behaviors. Confusion over role expectation and role perception is commonly observed. Moreover, frequently role conflict exists within a single individual: The role expectation may well clash with the individual personality needs of the role incumbent. A case in point is that of a school principal who was employed by a school district largely because of his innovative skill and strong leadership qualities; when a taxpayer revolt in the school district suddenly caused a sharp reversal of school board policy, the superintendent was dismissed and the school board put strong emphasis on economy of operation and conformity to mediocre educational standards. The school principal was plunged into a role conflict situation in which he could not perform to his, or anyone else's, satisfaction and ended up seeking another job with a more manageable amount of conflict.

A common source of tension from role conflict results from the expectation that the incumbent, perhaps an administrator, will be empathetic and understanding in dealing with his subordinates and will still be expected to enforce the rules of the organization. Many administrators feel this sort of conflict when they zealously attempt to build trust, confidence, and high morale in the teaching staff and then are required to conduct a formal evaluation procedure that seems to be in conflict with those goals.

Somewhat similar to role conflict, but significantly different, is *role ambiguity*, a situation whereby the role prescription is contradictory or vague; the situation is not so much one of conflict as it is of confusion. Role ambiguity is rather commonly observed in the attempt to preserve the distinction between administration and supervision: the first is generally seen as "line" authority, whereas the other is thought to be a "staff" responsibility. Yet supervisors are often perceived as being in hierarchical authority over teachers; not infrequently supervisors feel that they are being maneuvered, against the spirit of their role, into the exercise of authority over teachers which threatens their more appropriate collegial relationship with them.

Tension sometimes arises from the fact that all people play what Lonsdale calls *concurrent roles* at any given moment. He describes as an illustration, ". . . the plight of the married woman teacher who at 4:30 may be torn between giving further help to a small group of students and going home to get an early supper for her husband who has an evening meeting." [4]

Role conflicts—some of which have been described above—produce tensions and uncertainties which are commonly associated with inconsistent organizational behavior. In turn, this inconsistent behavior, being unpredictable and unanticipated, often evokes further tension and interpersonal conflict between holders of complementary roles. Frequently, those who must perform their roles in the ambiguity and tension outlined here develop dysfunctional ways of coping with the situation.

Thus, we find such socially acceptable avoidance behavior as joking about the conflict or ambiguity. In organizations where this kind of avoidance is not acceptable, and schools are a case in point, rather elaborate and mutually understood avoidance patterns may exist. These can include a studied avoidance of any discussion of the problem or sub-

---

[4] Richard C. Lonsdale, "Maintaining the Organization in Dynamic Equilibrium," in Daniel E. Griffiths, ed., *Behavioral Science and Educational Administration*, The Sixty-third Yearbook of the National Society for the Study of Education, Part II (Chicago: The University of Chicago Press, 1964), p. 154.

stituting any kind of "small talk" instead. A common avoidance technique is found in ritualistic behavior which permits parties to get through their role performances with a minimum of actual conflict. The use of vagueness, pomposity, complex structure, clichés, and over-obscure vocabulary in communication is one popular avoidance technique.[5]

Role Set

The notion of *role set* is helpful for clarifying some of the concepts of role theory as they are found to be operational in organizations. If we were to observe a work group we would, of course, find it possible to sort out the participants into subgroups in a variety of ways. And one way would be in terms of role. In the case of the role set that will be used here as an illustration, the pivotal role player may be thought of as an administrator.[6] Naturally, he has superordinates in the hierarchy of the organization, people to whom he reports (see Figure 4–7). These are key people in his referent-group and they convey their role expectations to him in many ways. But the administrator does not only have superordinates, he also has subordinates, or people who report to him. As shown in Figure 4–8, subordinates also are significant persons in the administrator's group and they, too, communicate role expectations to him. Thus, the role player's position becomes pivotal, and it is obvious that the role expectations being communicated to him are likely to be somewhat in conflict. The role set is incomplete, however, until a third group of referents is added: the role player's colleagues. With their addition to the role set, as in Figure 4–9, we see the administrator in a pivotal position. When we realize that, in this example, twelve persons— two superordinates, four subordinates, and six colleagues—are acting as *role senders* (that is, they are communicating role expectations to him), it is evident that the interpersonal dynamics of his role are complex.

There will undoubtedly be some role conflict present in such a situation, as well as some role ambiguity. Robert Kahn and his colleagues have used this operational concept of role theory to describe and measure role conflict and role ambiguity and to correlate their presence with attitudes that members of the set have toward their work situation and to the behavioral functioning of these people in the work group.[7] Thus, the role set is an important concept in a consideration of the ecology of

---

[5] Robert Boguslaw, *The New Utopians: A Study of System Design and Social Change* (Englewood Cliffs, N. J.: Prentice-Hall, Inc., 1965), pp. 170–77.

[6] The material presented here on role set is based on Warren G. Bennis, *Changing Organizations* (New York: McGraw-Hill Book Company, 1966), pp. 193–96.

[7] Robert L. Kahn, Donald M. Wolfe, Robert R. Quinn, and J. Diedrick Snoek, *Organizational Stress: Studies in Role Conflict and Ambiguity* (New York: John Wiley & Sons, Inc., 1964).

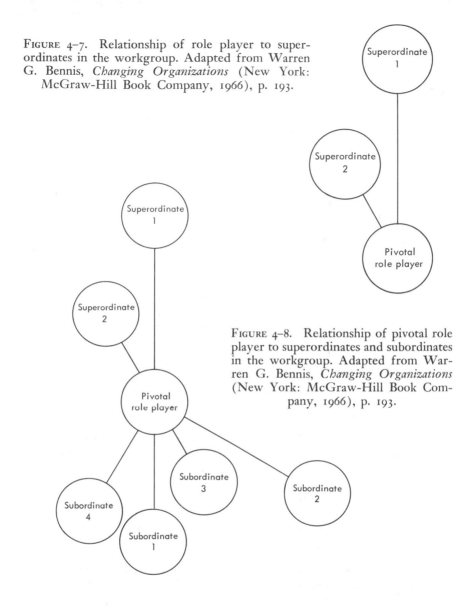

FIGURE 4–7. Relationship of role player to super-ordinates in the workgroup. Adapted from Warren G. Bennis, *Changing Organizations* (New York: McGraw-Hill Book Company, 1966), p. 193.

FIGURE 4–8. Relationship of pivotal role player to superordinates and subordinates in the workgroup. Adapted from Warren G. Bennis, *Changing Organizations* (New York: McGraw-Hill Book Company, 1966), p. 193.

the social setting in which the individual makes his contribution to the organization. It is a useful way of conceptualizing the connection between personality and the organization.

To possess knowledge of role theory and some of its concepts is, in itself, of little use. However, the construct can be useful in analyzing some of the interpersonal behavior that we encounter in the work groups of organizations. For example, leaders are concerned with facilitating the acceptance, development, and allocation of roles that are necessary for the group to function well.

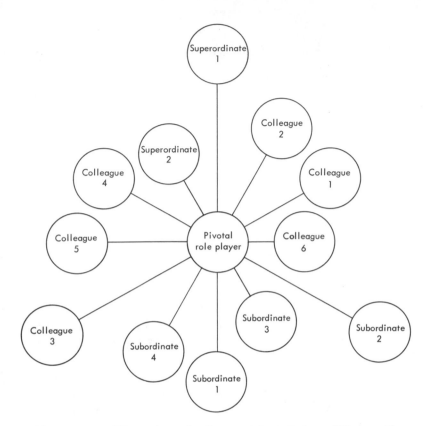

FIGURE 4–9. Illustration of role set. Adapted from Warren G.
Bennis, *Changing Organizations* (New York: McGraw-Hill Book
Company, 1966), p. 193.

Functional Roles in the Group

Benne and Sheats have pointed out that a group has three types of
roles that must be filled [8]:

1. *Group task roles.* These are roles which help the group select the
   problems to be worked on, define these problems, and seek solutions
   to these problems.
2. *Group building and maintenance roles.* These roles facilitate the development of the group and its maintenance over time.
3. *Individual roles.* These are the roles that enable group members to
   satisfy their own idiosyncratic needs as individuals.

Although we must be wary of too much labeling, let us consider Benne
and Sheats' further breakdown of possible specific roles that are available
to group members in each of the three types that must be filled:

[8] The following discussion of role allocation is based on Kenneth D. Benne and
Paul Sheats, "Functional Roles of Group Members," *Journal of Social Issues*, IV, No. 2
(Spring, 1948), 41–49.

1. *Group task roles:* (a) the initiator-contributor, (b) the information seeker, (c) the opinion seeker, (d) the information giver, (e) the opinion giver, (f) the elaborator, (g) the coordinator, (h) the orienter (with respect to group goals), (i) the evaluator-critic, (j) the energizer (who prods groups to action), (k) the procedural technician (who does routine "housekeeping" tasks for the group), and (l) the recorder.[9]

Benne and Sheats stress that each of these roles must be played by someone in the group; the leader must either assume these essential roles himself or see that they are allocated to other members of the group. Benne and Sheats contend that part of the leader's responsibility is to provide for the creation of an environment in the group in which these roles can be developed and carried out. Seven other specific roles are suggested under the second major category:

2. *Group building and maintenance:* (a) the encourager, (b) the harmonizer, (c) the compromiser, (d) the gatekeeper and expediter (who keeps communication channels open), (e) the standard-setter, (f) the observer and commentator (who provides the group with feedback on their actions), and (g) the follower.[10]

These seven roles are obviously quite different in their nature and function from the group task roles. Of course, it is possible that an individual group member will take on more than one role or that two or more members will share a given role. In addition to the above roles, Benne and Sheats suggest eight additional roles that can be useful in satisfying the individual needs of members:

3. *Individual roles:* (a) the aggressor (who attacks the problem or the group that is working on it), (b) the blocker (who is negative and tends to resist), (c) the recognition seeker, (d) the self-confessor (who provides subjective feelings, insights, and intuition), (e) the playboy (who is not really involved in the group's functioning), (f) the dominator, (g) the help-seeker (who seeks comfort from the group), and (h) the special-interest pleader (who speaks for a subgroup).[11]

The Concept of Role Related to Social Systems Theory

The foregoing discussion enables us to return to the social systems model which was presented in Chapter 3 with somewhat more insight.

---

[9] *Ibid.*, pp. 43–44.
[10] *Ibid.*, pp. 44–45.
[11] *Ibid.*, pp. 45–46.

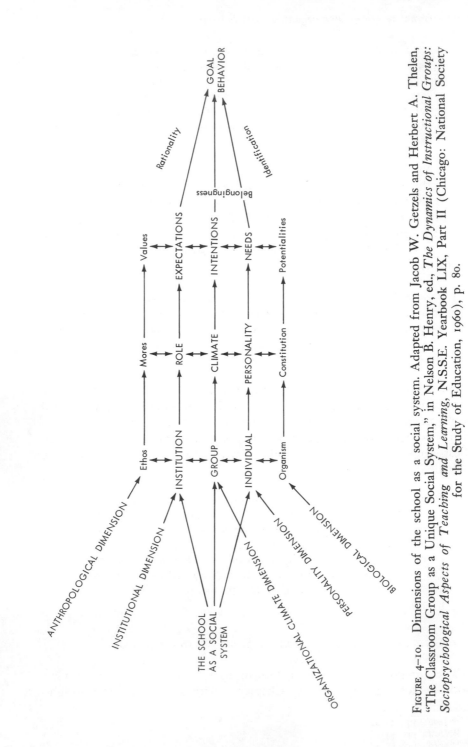

Figure 4-10. Dimensions of the school as a social system. Adapted from Jacob W. Getzels and Herbert A. Thelen, "The Classroom Group as a Unique Social System," in Nelson B. Henry, ed., *The Dynamics of Instructional Groups: Sociopsychological Aspects of Teaching and Learning,* N.S.S.E. Yearbook LIX, Part II (Chicago: National Society for the Study of Education, 1960), p. 80.

We have seen that the school, as an organization, has certain role structures and expectations (see Figure 4–10); these represent the so-called *nomothetic* dimension of the organization. As an institution, an organization establishes roles; and the incumbents of these institutional roles are expected by the organization to exhibit the kind of behavior which will contribute to the goals of the organization. But we are dealing with individual persons who have their own personality structures and needs; and these people occupy the various institutional roles which represent the *idiographic* dimensions of the organization. The mechanism by which the needs of the institution and the needs of the individual are modified so as to come together is the workgroup. There is a dynamic interrelationship in the workgroup, then, not only of an interpersonal nature, but also between institutional requirements and the idiosyncratic needs of individual participants. The shaping of the institutional role, the development of a climate within the social system, and the very personality of the participants all dynamically interact with one another. Organizational behavior can be viewed as the product of this interaction or, as was pointed out in Chapter 3, $B = f (R \times P)$, where B = organizational behavior, R = role, and P = personality.

How much organizational behavior can be ascribed to role expectation and role prescription and how much is traceable to the personality needs of the role incumbent? In other words, if $B = f (R \times P)$, what values can be assigned to R and P, respectively? Although much attention has been paid to attempts to make the above distinction, our present solutions must be highly speculative for any specific situation. A useful way of picturing the problem is shown in Figure 4–11. We can see that for some

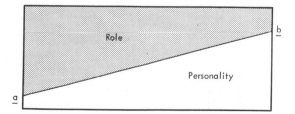

FIGURE 4–11. Concept of the interplay of role and personality in organizational behavior in which behavior is viewed as a function of organizational role and personality, or $B = f (R \times P)$. Adapted from Jacob W. Getzels, "Administration as a Social Process," in Andrew W. Halpin, ed., *Administrative Theory in Education* (Chicago: Midwest Administration Center, University of Chicago, 1958), p. 158.

people a role can have far greater influence in prescribing behavior than for others. We can think of relatively timid principals who are anxious to do what they feel is required or expected of them rather than boldly taking charge and infusing their role with dynamic personalities. But such thinking can be misleading. The need dispositions of individuals vary a great deal, and we must be careful not to suggest that only those individuals with an aggressive, outgoing nature will be successful in expressing their personality needs through their organizational behavior. Indeed, there is much in the research literature to suggest that in many cases it is the timid individual, who needs the security of a well-structured role, who aspires to a school principalship. The bureaucrat who is resigned to the belief that he will play only a small part in making decisions, and who thus cites "regulations" and the expectations of superiors, may be infusing a great deal of his own personality into his interpretation of his role. Presumably, everyone shapes his own role to *some* extent; hence, as shown in Figure 4–11, point *a* would not ordinarily be at zero; on the other hand, in any organization everyone plays some sort of institutional role and, therefore, point *b* is somewhat below the 100 per cent mark. The line *ab*, however, suggests the range of the function of role and personality that would normally be encountered in organizations.

Different kinds of roles in different kinds of organizations do suggest that some role players will be closer to point *a* (that is, will permit very little infusion of personality into the role). Conversely, we know that some kinds of roles demand greater personality involvement, as illustrated in Figure 4–12. One generally supposes that the role of an Army private is very largely prescribed and clearly limits the extent to which the private can meet his individual personality needs. Closer to the other

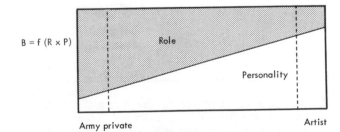

$B = f (R \times P)$ Role   Personality

Army private   Artist

FIGURE 4–12. Personality and role factors in organizational behavior of Army private and artist (proportions are approximate). Adapted from Jacob W. Getzels, "Administration as a Social Process," in Andrew W. Halpin, ed., *Administrative Theory in Education* (Chicago: Midwest Administration Center, University of Chicago, 1958), p. 158.

extreme would be an artist who exhibits highly creative behavior, with a minimum of organizational constraint, and who expresses his personal idiosyncratic needs to a great degree.

The Concept of Equilibrium

Earlier in this book we discussed the notion that people participate in organizations in order to satisfy certain physical and psychological needs. McGregor's *Theory X* and *Theory Y* illustrate this viewpoint, as do Maslow's *hierarchy of needs theory* and Herzberg's *motivation-hygiene theory*. And, presumably, the organization has needs of its own which are served by the participants who function in its various roles, as illustrated by the Getzels-Guba social systems model with its stress on the interplay between the *nomothetic* (organizational) needs and the *idiographic* (personal) needs of the "actors" who fill the various roles. There is obviously a *quid pro quo* relationship between the role-player and the organization, the maintenance of which can be thought of as a state of equilibrium between the needs of the organization and those of the individual. As long as this state of equilibrium exists, the relationship will presumably be satisfactory, enduring, and relatively productive. On its simplest level, this view is illustrated by the relationship between the unskilled day laborer and his employing company.

Perhaps, on a very rudimentary level, the notion of equilibrium between the needs of the organization and its participants is illustrated by the well-known case of Schmidt at Bethlehem Steel. Schmidt, as he was called in Frederick W. Taylor's description,[12] was a pig-iron handler: one of a crew of men who picked up, carried, and loaded pig iron— 12.5 tons in a ten-hour day for \$1.15 per day. Schmidt and his co-workers must have needed more money than the average worker—a need which was met by the inducement of wages the company offered these men in their role as pig-iron handlers. Obviously, the company needed men to do the pig-iron handling and this need was satisfied by the men whose role was that of "handler." Presumably, as long as the needs and satisfactions exchange was in a state of balance or *equilibrium*, the organization functioned adequately. In his account Taylor described how he applied his "scientific principles" to the task of rigorously training Schmidt to increase his daily work load to 47.5 tons. The needs-inducements balance was maintained by boosting the pay by 60 per cent to \$1.85 per day. Schmidt and the company apparently found the needs-

---

[12] Frederick W. Taylor, *The Principles of Scientific Management* (New York: Harper & Row, Publishers, 1911), pp. 42–43.

inducements arrangements mutually satisfactory because Schmidt was described as staying on the job for "some years."

Barnard discussed equilibrium as ". . . the balancing of burdens by satisfactions which results in continuance" of participation of both the individual and the organization in the mutual relationship. In his lexicon, the term "effectiveness" was the ". . . accomplishment of the recognized objectives of cooperative action." [13] "Efficiency" referred to the ability of the organization to sustain the continued participation of individuals by offering adequate satisfactions to them. Barnard described the organization as inducing cooperation by distributing its "*productive* results" to individuals. "These productive results," he wrote, "are either material or social, or both. As to some individuals, material is required for satisfaction; as to others, social benefits are required. As to most individuals, both material and social benefits are required in different proportions." [14] He points out—and this is familiar to us all—that the definition of what constitutes "adequate satisfactions" to individuals in the organization varies, depending in great measure on the makeup and circumstances of the individual involved. Some people certainly find great satisfaction in material reward, especially money, and their organizational role may thus be insecure, unpleasant, or strenuous; however, regardless of the many possible negative aspects of such a role, as long as there is high material reward such people will find the inducement satisfying. Others, for whatever reasons, might find a higher income not worth the price that must be paid. In the recent history of educational administration this can be seen in connection with the role of the superintendent of schools and, to a lesser degree, with that of high school principal. Although the salaries being offered to superintendents are reaching very high levels, many qualified people are not attracted to these roles and many incumbents have shifted to university teaching or other fields altogether. Long working hours, arduous demands, and enormous pressures are some of the drawbacks of the superintendency; in many cases there is little reward in terms of achievement or self-fulfillment. In order to attract and hold capable people as superintendents school districts must proffer a combination of material and psychological rewards which incumbents will find attractive. Not many years ago in the United States an important problem was attracting good teachers to rural areas and keeping them there in spite of the low pay, inadequate school facilities, and limited cultural opportunities which made teaching in such areas relatively

[13] Chester I. Barnard, *The Functions of the Executive* (Cambridge, Mass.: Harvard University Press, 1938), p. 55.

[14] *Ibid.*, p. 57.

unrewarding to many. Today, of course, the situation is reversed; other careers and schools in nonurban areas offer considerable reward to many teachers, whereas the bleak, hostile, frustrating environment of the teacher in the urban ghetto school is barely adequate—both in terms of money and a sense of fulfillment—for many capable teachers.

In discussing organizational equilibrium from the systems theory point of view, we must remember that there is not only a needs-inducements relationship between the individual participant and the organization; the organization itself is part of a larger system. Further, if the system is "open"—as in the case of schools and school systems—the organization will interact actively with the external systems that comprise its environment. Presumably, changes in the environment will stimulate a reaction by the organization, either *static* or *dynamic*. If the reaction is static, the system responds so as to restore relationships to their original state, i.e., the *status quo* is maintained. Dynamic equilibrium, however, is characterized by a rearrangement of the organization or a change in its goals. Lonsdale explains three useful terms which are found in the literature and which help in discussing organizational equilibrium:

1. *Homeostasis.* This is actually a biological term that has been applied to organizations and which refers to the tendency of an open system to regulate itself so as to stay constantly in balance. The biological organism tends to retain its own characteristics, to maintain itself, to preserve its identity, but, at the same time, it has compensatory mechanisms which enable it to adapt to and survive environmental changes within certain limits. Lonsdale describes, as homeostatic processes in human beings, processes such as the body's tendency to maintain a constant temperature and to maintain blood pressure by repairing a break in the circulatory system through coagulation.[15]

2. *Feedback.* A popular description of feedback is given by Pfiffner and Sherwood:

In its simplest form, feedback is the kind of communication an actor receives from a live audience. If the crowd is enthusiastic, the performer reacts with similar enthusiasm. There is in a way a closed circuit between performer and audience with continuing interchange of information. . . . Essential to feedback is the notion that the flow of information is actually having a reciprocating effect on behavior. This is why the term *loop* is frequently associated with feedback. This circular pattern involves a flow of information to the point of action, a flow back to the point of decision with information on the action, and then a return to the

---

[15] Lonsdale, *op. cit.*, p. 172.

point of action with new information and perhaps instructions. A primary element in this process is the sensory organ, the instrument through which information is obtained.[16]

Systems, which do not have sensitive antennae picking up accurate feedback information, or—perhaps worse—which do not provide for the accurate transmission of feedback information to decision makers, find it difficult to react appropriately to environmental changes.

3. *Entropy.* This is described "as a measure of ignorance, disorder, disorganization, randomness, or chaos. . . . Thus, maximum entropy is zero organization, and zero entropy is maximum organization."[17] The degree of entropy in an organization, from the systems theory point of view, would be an indicator of the state of equilibrium existing between the organization and its external environment.

We have, then, in the social system view, an organization which is—by definition—an open system. This means, in part, not only that the organization has internal subsystems but that it is also part of a suprasystem. Moreover, the organization is in interactive relationship to this suprasystem: it exchanges inputs and outputs with it. And, to some extent, the organization affects its environment (the suprasystem) and is also affected by changes which occur in the suprasystem. It can resist and deny changes in the suprasystem or environment by ignoring or fighting them or by attempting to insulate itself from them. It can attempt to accommodate to environmental change by homeostatic adaptation—"business as usual." Or, finally, the organization can adapt to environmental changes by developing a new balance, a new equilibrium. In a world such as ours, dominated by rapid and extensive change, it would appear that the organization with poor feedback mechanisms or weak homeostatic characteristics will evidence an increasingly high level of entropy. Chapter 9, "Change in an Organizational Setting," deals with some of these concepts at greater length; the section in that chapter that deals with organizational health relates particularly to the insights being discussed here.

The emphasis of this book is on organizational behavior and, so, we shall now turn from consideration of organizations relating to their larger environments to human involvement in organizations. Even a superficial consideration of this problem area raises normative questions: What is the best kind of organizational behavior? How can the organiza-

---

[16] John M. Pfiffner and Frank P. Sherwood, *Administrative Organization* (Englewood Cliffs, N. J.: Prentice-Hall, Inc., 1960), p. 299.

[17] Lonsdale, *op. cit.,* p. 174.

tion foster the most effective organizational behavior? There have been two major approaches to such questions.

Normative Approaches to Interpersonal Relations in Organizations

Warren Bennis provides a succinct listing of the "human problems confronting contemporary organizations." It would be appropriate for us to consider them at this point.[18]

Problem 1: *Integration.* This is the problem of how to integrate individual needs and management goals. Conceptually, it brings us back to the idiographic-nomothetic dichotomy of Getzels and Guba. In a bureaucratic organization, Bennis argues, there is no solution to this problem because there is no problem. According to bureaucratic theory, the individual is vastly oversimplified, being either disregarded as a person or seen as an essentially passive instrument. Three significant "new twentieth-century conditions," as Bennis calls them, tend to underscore the importance of this problem:

a. The emergence of the human sciences, such as psychology and sociology, and their contribution to the understanding of man's complexity
b. Rising aspirations of individuals
c. The development of a humanistic-democratic ethos

Problem 2: *Social influence.* This deals with the problem of the distribution of power and the sources of power and authority. Bureaucratic solutions, Bennis states, are centered on legal-rational (largely coercive) power, ". . . a confused, ambiguous, shifting complex of competence, coercion, and legal code." Recent challenges to such solutions have emerged from the general increase in educational level, the development of unionism, and the unintended negative effects of authoritarian rule.

Problem 3: *Collaboration.* This is the problem of managing and resolving conflicts. Conventionally, bureaucracies have handled this problem by applying the "rule of hierarchy" to the resolution of problems between ranks and the "rule of coordination" to the resolution of conflict between horizontal groups. If all else fails, the bureaucracy has conventionally invoked loyalty to the organization as a means of inducing collaboration. Modern conditions, however, emphasize high levels of

---

[18] Bennis, *op. cit.*, pp. 190–91.

collaboration between specialists and professionals; this creates too complex a situation for bureaucratic concepts to be effective.

Problem 4: *Adaptation.* This is the problem of responding appropriately to changes induced by the environment of the organization. The concept of bureaucratic organization, Bennis suggests, envisioned a stable environment which was rather simple and predictable and organizational tasks which were rather routine. Adaptation was haphazard and resulted in frequent unanticipated consequences. Under present conditions, however, organizations are finding themselves in far more turbulent circumstances and are confronting an "unprecedented rate of technological change." Newer, more adaptive organizational forms are needed.

Problem 5: *Revitalization.* This is the problem of growth and decay of organizations, for which, according to Bennis, bureaucratic theory has no solutions to propose. The literature on bureaucratic theory, in fact, gives the impression that little provision has been made to deal with twentieth-century conditions such as "rapid changes in technologies, tasks, manpower, raw materials, norms and values of society . . .," all of which constantly make revitalization of the organization imperative.

If these are the problems, what are the likely solutions? Presentday efforts to find solutions are largely guided by insights that emerged from the breakthrough researches of the Western Electric studies, with which we associate Mayo, Roethlisberger, and Dickson and, also, the work of Lewin and his associates. Let us consider the work of Frederick W. Taylor and his associates as a basis for gaining some clearer insight into the significance of the "new" line of thought that research such as the men just mentioned have conducted. Here are Taylor's instructions to Schmidt, the pig-iron handler, as he retrained him to be more productive, in keeping with the principles of scientific management:

> [Y]ou will do exactly as this man [the foreman] tells you tomorrow, from morning to night. When he tells you to pick up a pig and walk, you pick it up and walk, and when he tells you to sit down and rest, you sit down. You do that straight through the day. And what's more, no back talk.[19]

The Western Electric studies paved the way for a behavioral theory which pictured radically different norms for interpersonal relations between superordinate and subordinate. Essentially, this theory proposed that the organization is a social system and that involvement is important to effective organizational behavior. Not only was this theory developed as a direct result of the Western Electric researches, but two specific,

---

[19] Taylor, *op. cit.,* p. 46.

significant programs were undertaken as well, which were pioneer efforts by which the theory was made operational:

1. A counseling program was developed for employees, structured in such a way that employees would be listened to with acceptance; they could express their concerns, communicate ideas, and "talk over their problems." However, there was no promise that management would necessarily take any action.
2. A training program—or, rather, a retraining program—was established to teach supervisors the new theory and help them develop the skills that were needed to implement this theory.

The counseling program was very much like that advocated by Rogers, although the two programs were independently developed. The concept, to use Rogers' term, was that of a "helping relationship" [20] in which the internal self—one's feelings, needs, and motivations—affect the establishment of more productive interpersonal relationships in the organization. Attempts to make behavior more effective are educative, rather than coercive, and emphasize (1) the intrinsic satisfaction that the participant gets from being involved in decision making responsibility and (2) the idea that, to develop maximum satisfaction, individual participation must be varied according to a number of factors, including personalities of the participants, their values, and specific factors in the particular work-situation.

Kurt Lewin and his associates have contributed another significant theory concerning interpersonal behavior in organizations which is generally the approach that is widely associated with "group dynamics." Briefly, Lewin posited that important determinants of behavior are (1) the characteristics of the individual, (2) the characteristics of the group, and (3) the cultural norms. Together, these determinants form a field of forces which—as in the classic three-part Venn diagram—overlap; it is within this field that the individual "behaves." According to this conceptualization, efforts to change behavior must recognize that if meaningful change in organizational behavior is to be accomplished the group and cultural norms must adapt to and be supportive of the individual in his changed behavior. To try to change the individual's organizational behavior without providing support from his group and the culture could put the individual in a conflict situation which might well hinder, rather than than develop, better interpersonal behavior and, thus, organizational effectiveness. In Chapter 5, research reported by Coch and French which supports this theory is discussed.

---

[20] Carl R. Rogers, "The Characteristics of a Helping Relationship," *Personnel and Guidance Journal*, XXXVII, No. 1 (September, 1958), 6–16.

Summary

In this chapter selected theories which are currently being found useful for viewing organizational behavior were discussed. Interrelating these theories provides a more comprehensive way of viewing organizational behavior than any one theory would afford. Aspects of social system theory and role theory—which are among the foremost theories dealing with organizational behavior—were stressed and interrelated. The chapter has emphasized the historical trend toward the ". . . democratic-humanitarian values exemplified by McGregor's Theory Y." [21] The development of the social systems view of organizational behavior—beginning with Mayo and Roethlisberger's Western Electric researches in the 1930's and continuing through the work of Getzels in the late 1950's—has underscored the intimate interrelationship between the individual person and the organization and has pointed up the importance of role in the organization. And Lewin's stress on the importance of the individual's participation in decisions which affect him has aided the development of a concept with which names such as Argyris, McGregor, Maslow, and Herzberg are associated. Essentially, this concept is that organizational behavior is strongly affected by social influence and the need for the individual to control *himself*. Thus, the trend is not only away from the arbitrary, coercive, autocratic exercise of power, but toward more effective personal involvement—as reflected in organizational behavior.

Having set the stage in terms of the historical development of theory and concept, we shall, in the following chapters, deal more specifically with some of the functional areas of organizational behavior in schools.

---

[21] Bennis, *op. cit.*, p. 197.

⚜ 5 ⚜

decision making

The task of "deciding" pervades the entire administrative organization quite as much as the task of "doing" . . . a general theory of administration must include principles of organization that will insure correct decision-making, just as it must include principles that will insure effective action.

—Herbert A. Simon [1]

Generally speaking, administration has been interpreted in terms of tasks to be performed; administrator behavior has been seen in the light of *functions* that are essential to the performance of the tasks. For example, Fayol identified the "elements of management" as planning, organizing, commanding, coordinating, and controlling.[2] There have been numerous other efforts to discover the basic action components of administration. For example, Gulick produced a famous catalog of components based upon his study of the United States Presidency: planning, organizing, staffing, directing, co-ordinating, reporting, and budgeting.[3] (For many years students of public administration memorized this list by using the mnemonic POSDCoRB.) These efforts at analysis—and other lesser ones—were made chiefly by scholars concerned with business

---

[1] Herbert A. Simon, *Administrative Behavior*, 2nd ed. (New York: The Macmillan Company, © 1961), p. 1.

[2] Henri Fayol, "Elements of Management," in *General and Industrial Management*, trans. Constance Storrs (London: Sir Isaac Pitman & Sons, Ltd., 1949), Chap. 5.

[3] Luther Gulick and L. Urwick, eds., *Papers on the Science of Administration* (New York: Institute of Public Administration, 1937).

administration and public administration. Educational administration encouraged almost no scholarship in these fields for at least the first half of this century. However, by 1950 Jesse Sears had adapted Fayol's and Gulick's ideas to education by suggesting that administrative activity was comprised of planning, organization, direction, coordination, and control.[4]

By 1955 the American Association of School Administrators enumerated the following as the significant activities for administrators: planning, allocation, stimulation, coordination, and evaluation.[5] But, of course, by that late date students of behavioral sciences who were concerned with business administration and public administration were already exploring a fresh, newly discovered, and powerful element of administrative behavior: decision making.

Administration as Decision Making

Contemporary thinking about the nature of administration, both within and out of education, places decision making in a central position. It may be that decision making is the core process of administration to which all other activities can be subordinated. Or, it may be that administration and decision making are synonymous. However, a more generally accepted notion is that decision making is *the* key function or activity of administrators. Litchfield, for example, sees administration as a cycle of activities which begins and ends with decision making: (1) decision making, (2) programming, (3) communicating, (4) controlling, and (5) reappraising. This cycle which, for Litchfield,[6] comprises the "administrative process," involves the administrator not only in the making of decisions, but in the establishing of arrangements to implement these decisions (programming), to keep the organization informed (communicating), to adhere to the plans decided upon (controlling), and to evaluate results (reappraising). Presumably, a new cycle of administrative process will flow from a reappraisal.

The focus on decision making as a vital element of administration has produced a large body of literature, including scholarly speculation and research. Much of the literature focuses, of course, on the problem of making better decisions—better in that decisions should be more rational

---

[4] Jesse B. Sears, *The Nature of the Administrative Process* (New York: McGraw-Hill Book Company, 1950).

[5] American Association of School Administrators, *Staff Relations in School Administration* (Washington, D. C.: The Association, 1955), Chap. 1.

[6] Edward H. Litchfield, "Notes on a General Theory of Administration," *Administrative Science Quarterly* I, No. 1 (June, 1956), 3–29.

and more creative. Herbert A. Simon's book *Administrative Behavior* [7] is credited with having ". . . opened a whole new vista of administration theory" [8] when it appeared in 1945. Subtitled *A Study of Decision-Making Processes in Administrative Organization,* this book spelled out a number of concepts which are presently having significant impact on thinking in educational administration: its practice, its research, and its teaching. One of these concepts concerns the division of labor and specialization.

Simon pointed out that, traditionally, the emphasis on specialization is horizontal in an organization. In a school, for example, faculty members are generally considered to be equals although all of them are actually specialists: French teachers, math teachers, guidance counselors, elementary classroom teachers, and so on. But, as Simon pointed out, there is another division of labor: *vertical* specialization. This type of specialization focuses on decision making behavior. All people in an organization make decisions, but they specialize in (1) the kinds of decisions they make and (2) the amount of time devoted to decision making. Teachers, for example, make crucial decisions which actually determine to a large extent the impact the school will have on the learner. The principal, however, is responsible for little or no teaching, and he makes few decisions of the type required of a teacher. Yet the principal is in a position in the organizational hierarchy which demands that more of his time be spent on decision making, although of a different kind.

"With general policy making concentrated at the top, policy specification carried out at the middle ranks, and actual work performance carried out at the lower ranks," [9] the organization becomes an efficient tool for the making and implementation of decisions. The organization requires that the individual yield some of his individual decision making autonomy, and it decides for him what the nature and limits of his duties are and how much power and authority he shall have over others. Simon gives three reasons for this kind of vertical specialization in the organization:

First, if there is any horizontal specialization, vertical specialization is absolutely essential to achieve coordination among the operative employees.

Second, just as horizontal specialization permits greater skill and expertise to be developed by the operative group in the performance of their tasks, so vertical specialization permits the greater expertise in the making of decisions.

---

[7] Simon, *op. cit.*

[8] Amitai Etzioni, *Modern Organizations* (Englewood Cliffs, N. J.: Prentice-Hall, Inc., © 1964), p. 30.

[9] *Ibid.*

Third, vertical specialization permits the operative personnel to be held accountable for their decisions. . . .[10]

Decision Making in Educational Administration

Nothing that the behavioral sciences had to offer caught the imagination of the pioneers of the "new" educational administration of the 1950's more than the literature on decision making. Although school administrators have always been expected to "be decisive" and to make reasonably adequate decisions, little attention had been devoted to systematic study and teaching in this area. In recent years, however, some research and considerable discussion of decision making has appeared in the literature; increased attention is also being devoted to decision making in university courses in educational administration.

The best-known research work in this field among school principals is often called the Whitman School study.[11] In terms of method alone, this study is fascinating to most school administrators. The researchers were basically interested in finding out whether a systematic relationship existed between certain personality characteristics of principals and the way they performed their jobs. Although no clear-cut relationship was found to exist, the study made two major contributions of long-term significance to the practitioner: (1) it introduced the American school administrator to *simulation* as an in-service training technique and (2) it gave him a valuable beginning (if not actual cause-and-effect relationships) for understanding some of his own role behavior. The power of this research in stimulating more research and study at the university level has been very great and is still being felt.

The Whitman School study derives its title from the school in Jefferson Township, in the state of Lafayette, where researchers devised a simulation in which participants took the role of Marion Smith, principal of the school. Of course, as is usually true in simulation, the Whitman School was patterned after an existing school and events that occurred were drawn from actual events. To enhance the plausibility of the simulated situation, "Marion Smith" was provided with motion pictures, documents, background readings, and other materials which gave him (or

---

[10] Simon, *op. cit.*, p. 9.

[11] For a description of this study see John K. Hemphill, Daniel E. Griffiths, and Norman Frederiksen, *Administrative Performance and Personality* (New York: Teachers College Press, 1962). For an excellent twenty-page digest of the highlights of the study and its findings, see John K. Hemphill, "Personal Variables and Administrative Styles," in Daniel E. Griffiths, ed., *Behavioral Science and Educational Administration*, The Sixty-third Yearbook of the National Society for the Study of Education, Part II (Chicago: The University of Chicago Press, 1964), pp. 142–77.

her) considerable information about the school, its faculty and the community. In the original experiment, 232 "Marion Smiths" sat at the simulation of a principal's desk in Whitman School, receiving mail and other inputs in the "in-basket" and reacting to them. All reactions were put in writing so that the researchers were able to analyze the performance of each principal and relate it to some of his personal characteristics and to the actual perceptions that people had of him as a principal in his real, "home" school.

Essentially, the "Marion Smiths" who participated as "principals" of the simulated Whitman School were most clearly differentiated by two factors:

1. *Factor X*, the preparation that they put into the making of a decision
2. *Factor Y*, the amount of work done in a fixed period of time

In general, principals in this study who are rated highly effective by both superiors and teachers devote much time to preparing for decision making. They seek more information, they seek clarification, and they obtain opinions of others. It would appear from this research that principals at the other end of the spectrum who make quick "yes" or "no" decisions without much (if any) preparation, tend to be regarded less favorably in their professional role. Of course, there is a continuum between these extremes which includes those who exhibit more moderated behavior.

From the Whitman School research data, eight "administrative styles" were identified:

1. *High communication style.* Principals characterized by this style of work stressed communicating with others about the problems they encountered in their work.
2. *High discussion style.* Principals characterized by this style placed unusually high emphasis upon the use of face-to-face discussion in administration.
3. *High compliance style.* This style characterizes principals who generally followed suggestions made by others.
4. *High analysis style.* Principals who were high with respect to this style spent relatively more effort than others in analyzing the situation surrounding each administrative problem.
5. *High relationships style.* This style refers to a high concern with maintaining organizational relationships, especially relationships with superiors.
6. *High work-organization style.* This refers to the principal's emphasis upon scheduling and organizing his own work.
7. *High outside-orientation style.* Principals high on this style of admin-

istrative performance displayed greater readiness than others to responding to pressures from outside the school.
8. *High work-direction style*. Principals who followed this style tended
   to stress giving directions to others as an important part of their
   work.[12]

The researchers in this study concluded that the principal who is seen
as effective by his superiors and his teachers will tend to emphasize frequent and full communication and will devote careful attention to his
relationships to others in the organization. Such a principal will probably
be sociable, relaxed, sensitive, confident, and will have considerable verbal
fluency.[13]

The RAND air defense simulation experiments of 1952–1954 [14] were
basically different from the Whitman School study. One essential difference was that the RAND experiments, which dealt with the early warn-
ing system of radar surveillance that protected this country from enemy
air attack, was a "man-machine" simulation. This means, essentially, that
the simulated environment in which the situation was set included a large
amount of material stored in a computer. Although such a simulation is
complicated to devise, it can provide some reaction, or feedback, to the
participants, giving them clues as to how their decisions affect the simulated environment. This heightens the plausibility of the simulation for,
as every administrator knows, every action that one decides to take
changes a situation somewhat and subsequently presents one with a new
array of choices. However, an unforeseen and unexpected discovery that
emerged from both the RAND air defense and Whitman School experiments was that the simulation exercises were excellent training devices.
After the initial experiments were over, the RAND Air Defense Simulation was used hundreds of times by the Air Force to train and retrain
the crews of its air defense direction centers. Similarly, after the original
research data had been gleaned from the 232 experimental subjects, the
Whitman School simulation was used to train literally thousands of
people. It has been used at conventions, in summer seminars, in university
courses, and in countless other situations. Indeed, interest in the use of
these materials for training purposes has been so great that revised simulation materials were published in 1967 which deal with problems of the
"Madison Schools" in the state of Lafayette and provide simulated
problems for the positions of elementary school principal, high school

---

[12] Hemphill, *ibid.*, pp. 197–98.
[13] *Ibid.*, pp. 192–93.
[14] R. L. Chapman, J. L. Kennedy, A. Newell, and W. C. Biel, "The Systems
Research Laboratory's Air Defense Experiments," *Management Science*, V (1959),
250–69.

principal, assistant superintendent for business management, assistant superintendent for instructional service, and superintendent.[15]

Thus, a research technique for the *study* of decision making behavior—simulation—is being exploited as a *training technique* to develop more effective decision making skills. For example, one set of simulation exercises is designed expressly for training members of school boards to be more effective in decision making.[16] Simulation exercises are also available for training both school board members and administrators in the processes of collective negotiation.[17] Alexander *et al.* have developed a technique for producing simulation exercises specifically to meet the requirements of local school districts in training administrators; they have demonstrated the application of this technique to elementary school principals in a large city.[18] In the world of business, a man-machine simulation called the Carnegie Tech Management Game has been designed expressly for the training of business managers in the making of decisions.[19] When they are used as training devices, rather than data-gathering research tools, simulations are often thought to be analogous to the famed Link trainer which is used to train aircraft pilots. The use of artificial settings such as simulation, in-baskets, and gaming seems to be as promising for training in educational decision making as it is for research. Because of recent technological developments educators hope that, by employing computers and other man-machine techniques, simulations will soon be devised with more reactive environments which will be useful in improving the decision making of school administrators in nonthreatening environments.

Practical Problems in Educational Decision Making

Decision making, of course, involves the selection of a course of action from among available alternatives. One can impulsively take the first

---

[15] For information regarding the availability of these and other related materials, write the University Council for Educational Administration, 29 West Woodruff Avenue, Columbus, Ohio 43210.

[16] Robert G. Owens, *A Regular Meeting of the Board* (Albany, N. Y.: State Education Department, 1968).

[17] John J. Horvat, *Professional Negotiations in Education: A Bargaining Game with Supplementary Materials* (Columbus: O.: Charles E. Merrill Books, Inc., 1968).

[18] Lawrence T. Alexander, Steven Lockwood, Robert G. Owens, and Carl Steinhoff, *A Demonstration of the Use of Simulation in the Training of School Administrators* (New York: Office of Research and Evaluation, Division of Teacher Education, City University of New York, 1967).

[19] K. J. Cohen, W. R. Dill, A. A. Kuehn, and P. R. Winters, *The Carnegie Tech Management Game: An Experiment in Business Education* (Homewood, Ill.: Richard D. Irwin, Inc., 1964).

course of action that appears, or one can endlessly consider every possible alternative and thus never make a decision at all. Naturally, it is desirable to seek a balance that will be effective in a given situation; this has been the subject of considerable speculation and study. Some of the most frequently noted factors that relate to this balance will now be considered.

FACTS AND VALUES

There seems to be little disagreement that facts are—or ought to be—important in decision making. The role of values, however, has been subject to conjecture and debate. At a time when people are wary about having certain values foisted on them against their will or without their consent, many administrators shrink from the exercise of value judgments in making decisions. The truth is, of course—and Simon stated it with classic clarity [20]—that facts and values are inextricably intertwined in the choosing from alternative courses of action. Some element of what "ought to be done" is always present.

Of course, values are embodied to some extent in laws, traditions, customs, school board policies, and other guides to public acceptance of what ought to be. Laws, policies, and customs change, of course, and the administrator bears responsibility for being sensitive to these changes. Ethical questions are apt to crop up when the administrator (or the school as a decision making organization) begins to substitute personal values in decision making for those values held by the community, the latter of which ought to establish the objectives of the school.

A common example of substitution, frequently reported in the press in recent years, has been concerned with the dress and general physical appearance of public school students. Court decisions have never been very specific about the power of schools to control the dress and appearance of students [21]; much has been left to the discretion of the principal. However, with trends toward longer hair and casual dress for boys and short skirts for girls, trends which picked up popular support in the late 1950's and into the 1960's, many a principal found that he had observed facts correctly but had been less sensitive to the emphasis that society was placing on nonconformity and the right to peacefully express individuality.

JUDGMENT

The exercise of judgment in making decisions hinges not only on a sensitive interpretation of values, but also on the nature of "facts." In his

---

[20] Simon, *op. cit.*, Chap. 3.
[21] Newton Edwards, *The Courts and the Public Schools* (Chicago: The University of Chicago Press, 1951), pp. 530–36.

professional world the administrator is almost never in possession of all the facts. From his vantage point he can at best view only portions of whatever is happening; he receives fragments of information which must be evaluated and pieced together. He is never sure that what he *does* have by way of facts is accurate because his own value judgments may well affect his *perception* of what really is. We may attempt to improve our understanding of facts by using the following definition of a fact: "a statement about a condition, object, or event that would be accepted as accurate by two or more observers." [22] Unfortunately for the administrator today, however, the accuracy rendered by such "triangulation" depends upon the perceptions of the observers on whom he depends. In the present social situation, with schools thrust firmly into the rough-and-tumble of racial unrest, teacher militancy, and other emotionally charged turmoil, it is difficult to feel assured that one's judgment of facts and values is reasonably accurate. The resignation of Washington, D. C.'s Superintendent of Education, after nine years in office, underscores the problem.

In 1958, Dr. Carl F. Hansen introduced the famous "track system" in Washington's schools, a system which was heartily endorsed by civil rights advocates because it was "color blind." By 1967, however, Hansen's judgment that the track system was still the best way to obtain quality public education in a school district with a 93 per cent Negro population was successfully attacked as "a symbol of a past era," [23] and was overturned by a United States Court of Appeals and—in effect—the District of Columbia Board of Education. It now appeared that the community felt that "if poor Negroes were to have equal educational opportunities, they must, in effect, be given special treatment to overcome their social and economic handicaps. . . ." [24] The value system—what *ought* to be —had changed considerably and on this basis, rather than "facts," new decisions were made.

INFORMATION FLOW

If one makes a decision upon the receipt of some kind of communication, then decision making involves "a complicated process of combining communications from various sources, and it results in the transmission of further communication." [25] It is evident, then, that the administrator

---

[22] Jack A. Culbertson, Paul B. Jacobson, and Theodore L. Reller, *Administrative Relationships: A Casebook* (Englewood Cliffs, N. J.: Prentice-Hall, Inc., © 1960), p. 462.

[23] *The New York Times* (July 9, 1967), Sec. 4, p. 9. © 1967 by the New York Times Company. Reprinted by permission.

[24] *Ibid.*

[25] John T. Dorsey, Jr., "A Communication Model for Administration," *Administrative Science Quarterly*, II, No. 3 (December, 1957), 309.

has more than a casual interest in the flow of information throughout the organization. The amount of information available to a decision making group such as a school's faculty has been shown to affect the quality of decisions that the group makes.[26]

It is important that we stress exactly what we mean when we speak of information being available to a group; for we must bear in mind that the quality of the group's decisions depends to a great extent on *who* has the information. The likelihood that useful decision making information will reach the decision makers and be believed, accepted, and respected depends to a great extent on the status that the holder of the information has with the group. In one study, for example—and this has been a very active area for research—poor suggestions by aircraft pilots were more readily accepted by a group of flight crew personnel than were good suggestions by gunners.[27] The group member who has low influence, whether because of his official status or his informal position in the group, may not be able to make the group believe and accept his information. However, the more the information is generally known by members of the group, the greater the chance that it will be accepted and acted upon.

In practical terms, the administrator is concerned with facilitating the free flow of information up, down, and laterally within the organization. Researchers refer to communication networks, or nets, in the organization. An understanding of the nature of such nets, what their patterns are, and how they work can be useful in improving the decision making performance of the school. Although official, legal channels of communication are absolutely vital to the school—particularly in defining legal boundaries and expressing chain-of-command orders—the extralegal communications channels of the informal organization are also vital. For example, even though the administrator occupies high official status in the school, it is likely that—on occasion—he will not have the information that the group needs to make a decision or, if he does, he will not be able to communicate this information effectively to the decision making group.

Much of the flow of information in the school occurs in informal settings—during kaffee klatsches and within friendship groups and cliques. Formal organization charts depict the channels through which information "should" flow. And, in the same way, informal communication nets are more readily understandable if they are diagrammed; such a dia-

---

26 Marvin E. Shaw and William T. Penrod, Jr., "Does More Information Available to a Group Always Improve Group Performance?" *Sociometry*, XXV, No. 4 (December, 1962), 377–90.

27 E. Paul Torrance, "Some Consequences of Power Differences on Decision Making in Permanent and Temporary Three-Man Groups," in A. Paul Hare, Edgar F. Borgatta, and Robert F. Bales, eds., *Small Groups* (New York: Alfred A. Knopf, Inc., 1955).

gram for a school faculty usually resembles a sociogram. Typical findings show that (1) communications nets center around certain "key" people; (2) there are people who are members of more than one net and serve to link nets together; (3) some people are members of only one net and therefore are out of communication with people not in that net; and (4) the membership and pattern of the nets will shift according to what is being communicated. The administrator who wants to send and receive as much information as possible will be interested in identifying and retaining a role in the informal communications networks in the school. However, he should not be surprised at the reluctance of subordinates to be open, candid, and free in communicating with him.

In a study of some causes of ineffectiveness of the United States Department of State, Argyris found that competent, hardworking Foreign Service officers expressed the need to be careful, indirect, and withdrawing; it seemed important "not to make waves." [28] The result of this behavior was that officers withheld information from superiors in the organization, as well as insights and feelings that could have made decisions in "Foggy Bottom" more effective. Even in situations where key people had information which enabled them to predict unhappy consequences of a decision made above them in the hierarchy, Foreign Service officers often felt it was too risky for them, personally, to speak up.

It would appear that in a school, as in the Department of State, the free flow of useful decision making information depends more on interpersonal relationships between people in informal communication nets than the formal structure of the organization would indicate. This is consonant with the findings of numerous behavioral scientists who, working with corporate executives in attacking the decision making problems of business and industrial organizations, stress as principles for improving decision making interpersonal factors such as:

1. *Genuineness,* or authenticity, which involves accepting others without threat and being receptive to their ideas and beliefs
2. *Descriptive nonevaluative feedback,* a process by which one tells others what effect he perceives a behavioral act is having on the group, without expressing a value judgment of that behavior
3. Increased *sensitivity* by the executive to the effect that his own behavior has on the other people in the group
4. *An unemotional, rational response* to and acceptance of the emotions of others in the group [29]

---

[28] Chris Argyris, *Some Causes of Organizational Ineffectiveness within the Department of State* (Washington, D. C.: Department of State, 1967).

[29] For a detailed account of one attempt to apply principles such as these in a large business firm, see Chris Argyris, *Interpersonal Competence and Organizational Effectiveness* (Homewood, Ill.: Richard D. Irwin, Inc., 1962).

The effect of principles of interpersonal behavior such as those suggested above is to encourage the development of an emotionally free, nonthreatening atmosphere in the organization where information will flow freely and the threat of power struggles and interpersonal conflicts will be reduced, promoting more effective decision making in the organization.

SEARCH BEHAVIOR

An organization does not search endlessly and relentlessly for better ways of achieving its goals, but normally utilizes its decision making procedures to find rational alternatives for achieving goals only when the organization's performance seems to be falling below an acceptable level. It is unrealistic to expect an organization to continue to sift alternative courses of action until it achieves near-perfect rationality between its behavior and its goals or objectives. Rather than strive for an optimum solution or decision, an organization will tend to accept a satisfying solution, one that is good enough to fit the organization's perception of reality and values.[30] When a reasonably intelligent course of action is decided upon, the organization can be expected to accept it even though it may not be completely rational. Until the decision is seen by the organization to be no longer adequately satisfying, the search for another course of action to follow will not be renewed.

The complicated pattern of values, perceptions, feelings, and belief systems which underlies an organization's feelings of satisfaction with a decision is not easy to describe, especially when—as with the school—problems can appropriately be described as "ill-structured." Unfortunately for the school administrator, few of the important problems faced by his organization meet the three criteria of a well-structured problem:

1. It can be described in terms of numerical variables—scalar and vector quantities.
2. The goals to be attained can be specified in terms of a well-defined objective function—for example, the maximization of profit or the minimization of cost.
3. There exist computational routines (*algorithms*) that permit the solution to be found and stated in actual numerical terms.[31]

The significant problems in educational administration are not only ill-structured, but tend to be emergent in nature as well, that is, the orga-

---

[30] James G. March and Herbert A. Simon, *Organizations* (New York: John Wiley & Sons, Inc., 1958).

[31] Herbert A. Simon and A. Newell, "Heuristic Problem Solving: The Next Advance in Operations Research," *Operations Research*, VI (1958), 4–5.

nization is rarely confronted with a complete problem at any given moment; the administrator is not often in full possession of the facts regarding the organization's problems. Rather, these problems are dynamic—they usually involve complex issues which are related in unseen ways, and their dimensions tend to unfold over time. Let us thus remember that schools deal largely with ill-structured emergent problems, a fact which has significant implications for the search behavior pattern of these organizations and the feelings of satisfaction that they derive from decisions that they have made.

Decision Making in the Professionally Staffed Organization

Organizations which are staffed with professional personnel engage in somewhat different decision making processes than organizations which have nonprofessional staffs. As a result, we must be careful when we attempt to describe behavior observed in one type of organization in the same way as that observed in another. For example, we must bear in mind dissimilarities in staffing when we compare findings from studies of business or the military to the public school situation. Basically, these differences are dimensions of the extent to which the staff are involved in the decision making processes and the closeness with which the staff members are supervised to insure precise execution of the decision.

An army is popularly regarded as a nonprofessionlly staffed organization wherein the individual soldier plays little or no role in decision making. Typically, an army is seen as an organization in which decisions are made in the hierarchy and then handed down to be followed closely by the soldier. Critical decisions, frequently involving even matters such as whether a soldier should fire his weapon and if so, precisely where, are commonly not the individual soldier's prerogative. Such decisions are made for the soldier and communicated to him; his subsequent execution of these decisions is closely supervised.

And, at the other end of the spectrum, the hospital is an illustration of a professionally staffed organization. The most crucial decisions in a hospital are made *and actually carried out* by the same persons—the physicians themselves, acting in a relatively free and responsible capacity as professionals. Supervision over physicians, although very real, is rather general in recognition of the professional prerogative of doctors to elect certain available alternatives and forego others. The hospital is an interesting place for students of organizational decision making in another sense as well—it includes participants who are considered to be semiprofessional and nonprofessional. The handling of decision making as it involves nurses,

nurses' aides, orderlies, cleaning women, and other groups in the hospital organization, coupled with the kind of supervision these groups receive, tends to underscore the differences in the way that organizations with professional staffs handle decision making as compared to nonprofessionally staffed organizations. In short, the influence of administrative authority is stronger in decision making in nonprofessional organizations than it is in professional organizations.

Is a school a professional organization or a nonprofessional organization? A clear-cut answer to this question would enable one to make some useful generalizations about how to obtain better decisions in the school situation. Unfortunately, there is no clear-cut general answer, for, in the first place, much depends upon how one defines professional status, and there is far from universal agreement on any definition. Second, much depends upon one's *perception* of the activities that teachers engage in. For example, if one's definition of professionalism includes *applying* knowledge and if one considers elementary school teaching to be the *communication* of knowledge, one may conclude that the elementary school is not staffed by professionals. Many elementary school teachers, however, would insist that their professional work consists basically of applying specialized knowledge of the process of child growth and development and the psychology of learning—thus qualifying them as "professionals." This particular question is quite relevant to administrative decision making because it involves a very urgent issue in our schools today.

In a nonprofessionally staffed organization, the administrative hierarchy dominates the making and execution of crucial decisions, and close supervision is necessary to assure precise implementation of these decisions. In a professional organization, there are two types of authority: the central one is based on professional qualifications and a secondary one includes nonprofessional supporting services (administrative, clerical, custodial, maintenance, etc.). In the professional organization only supporting services can be organized into a bureaucratic hierarchy in which administrative authority dominates the decision making processes. However, as one might expect, there are other types of organizations which can be described as semiprofessional; the elementary school is a good example. In such an organization, workers have more autonomy than, say, factory workers, but they still do not have full-fledged professional autonomy (see Figure 5–1). Etzioni claims that the people staffing such organizations, including schools,

have skills and personality traits more compatible with administration, especially since the qualities required for communication of knowledge are more like those needed for administration than those required for the

DECISION MAKING DIMENSION

High participation ——————⟶ Some participation ——————⟶ Little participation

Professionally staffed organizations	Semiprofessionally staffed organizations	Nonprofessionally staffed organizations
Hospitals University faculties Service research organizations	Public schools Social work agencies Professional research organizations	Factories Businesses Military organizations

General (collegial) ——————⟶ Fairly close (hierarchical) ——⟶ Close (markedly hierarchical)

SUPERVISION DIMENSION

FIGURE 5-1. The extent of participation in decision making and the nature of supervision in three types of organizations.

creation and, to a degree, application of knowledge. Hence these organizations are run much more frequently by the semiprofessionals themselves than by others.[32]

Today the goals of the schools are becoming more numerous and more complex. The traditional role of the principal as the master teacher, competent enough to supervise knowledgeably all phases of instruction and curriculum, seems untenable; a new role is emerging.[33] Teachers are increasingly demanding greater professional autonomy and authority in the making of decisions regarding instruction and curriculum and freedom from bureaucratic domination. In this context, it could be useful for the school administrator to review and clarify his own understanding of the kind of organization he belongs to and to spell out the strategy by which the best decisions may be made in his own school.

To a great extent, the administrator's approach to developing decision making processes in the school will depend on (1) the value judgments he holds with regard to the participation of others besides himself in shaping the school's decisions and (2) the skill with which he organizes this participation into a decision making process within the school. We know that the administrator can influence the school to move toward

---

[32] Etzioni, op. cit., p. 87.
[33] For one discussion of this, see James M. Lipham, "The Role of the Principal," The National Elementary Principal, XLIV, No. 5 (April, 1965), 28-33.

professional status or away from it, depending upon the skill and energy with which he encourages meaningful participation of teachers in the decision making process.

In summary, it seems clear that the role of an organization's participants in the decision making processes of the organization is related to the extent to which the participants are perceived as members of a professional staff. It is equally clear that there is far from universal agreement as to whether school teachers may be properly considered to be professionals. There is, therefore, a great deal of confusion over the extent to which teachers "ought"—as autonomous professional persons—to participate with administrators in the central decision making processes of the school. Moreover, there is another, more compelling, reason for encouraging shared decision making processes in schools and all kinds of organizations: the hope that better decisions will be the result. We shall now turn to a discussion of two vital questions:

1. Does shared decision making produce better decisions in an organization?
2. What are some effective ways of organizing the processes of shared decision making in a school?

Shared Decision Making in the School

We have seen that one of the administrator's major activities is decision making, for example, as included by Campbell and his colleagues in their list of five steps in *the administrative process:* (1) decision making, (2) programming, (3) stimulating, (4) coordinating, and (5) appraising.[34] Decision making—the search for rational alternatives of action—may be thought of as either the decision making of an individual, as Griffiths emphasizes,[35] or as an essential activity of the organization. The present author stresses the latter connotation, with particular consideration of the role of the administrator as an effective participant in the activity, because a school is not a nonprofessionally staffed organization and, therefore, its staff will expect to be effectively involved in the professional questions which affect them. Perhaps more important, the school organization is viewed here as a decision making tool which probably does not engage in any more significant activity than choosing from among the educational alternatives within its jurisdiction.

---

[34] Roald F. Campbell, John E. Corbally, Jr., and John A. Ramseyer, *Introduction to Educational Administration,* 3rd ed. (Boston: Allyn & Bacon, Inc., 1966), pp. 144–45.

[35] Daniel E. Griffiths, *Administrative Theory* (New York: Appleton-Century-Crofts, 1959), Chap. 4.

In practice, the boundary line between leadership and the administrator's role in organizational decision making is not as clear-cut as it might be in theory. For many years school administrators have been urged to be "democratic" leaders; this has frequently been expressed as a value judgment—the school "ought" to be democratically run. Not infrequently, the reasons advanced for urging "democratic" leadership on the principal have centered about the fostering of stronger subordination of teachers. To facilitate higher morale is sometimes given as a reason for giving teachers "the privilege of contributing their ideas to the formation of general policy structure of the school's operation." [36] Aware that they "ought" to involve teachers in the school's decision making, principals are often concerned that the teachers will end up "running the school." They are also concerned about knowing *when* to involve teachers (on what problems? at which point?) and *how* to involve them (do teachers *advise* or do they *decide?*).

A typical illustration of this confusion may be drawn from the recent experience of a New England elementary school which we will call Shady Lawn School. For many years, each of the fifteen elementary schools in the school district had enjoyed autonomy in the selection of textbooks. The principal of Shady Lawn School, in turn, had allowed his teachers great latitude in selecting their textbooks; in reading, for example, several different publishers' basal texts were in use in various Shady Lawn classes, based on the discretion of individual teachers. The advent of "busing," however, with its concomitant shifting of groups of pupils from school to school, caused a swift policy change in the district. The superintendent quickly endorsed a curriculum committee recommendation that each elementary school be required to adopt a single basal reading text. After reporting this decision to his faculty, the principal of Shady Lawn School then asked his teachers to select one reading series they wished to adopt. The faculty studied the problem for a full school year and ultimately voted to adopt a compromise: one series for grades 1 through 3 and a different series for grades 4 through 6. The following fall, the principal explained that such a decision by the faculty was unacceptable because a *single* adoption was required. The reaction of the teachers was swift and bitter; they had made a professional decision and they were not going to change it to conform to the thinking of the principal or any other administrator. This was, they said, a professional matter that had been democratically decided and for the teachers to submit would reveal what a farce their "democratic" participation had been in the making of the decision at Shady Lawn. With reluctance, the staff was persuaded to

---

[36] Paul J. Misner, Frederick W. Schneider, and Lowell G. Keith, *Elementary School Administration* (Columbus, O.: Charles E. Merrill Books, 1963), p. 370.

consider the problem for a second year of study; however, the second year produced only further wrangling and disillusionment which finally resulted in a vote to reaffirm the decision of the previous year. With the teachers adamant, the principal unwilling to "dictate," and the school district policy unfulfilled, the situation was at a stalemate. After an administrative reshuffle, a new principal took control at Shady Lawn School, only to learn that it would take much time before the sullen, divided, and suspicious group of teachers would ever listen to talk about "democratic participation" again.

Situations like the one described above are constantly encountered in various guises by school administrators. In order to make practical, workable suggestions which can be utilized in improving the decision making processes in schools, we will emphasize only five generalizations drawn from the vast research literature on organizational decision making:

1. *Effective participation by teachers in meaningful organizational decisions does "pay off."*
2. *Teachers do not want to be involved in every decision, nor do they expect to be.*
3. *An important task of the principal is to distinguish between the decisions in which teachers should be involved and those which should be handled in other ways.*
4. *The roles and functions of teachers in decision making can be varied according to the nature of the problem.*
5. *The points in the decision making process at which teachers are involved can be varied according to the nature of the problem.*

We will discuss these generalizations as they apply to schools and then incorporate them into a pattern which principals can modify for their own use to "flow-chart" the decision making process in their schools.

Research on Shared Decision Making

A great deal of research on democratic leadership and participation in decision making was triggered by management's feeling that employees were *resisting* change and improvement. This was the problem when Coch and French did their famed series of experiments in the Harwood Manufacturing Corporation plant.[37] Harwood manufactured pajamas and was considered to be one of the more enlightened firms in its industry;

---

[37] L. Coch and J. R. P. French, Jr., "Overcoming Resistance to Change," in G. E. Swanson, T. M. Newcomb, and E. L. Hartley, eds., *Readings in Social Psychology* (New York: Holt, Rinehart & Winston, Inc., 1952), pp. 474–90.

it provided background music, good working conditions, recreation programs, and other fringe benefits for its employees in order to foster good labor relations. However, as the company introduced new methods and technological developments in an effort to control production costs and remain competitive in their market, they encountered some problems. Suspecting that pressure from workgroups in the informal organization intended to resist change in work habits and job patterns, the experimenters kept data on three carefully matched groups of workers:

1. The first group received only a short, routine announcement that there would be some change on the job.
2. The second group was told that a change was coming, why it was necessary, what it would be like, and, further, this group was then asked to pick some representatives to help develop a retraining program.
3. The third group was treated much the same as the second group except that *everybody* helped plan the new jobs themselves, as well as develop the retraining program.

When the new system was introduced, production of group 1 fell, whereas production of groups 2 and 3 rose (with group 3 production not much greater than that of group 2). In addition, absenteeism, employee turnover, and number of grievances increased in group 1 but were virtually absent in the other two groups. The next experimental step was taken about two and one half months later—a time lapse which makes this particular research quite valid. Then the first group was required to change jobs again, but they used the participation pattern originally developed for group 3. The favorable reaction originally observed for group 3 was evidenced for this group of workers; since the only known variable was the extent and nature of the part the workers played in deciding what happened to them, it follows that the *way* decisions are made in an organization can have significant impact on the results of these decisions.

However, the foregoing occurred in a factory—a setting hardly comparable to a school. Therefore, how can we be sure that the findings of such research can indeed be applied to a school? There are two answers:

1. A pajama factory, such as the Harwood Manufacturing Corporation, is a nonprofessionally staffed organization. The workers do not expect to participate to a great extent in decision making, yet the participation that was allowed seems to have produced markedly positive effects. In a school, which is staffed by at least semiprofessionals, the expectation of autonomy is greater.
2. This research corroborates and "fits in" with the findings of many

other studies and surveys which have been conducted in all kinds of organizations, including schools.[38] In fact, research on the participation of teachers in decision making suggests that the extent and nature of participation affects (a) the satisfaction gained from teaching as a profession, (b) the enthusiasm of the teacher for his particular school, and (c) the attitude the teacher has toward his principal.

Even though research has shown that participation by teachers in decision making "pays off," it is equally clear that such participation can be overdone. Excessive involvement of teachers can produce resentment and resistance; teachers want the administrator to settle his own problems and they do not want to be excessively tied up in committee work.[39] Chester Barnard, a seasoned top-level telephone company executive, recognized this fact as a general organizational truth and commented lucidly on it in his classic *Functions of the Executive* in 1938. Barnard's term, "zone of indifference," may seem a bit stiff today, but he used it to refer to the observation that there are some areas in which the administrator's decision will be accepted without question. In fact, there are some decisions which teachers feel the administrator must make for himself, because he is paid to make them. For an administrator to confront teachers with a problem that they feel is within their zone of indifference is to court irritation and resentment.

If the administrator attempts to make decisions which teachers feel are outside their zone of indifference (i.e., decisions that teachers are naturally concerned about), he will undoubtedly encounter resistance and negative feelings. Administrators who attempt to create a facade of staff participation by permitting teachers to deal with minor problems while reserving significant decisions for themselves tend to run into this problem. Clearly, one of the first decisions that the administrator must make is to identify which decisions should involve the staff.

Bridges has suggested two rules of thumb for the school administrator to use in identifying decisions in which teachers will want to share [40]:

---

[38] The literature is extensive. For example, see Robert H. Guest, *Organizational Change: The Effect of Successful Leadership* (Homewood, Ill.: Richard D. Irwin, Inc., 1960). A typical specific piece of research is Margaret Carlson Browne, "Job Attitudes of Middle Management in Three Cooperative Extension Services" (unpublished doctoral dissertation, University of Wisconsin, 1959). In the field of education, *The Administrator's Notebook* (published monthly during the school year by The Midwest Administration Center at The University of Chicago) has reported several interesting studies, including Francis S. Chase, "The Teacher and Policy Making," I (May, 1952); Chiranji Lal Sharma, "Who Should Make What Decisions?" III (April, 1955); and Edwin M. Bridges, "Teacher Participation in Decision Making," XII (May, 1964).

[39] Edwin M. Bridges, "A Model for Shared Decision Making in the School Principalship," *Educational Administration Quarterly*, III, No. 1 (Winter, 1967), 51.

[40] *Ibid.*, p. 52.

1. *The test of relevance.* "[W]hen the teacher's personal stakes in the decision are high," Bridges states, "their interest in participation should also be high." [41] Problems which clearly meet this test concern teaching methods and materials, discipline, curriculum, and organizing for instruction.
2. *The test of expertise.* It is not enough for the teacher to have a stake in the decision; if his participation is to be meaningful and significant the teacher must be competent to contribute effectively. In dealing with the Physical Education Department's program schedule, for example, English teachers may be fitted by training and experience to contribute little or nothing.

There is a significant third test that administrators can use in attempting to decide what problems to consult their teachers about:

3. *The test of jurisdiction.* Schools are organized on a hierarchical basis; the individual school and staff have jurisdiction only over those decision making areas that remain, either by design or by omission. In the case of the Shady Lawn School mentioned above, the key factor that the principal and his staff failed to recognize was that their jurisdiction had been curbed by higher authority. The problem was *relevant* to teachers; and the teachers had the requisite *expertise;* but—right or wrong—they no longer had the jurisdiction that they had enjoyed for so long. Participation in the making of decisions which the group cannot implement can lead to frustration at least as great as simple nonparticipation.

After determining that a given problem meets these three tests sufficiently to warrant teacher participation in a decision, the administrator is then faced with two further questions: (1) at what point in the decision making process should teachers be included and (2) in what way should the teachers participate when they *are* included? The choices made by the administrator with regard to these two points will largely determine how much freedom and power the teachers will actually possess for materially affecting the selection of possible alternative actions.

The Function of Teachers in Decision Making

Teachers can participate appropriately in decision making with a principal in a variety of ways from the discussion of a problem face-to-face with a single staff member to an assembly of the full faculty. Such deci-

---

[41] *Ibid.*

sion making can be anything from a simple discussion through higher
steps of increasing involvement to a point where the participants legislate
a decision which is binding on them. Although there has been little
research on the relative merits of various ways of involving teachers as
participants in the decision making process, we will describe briefly five
of the major techniques that administrators have been found to utilize [42]:

1. *Discussion.* Perhaps the simplest level of participation, the discussion
   of a problem with teachers, is widely used to ascertain that teachers
   are aware of a problem and that a decision about this problem must
   be made. When participation is limited to discussion, the administrator makes the decision, but he hopes that the teachers will accept his
   decision more readily than if he were to communicate his decision to
   them *before* discussion.
2. *Information-seeking.* This technique of teacher participation is more
   than mere discussion; it also involves the administrator's obtaining of
   information (or bits of information that may be pieced together) so
   as to place him in a better position to make a more rational, logical
   decision.

These types of teacher participation are most useful for decisions that
fall within the teachers' zone of indifference; presumably, the decisions
involved would not be of vital interest to them and each actual decision
would be made by the administrator. The essential purposes of involving
teachers at these levels would be (1) to help the administrator make a
better decision, and (2) to enhance the liklihood that the decision will
be accepted by the group when it is made. To decide matters outside the
teachers' zone of indifference—and allow them to participate actively—
other forms of involvement will be used:

3. *Democratic-centralist.* Undoubtedly the most commonly used procedure, this method consists of the administrator's presenting of the
   problem to the staff and asking for suggestions, reactions, and ideas.
   The administrator will make the decision, generally, because he legally
   must, but he will try to reflect the staff's participation in his decision.
4. *Parliamentarian.* When the teachers are to actually make a decision,
   but it does not appear likely that unanimity or even consensus will
   prevail, the parliamentarian technique is often used. It offers the great
   advantage of specifically providing for minority opinions, conflict of
   ideas and values, and shifting positions in time as issues, facts, and
   values change.
5. *Participant-determining.* The essential characteristic of this proce-

---

[42] The five types of teacher participation discussed here are adapted from Bridges,
op. cit., pp. 52–59.

dure is that consensus is required of the group. It is one that would be used when (1) the issues are considered very important to the teachers, and (2) when it appears that consensus probably will be reached. Because consensus for the faculty is not always easy to obtain, and administrative insistence on obtaining consensus can be looked upon as pressure, the participant-determining method would probably not be used frequently. However, when it is used successfully, it is a powerful decision making procedure.

A Paradigm for Decision Making

Confusion can be a very real hazard in organizational decision making. Unless participants know just what procedures the organization is using to arrive at decisions and what their own role and function will be in the procedures, the very advantages ascribed to "democratic" or participatory decision making may well be nullified. There is no research support for the possible contention that ambiguity about the decision making processes in a school is somehow a virtue. In addition to knowing *how* teachers are to participate in decision making, that is, what their roles and functions will be, we must know *just when* they will participate.

It is also important that teachers understand the orderly steps of the decision making process as the organization moves toward a decision. These steps can be charted; in so doing, some of the critical choices to be made can be seen more readily. We suggest that school administrators consider the adoption of a very simplified version of the famous PERT technique developed by the Navy's Special Projects Office for the management of the huge Polaris program.[43] Essentially, PERT calls for a flow-chart on which every step of a particular sequence is placed; it is important that what is to be done in each step, by whom, and when, be clearly specified.

For decision making in the schools, a skeleton of a proposed decision making paradigm might resemble the one shown in Figure 5-2, which incorporates Bridges' suggestion that four steps are typically involved in reaching a decision: (1) defining the problem, (2) identifying possible alternatives, (3) predicting the consequences of each reasonable alternative, and (4) choosing the alternative to be followed.[44] In Figure 5-2 these four steps are identified by the numbers along the *time* dimension. In practice, individual administrators and their staffs might employ an-

[43] For a popular description of PERT, see Howard Simons, "PERT: How to Meet a Deadline," *Think* (May, 1962), 13–17.

[44] Bridges, *op. cit.*, p. 53.

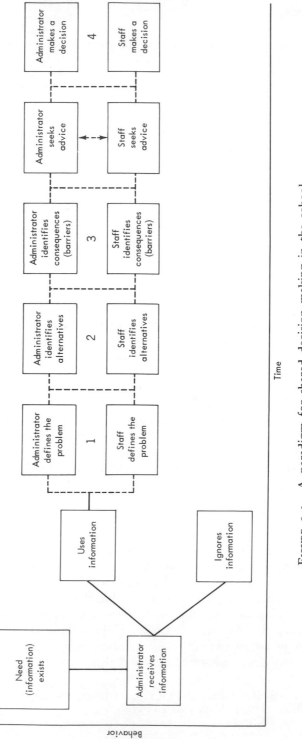

FIGURE 5-2. A paradigm for shared decision making in the school.

other series of steps, perhaps labelled differently; the suggested paradigm is readily adapted to any sequence of decision making behavior. Along the *behavior* dimension, a choice must be made as to who is going to perform each necessary decision making function. Here, broken lines indicate choices of action which the administrator can elect to make; he can involve the staff at any one step, at all of them—or, indeed, he need not involve them at all.

In other words, when the administrator receives (or becomes aware of) information indicating the need for a decision, his choice is clear: he can either use the information or he can ignore it. If he decides to act on the information, again, he can logically proceed in one of two ways: (1) he can proceed to define the problem or (2) he can give the information to the staff and ask them to define the problem. From then on, the process of decision making can comprise any combination of participation that the decision makers desire. The administrator can handle every phase of the process by himself or utilize any combination of participation by his staff.

How an administrator handles the responsibility for a particular decision will depend primarily on two factors: the extent to which staff participation is desired and the complexity of the problem. The flow chart for a complex problem that requires long-term consideration involving many factors and a series of "what if" decisions will be quite detailed and very functional. The advantages of flow-charting the proposed course for making a decision in the school are: (1) the course to be followed, including the timing and nature of staff participation, can be clearly and unemotionally planned, and (2) the administrator can keep in touch with all the interrelated parts of the decision making sequence as the process proceeds. Such a system can be a practical aid in assuring that the necessary decisions will be made in an orderly way, on time, and with as much staff participation as the organization wants to allow. If the staff participates in the flow-charting of the school's decision making processes, the likelihood that greater interest in and understanding of these processes will be generated will be enhanced.

The Outside Consultant in Decision Making

We have seen that the great power, influence, and status of the administrator affects group decision making in the school. An administrator's presence in a decision making situation can provide leadership, guidance, and counsel. Research has shown that, despite evidence to the contrary, the administrator's participation in group decision making can also lower efficiency, productivity, and creativity of the group. Torrance's study of aircraft crews, mentioned earlier, revealed that the best suggestions were often ignored if they conflicted with suggestions of pilots with higher status.

This is a commonplace and observable phenomenon. Recently, in a large city, an in-service project was undertaken by a group of elementary school principals at the urging of their district superintendent. The general objective of the project was to improve the principals' understanding of the school as a living social system. As a part of this project, and with the assistance of two university professors, an objective assessment of some specific factors of the "climate" of the schools was undertaken. By the time the data from the schools was ready for interpretation and study, the district superintendent had gone on sick leave and could not meet with the principals. The sessions in which the principals studied the "climate" assessment data from their own schools were lively ones; discussion was free, questions flowed, and ideas for utilizing the newly gained insights flourished. The district superintendent was able to return to work in time to attend the final project session of the year. And, since he was, of course, interested in this project, he began to ask questions and contribute ideas, some of which ran counter to interpretations that principals had become interested in. As the meeting continued, principals became silent, and some even became critical of the project itself; in a few minutes the group went "dead"—and the in-service project died with it. Here was a group of seasoned principals, all on tenure, each successful enough to be running a "model" school in an inner-city ghetto; yet, when the superintendent appeared on the scene, the group quickly attempted to adjust its thinking to conform to *their perception* of the superintendent's thinking.

Teachers, by training and experience, are sensitive to the "hidden agenda" present in every discussion group and decision making gathering. They feel that administrators—despite their most earnest efforts to keep communication open and the atmosphere free—often favor decision making procedures which produce "safe," conformist, unimaginative results: decisions which do not "rock the boat" too much. To some extent, this behavior of administrators is prompted by their desire to mediate the conflicts of power and influence which exist in the dynamic, interpersonal relationships between people in the organization. One way to render these internecine conflicts manageable without always putting the administrator in the position of steering a careful middle course is to utilize "outside" consultants to help the decision making group set and attain its own goals.

A consultant who is skilled and qualified becomes a temporary participant in the school's social system; and this status is highly significant in terms of what he can do. As an "outsider" he will never really be a part of the power structure, but he is privileged to raise questions, to suggest procedures, and generally to facilitate the operations of the group more candidly and objectively than he could if he were an "insider." Because his participation is temporary, the consultant's presence—in effect —creates a new *temporary social system* which should be expected to function somewhat differently than the permanent social system.

The consultant, of course, must be a skilled group leader and one who is familiar with the special problems faced by the organization that hires him. Just what the organization wants the consultant to help it accomplish must be carefully explained before he is hired. In Chapters 9 and 10, the role of the consultant in facilitating change in the school is discussed in more detail. However, let us briefly consider the appropriateness of using "outside" consultants. Some administrators may still feel that their job demands that they "stand on their own two feet," or that to call upon outsiders is a sign of weakness and/or lack of ability. Today, however, most administrators of all kinds of organizations—government, military, business, industrial, and educational—recognize that skilled consultants can be very helpful to the organization in its search for more effective decision making procedures. The school administrator who seeks consultant help for his organization in developing better decision making procedures is demonstrating his genuine concern in facilitating better decision making in his school.

The "Team System" of Decision Making

When the staff is to participate in decision making in a school, the typical practice is to call a meeting for discussing how to proceed. There is much literature that reports studies of what happens in such groups. Among the phenomena that have been observed are power struggles, expressions of status differences, emergent leadership, influences of informal groups within the total group, and a host of informal social interactions that affect the outcome. Generally, some sort of homeostasis is observed; such groups do not often proceed in bold imaginative new directions, but tend, instead, to modify existing decisions enough to satisfy the organization's needs. A principal searching for a point of departure, a decision relatively unhampered by the "here and now," might want to emulate some of the proceedings of *Project Strat-X*.

Project Strat-X was the code designation for an "effort to guide the Pentagon in its selection of a new breed of large, long-range missiles to succeed the force of 1,000 Minuteman missiles" [45] that in 1967 constituted

---

[45] *The New York Times* (July 17, 1967), pp. 1, 3. © 1967 by the New York Times Company. Reprinted by permission.

the cornerstone of America's nuclear arsenal. The decision to proceed, in this case, had to be made by the Pentagon; it could not be made by anyone else. However, the top military planners wanted to be sure that they were aware of all reasonable alternatives before they made their recommendations. Outside temporary specialists were called in to determine the alternatives for Project Strat-X and reach a decision; however, the technique could have been utilized by the Pentagon's own staff.

The technique used was to divide the group into three teams:

1. *Blue Team* prepared a number of different proposals for basing ICBM's which ranged from hiding missiles under artificial lakes to storing them in constantly flying, long-endurance aircraft; from shuttling the missiles around the country in boxcars to hiding them in merchant ships. Not only did Blue Team consider an array of proposals—40 or 50 in all—they also prepared *detailed* plans and specifications as to how each method might be implemented in practice.
2. *Red Team*, meanwhile, played the role of Russian planners and did their best to thwart each system that Blue Team proposed. Each team found it had to deal with more than "ideas"; specific, detailed proposals had to be considered.
3. *Evaluation Team* had the job of weighing the claims and counterclaims of Blue Team and Red Team, and it took into consideration practical matters such as cost and effectiveness.

The result of using the above technique was that Pentagon officials had available to them an array of evaluated proposals, with costs and other details, that they could use in making their decision. The decision as to what to recommend to Congress was still theirs to make, but the officials had been given assistance in avoiding stereotyped, conventional thinking as they faced their decision.

Although schools and their administrators may not be faced with problems approaching the magnitude or significance of the decision described above, schools *are* in need of new, fresh, and promising—perhaps even innovative—alternatives from which to make choices. By using the techniques developed for the Pentagon on appropriate occasions, imaginative administrators can discover new alternatives to improve the quality of their decisions. For example, if the school receives "feedback" which indicates the need for more effective community relations, how can the school improve the existing community relations? A decision must be made; what alternatives—reasonable, workable, and effective—are available? And of these, which seems likely to "pay off" most? Conventional procedures for moving toward such decisions have tended to produce conventional decisions. It is possible that by dividing the school staff into teams—one to make proposals, one to predict community reaction, and one to evaluate each proposal and its probable reaction—the administrator will be able to make better decisions and foster a more effective level of staff participation.

Summary

In this chapter selected insights regarding organizational decision making that have emerged from behavioral research were discussed. The decision making behavior of individuals was treated mainly in terms of the administrator's sharing of organizational decisions with the staff. Emphasis in this chapter has been on the decision making behavior of schools as organizations and specific suggestions have been made to the administrator to consider flow-charting, the use of consultants, and team approaches as techniques for improving the quality of decision making in his school organization.

❧ 6 ❧

leadership
in the school

*I am trying to puncture a myth—the myth that every man does in-
deed want to lead and innovate. Most administrators will proclaim
this as their purpose. Yet research on the behavior of administrators
repeatedly gives the lie to this proclamation.*
—Andrew W. Halpin.[1]

Leadership has occupied the mind and imagination of man for a long
time. Indeed, much of the record of human experience which the
civilized world has accumulated concerns leadership. If all the artistic,
literary, and scholarly works which deal with leadership were brought
together we would have a collection of mammoth proportions by any
standard. But a great deal of such a collection would be comprised of
speculation and folk wisdom. It has been the development of psychology
and sociology as human sciences only during the last half-century—
with their methodologies and accumulations of knowledge—that has provided us with a promising start in our efforts to understand leadership.

Ways of Studying Leadership

A popular concept of leaders, supported by years of philosophical
speculation and research effort, is that they are people who are endowed

---

[1] Andrew W. Halpin, "Escape from Leadership," *The Journal of Education*
(Faculty of Education, The University of British Columbia, Vancouver) XI (March,
1965), p. 63.

with certain traits or characteristics that especially fit them for their leadership roles. It is generally believed that intelligence, imagination, perseverance, and emotional stability are among the many personal traits which characterize the individual qualified to exercise leadership. This concept, of course, suggests that those who possess these traits must be sought out for their leadership potential. Training, according to this view, can be very effective in improving the skills of such people. However, let us remember that the selection of people who are to lead, or be trained to lead, will depend on the capacity of individuals to lead as defined by the presence of selected personal traits.

Ever since the beginning of the development of modern psychology as a discipline with an accompanying research methodology, considerable effort has been made to pursue psychological studies of leadership; typically, such studies attempt to identify the traits that contribute to leadership ability and to refine the ways of measuring these traits in people. Extensive surveys of the research literature do not reveal this method to be particularly productive or promising for understanding leadership at our present stage of knowledge and ability. Although long lists of traits that seem to be associated with leadership have been compiled by researchers, psychologists have been unable to clarify which traits are most important in specific leadership positions. Also, our present inability to measure accurately various personal traits makes it difficult to be very precise in specifying the perfect "mix" of personal attributes.

Leadership is found in some kind of group, and the leader functions, necessarily, in relationship to his followers. Viewing leadership as an interactive process between members of the group, especially as interaction between the leader and the rest of the group, has fascinated a number of scholars who have done many sociological studies of leadership. The most obvious point of departure is that groups differ; however, how various groups differ may not necessarily be related to the presence of leadership. Hemphill found, for example, that how groups differ from each other can be described in terms of specific characteristics such as size, homogeneity, flexibility, and stability. There were other "group dimensions," as Hemphill called these characteristics, of which two that seemed to be most closely associated with leadership in the group were *viscidity* and *hedonic tone*. Viscidity refers to the cohesion that group members feel, and hedonic tone refers to the feeling of satisfaction that individuals receive from being members of a group.[2] Such research—studies of decision making groups, conferences, and various kinds of work groups—can give the leader insight into the nature and workings of

[2] John K. Hemphill, *Situational Factors in Leadership* (Columbus, O.: Bureau of Business Research, College of Commerce and Administration, The Ohio State University, 1949).

groups. However, this research does not focus directly on the nature of leadership and how it is exercised.

Psychological studies of leadership have tended to focus on personal traits associated with leadership,[3] whereas sociological studies have focused on aspects of the situation in which leadership is attempted.[4] Thus, a *trait-situation* conflict arose because some scholars were convinced that the key to understanding leadership lay in better research on the personality traits of leaders and others were equally sure that the answer lay in better understanding of the interactions between leaders and followers. This trait-situation dichotomy is reminiscent of the nature-nurture conflict over learning theory which raged in academe a few years ago. In recent years, this seemingly fruitless conflict has been superseded by a more general *behavioral* approach to understanding leadership.

Behavioral studies focus on observed behavior, and, although they recognize that the people involved in leadership do possess personal traits and are functioning in a situation, these studies avoid making flat statements about causal relationships. Their emphasis is on observed behavior in certain situations—a behavioral approach to leadership. Researchers of such studies do not insist that the cause of behavior be pin-pointed, and they do not assume that the leadership behavior observed in one situation will necessarily be found in another.[5] The behavioral approach to understanding leadership is useful to the practical man of affairs, such as the school administrator, because it focuses attention on things that are *happening* (or appear to be happening) rather than on finding the supposed causes of observed behavior.

The Dimensions of Leadership

Numerous studies involving careful observation of leadership behavior have been reported by various types of organizations: military, educational, business, and others. These studies suggest that the things leaders do—the leadership behavior they exhibit—fall into two general categories called *dimensions*. Although no universally accepted labels for these two categories have yet appeared, the terms *structure* and *consideration* are widely used:

---

[3] For a highly respected scholarly survey of the literature in this field, see Ralph M. Stogdill, "Personal Factors Associated With Leadership: A Survey of the Literature," *Journal of Psychology*, XXV (1948), 35–71.

[4] Emory S. Bogardus describes this point of view in "Leadership and Social Situations," *Sociology and Social Research*, XVI (1931–1932), 164–70.

[5] Andrew W. Halpin has written a clear and succinct discussion of the behavioral approach in "How Leaders Behave," in *Theory and Research in Administration* (New York: The Macmillan Company, 1966), Chap. 3.

Structure includes behavior in which the supervisor organizes and defines group activities and his relation to the group. Thus, he defines the role he expects each member to assume, assigns tasks, plans ahead, establishes ways of getting things done, and pushes for production.

Consideration includes behavior indicating mutual trust, respect, and a certain warmth and rapport between the supervisor and his group. This does not mean that this dimension reflects a superficial "pat-on-the-back," "first name calling" kind of human relations behavior. This dimension appears to emphasize a deeper concern for group members' needs and includes such behavior as allowing subordinates more participation in decision making and encouraging more two-way communication.[6]

The researcher John K. Hemphill had long been known for scholarly studies of leadership when he and Alvin E. Coons developed the Leader Behavior Description Questionnaire at Ohio State University.[7] This instrument, which is often called the LBDQ, consisted of a series of short descriptive statements concerning the behavior of leaders. From their scholarly knowledge of leader behavior, Hemphill and Coons were able to include in the LBDQ a wide range of behaviors employed by leaders.

In order to use the instrument, members of the leader's group were asked to check the frequency with which they observed the leader using the kind of behavior described: *always, often, occasionally, seldom,* or *never.* Following are two of the 100 items on the LBDQ-Form XII, which was a 1962 revision of the original instrument:

1. He makes sure that his part in the group is understood by the group members.
2. He is friendly and approachable.[8]

Thus, a typical application of the LBDQ would be to ask members of the superintendent's staff to indicate the extent to which the superintendent engages in these two kinds of behavior.

When the LBDQ is applied, the researcher should watch for possible clusters of behavior patterns for a given leader such as a superintendent, and observe how the behavior patterns of various superintendents com-

---

[6] Edwin A. Fleishman and Edwin F. Harris, "Patterns of Leadership Behavior Related to Employee Grievances and Turnover," *Personnel Psychology,* XV, No. 1 (Spring, 1962), 43–44.

[7] John K. Hemphill and Alvin E. Coons, "Development of the Leader Behavior Description Questionnaire," in Ralph M. Stogdill and Alvin E. Coons, eds., *Leader Behavior: Its Description and Measurement* (Columbus, O.: The Ohio State University Press, 1957).

[8] *Leader Behavior Description Questionnaire-Form XII,* copyright © 1962 by the Bureau of Business Research, College of Commerce and Administration, The Ohio State University, Columbus, O.

pare. This raises the question: If we compare the leader-behavior of individuals thought to be effective with the leader-behavior of those thought to be somewhat ineffective, will we find consistent and significant differences? The LBDQ has been used by researchers for just such studies, and the results have been very useful for understanding how leaders behave.

The Korean conflict was in progress when the LBDQ was first found to be a valuable research instrument by students of leadership, and Andrew W. Halpin used it on the flight crews of B-29 bombers as a part of a study of leadership problems in the military.[9] Very briefly, this study was composed of two main phases of data collecting:

1. A 130-item form of the LBDQ that had been adapted to the military situation was administered to 353 members of 52 B-29 crews who were in training at MacDill Air Force Base in the fall of 1950.
2. The following summer, in Japan, three kinds of data were collected for 33 of the 52 airplane commanders:
   a. A shorter (80-item) form of the LBDQ was administered.
   b. The squadron and wing commanders of all 33 airplane commanders rated each of the latter on a 7-item scale of combat performance.
   c. Twenty-seven of the 33 crews were asked this question: "If you could make up a crew from among the crew members in your squadron, who would you choose for each position?"

Upon analyzing his data, Halpin found that two factors were clearly the most significant for describing differences in leader behavior of the airplane commanders:

1. *Consideration*, which Halpin then analyzed as "behavior indicative of friendship, mutual trust, respect, and a certain warmth in the relationship between the airplane commander and his crew." [10] Rather than being authoritarian and impersonal, the commander whose behavior rates high for this dimension is considerate of the men in his crew while he is performing his leadership functions.
2. *Initiating structure*, which refers to behavior in which the commander "defines the relationship between himself and the members of the crew . . . , [defines] the role which he expects each member of the crew to assume, and endeavors to establish well-defined patterns of organization, channels of communication, and ways of getting jobs done." [11]

---

[9] Andrew W. Halpin, "The Leadership Behavior and Combat Performance of Airplane Commanders," *Journal of Abnormal and Social Psychology*, XLIX, No. 1 (January, 1954), 19–22.
[10] *Ibid.*
[11] *Ibid.*

As is evident from the above, there is a "mix" of factors that seem to be important in the behavior patterns of leaders. It is tempting to speculate which "mix" is the best one, the one that will produce the most desirable leadership. We can ask: Should an administrator concentrate on the *consideration* aspects of behavior, or is it more important to *initiate structure*? Although a study such as this provides us with useful insights, let us bear in mind that by no means does it furnish us with prescriptions for the behavior of administrators who would be effective leaders.

Judging from the many studies of air crews in the Korean conflict such as the one described above, we can say that the leader who is evaluated as doing well will tend to be one who is behaving (as a leader) in such a way that consideration and initiating structure are *both* very much in evidence. The leader who overemphasizes either dimension is perceived by his referents in a less favorable light. In this connection, there is some reason to believe that there is a tendency for an airplane commander who emphasizes consideration to be regarded highly by crews but rated lower in performance by superiors; conversely, if he overemphasizes initiating structure, the crew sees him as less effective and his superiors tend to rate his performance in combat higher.

A more accurate and generally useful statement emerging from these studies might be: Commanders whose behavior was perceived as being above average in *both* dimensions—consideration and initiating structure—tend to be evaluated high in overall effectiveness as leaders. Curiously, there is evidence that there is little relationship between a leader's knowledge of effective leader behavior and the way he is perceived as behaving by his group. This suggests that it is not enough to learn *about* leader behavior; this knowledge must also be internalized and made behaviorally operational before it can affect actual practice.

Aircraft commanders are not academicians, of course, and we must question the validity that the findings of the Air Force studies have for school administrators. Are the leadership situations of B-29 bomber commanders in battle over Korea and school administrators in the United States (however embattled!) similar enough to warrant generalizing from one to the other? Happily, considerable research has been done in this problem area, and we find that there is indeed a remarkable similarity in the concepts of leader behavior that seem to be useful.

Not only have studies comparing leader behavior of school superintendents with that of airplane commanders been conducted,[12] but the leader behavior of superintendents has been investigated in terms of how it is perceived by boards of education, as compared to how it is seen by

---

[12] Andrew W. Halpin, *Theory and Research in Administration* (New York: The Macmillan Company, © 1966). See Chapter 3 for an excellent summary of the research literature in this field.

school staffs. The leader behavior of school principals has been studied in terms of the perceptions of teachers as compared with the rated effectiveness of the principals as seen by their superintendents. Let us bear in mind that when we discuss some of the major findings emerging from this research, we should note later definitions for initiating structure and consideration which Halpin offered in connection with studies of the leadership behavior of superintendents of schools:

1. *Initiating structure* refers to the leader's behavior in delineating the relationship between himself and the members of his workgroup, and in endeavoring to establish well-defined patterns of organization, channels of communication, and methods of procedure.
2. *Consideration* refers to behavior indicative of friendship, mutual trust, respect, and warmth in the relationship between the leader and the members of his staff.[13]

From the considerable data that have been assembled in numerous studies it seems clear that initating structure and consideration are dimensions that are essential to the behavior of leaders. Just what proportion of the two dimensions will make the best "mix" for leadership cannot be ascertained, but leaders who are perceived as being effective tend to be high in both consideration and initiating structure. Superiors tend to see the behavior of leaders differently than subordinates; in many instances, for example, boards of education think the superintendent is high in consideration toward the staff, but the staff does not always agree with this perception. Superiors also put more stress on initiating structure behavior of the leader than his subordinates do, whereas subordinates are more interested in the consideration behavior of the leader. This "leader's dilemma" is further complicated by the question of the "ideal" leader—how much of his behavior should be consideration and how much should be directed toward initiating structure. For example, in one study of 50 school superintendents, it was found that the actual behavior of the superintendents differed considerably from ideal behavior for superintendents as pictured by the superintendent himself, the staff, and the board of education.

Let us not forget that the dimensions of leader behavior being considered here are not scientifically tested; it is the observer's *perception* of the extent to which the leader exhibits the kinds of behaviors described in the LBDQ or in any other similar research instrument that forms the basis of the data. It is evident, of course, that even the most careful studies of this kind have many limitations and must be carefully interpreted.

---

[13] *Ibid.*, p. 86.

But it would seem reasonable to assume that the dimensions of leadership are more than a mere "spray-gun consideration," in Halpin's words, which for him is typified by "the P.T.A. smile, and by the oily affability dispensed by administrators at faculty picnics and office parties." [14] Something deeper is suggested, a combination of two behavioral dimensions which may be the most integral aspect of leadership. Yet, to be effective, and a more than superficial gesture, the behavior of leaders must be genuine.

Democratic Leadership

In 1939 Kurt Lewin, Ronald Lippitt, and Ralph White reported a study in the *Journal of Social Psychology* which has had profound effect on notions of leadership in American education for a long time.[15] This research involved a well-designed study of the reaction of boys to carefully portrayed examples of three leadership styles: democratic, autocratic, and laissez-faire. The boys in the study were ten-year-olds who were organized into hobby clubs of five boys each. The researchers observed what happened when adult leaders of the hobby clubs deliberately engaged in different leadership styles.

As is widely known in educational circles, the boys in the hobby clubs responded best in the "democratic leadership" situation. Under autocratic leadership, for example, considerable resistance and aggressive behavior was observed. Under laissez-faire leadership, there was frustration, lack of purpose, and indecision. But democratic leadership produced higher morale and greater achievement.

The notion of "democratic leadership" in education was largely developed from these studies. The behaviors described in the studies served for many years as models of what is good and what is bad in educational leadership. Unfortunately, as Lipham points out, "this loosely defined political concept [democratic leadership], which had been seized as a panacea, hindered more potential leaders than it helped." [16] Many a practical school administrator knows that, in actual practice, "democratic leadership" can be confused with a sort of shell-game that the administrator plays with the faculty. As Brickell has stated it, "The participation

---

[14] *Ibid.*

[15] Kurt Lewin, Ronald Lippitt, and Ralph K. White, "Patterns of Aggressive Behavior in Experimentally Created 'Social Climates,'" *Journal of Social Psychology*, X (1939), 271–99.

[16] James M. Lipham, "Leadership and Administration," in Daniel E. Griffiths, ed., *Behavioral Science and Educational Administration*, The Sixty-third Yearbook of the National Society for the Study of Education, Part II (Chicago: The University of Chicago Press, 1964), Chap. 6, p. 125.

patterns in widespread use are very often little more than enabling arrangements, organized after an administrator has decided the general direction (and in some cases the actual details) of an instructional change." [17] Phrases such as "democratic administration" and "shared decision making" are, Brickell believes "often used with the intention of hiding the great strength of administrative action." [18] Brickell was not alone in observing this problem. Cynicism and confusion regarding democratic leadership is rather common among administrators and other professional educators; it is common enough, in fact, to suggest that Brickell's opinion is rather widely—if cautiously—held.

Today, even though there is probably no lessening of interest in the exercise of leadership that is appropriate to the ideals and values of our society, the notion of "democratic leadership" by administrators is being reexamined. In retrospect, it now seems that the concepts proposed by the studies of Lewin, Lippitt, and White were badly distorted when they were applied to the operation of schools. After all, schools are not hobby clubs and teachers are not ten-year-old boys.

Schools are highly complex organizations, and this fact alone is enough to make us cautious in applying these concepts of leader behavior to schools. Schools are hierarchical in organization structure, and this alone signifies different leadership roles for school administrators as compared to leaders of small hobby clubs. Teachers engaged in their professional work differ in many respects from the subjects in the hobby clubs. Recent research on leadership takes these important realities into account. It is to be hoped that the concepts emerging from more recent scholarly work will, consequently, be more useful to the administrator in exercising effective leadership.

Administrative Leadership

An important source of role conflict for the principal is that he is expected to be both administrator and leader, although, by definition, the behaviors appropriate for each of these roles are mutually exclusive. Thus, it is misleading to use terms such as *administrative leadership* which merely blur the boundaries of the problem.

Administration is concerned with the smooth operation of an organization, here, the school. In his role as administrator, the principal facil-

---

[17] Henry M. Brickell, *Organizing New York State for Educational Change* (Albany, N. Y.: University of the State of New York, State Education Department, 1961), p. 24.
[18] *Ibid.*

itates the use of established procedures and structures to help the organization achieve its goals. Administrators are properly concerned with *maintaining* the organization, with keeping its interrelated parts functioning smoothly, and with monitoring the orderly processes that have been established to get things accomplished. When they are wearing their "administrative hats," principals tend to view themselves as executive-managers in the tradition of corporation executives. As such, they coordinate and regulate the small, specialized tasks which together make up the total operation of the school.

Administration, then, involves the processes which help the organization operate its mechanisms for achieving its goals. The administrator is a stabilizing force in the school, who clarifies its goals and helps people in the school play effective roles in achieving these goals. Leaders have quite a different role to play.

Leaders initiate changes in the organization: changes in either its goals or in the way the organization tries to achieve its goals. The emphasis here is upon *change*, as differentiated from the administrator's emphasis on *maintaining*. In other words, leaders tend to be "disruptive of the existing state of affairs." [19] This emphasis on change may very well affect the organization positively by helping it achieve its ultimate mission more successfully; but the behavior of leaders is probably governed more by broader, cosmopolitan personal goals than is the behavior of administrators. Actually, school principals are expected to be both administrators and leaders. It would be unrealistic to expect a principal to spend all of his time in leadership behavior, for he must devote careful attention to administrative matters. But the remarkable resistance that schools have shown toward change raises the question as to how effective principals can be as leaders. Herbert Thelen comments on this resistance to change thus:

Comparing classrooms now with classroms of 40 years ago, one notes that at both times there were numbers of students not much interested in what was being done; the typical teacher still presents material and quizzes the kids to see if they understand it; the amount of creativity and excitement is probably no greater now than then. The development of new materials and techniques has enabled us to spin our wheels in one place, to conduct business as usual in the face of dramatic changes in society and in the clientele of the school. The operation of the educational enterprise has encountered what only can be thought of as a very large number of increasingly serious obstacles and the new devices sustain the forlorn hope of protecting and maintaining, rather than changing, the

---

[19] Lipham, *op. cit.*, p. 122.

old orthodoxy in the face of the most important revolutions in the history of mankind.[20]

The tendency of schools to resist change has often been noted. There has been speculation that an underlying cause may be related to the *kinds* of people who occupy leadership positions in public schools. Steinhoff, for example, found that many principals are timid, submissive, and have "a personal disposition to support an administrative style which minimizes the likelihood of conflict or change."[21] Others speculate that the root of the problem may be in the nature of organizations themselves:

> All organizations possess built-in devices which tend to maintain stability. Acting as a gyroscope these devices seek to hold the organization in a steady state, or to return it to stability when buffeted from within or without. This tendency toward stability, seemingly inherent in all organizations, constitutes a powerful force against change.[22]

These points of view, of course, remind us, once again, of the trait-situationist confusion about the underlying causes of successful and unsuccessful leadership. The practicing administrator who needs useful approaches to the problem of leadership will find it helpful to use a behavioral approach.

The concepts of administration and leadership make phrases such as *administrative leadership* somewhat misleading, for they imply that the school administrator, being a wearer of two hats, is expected to emulate both Dr. Jekyll and Mr. Hyde. On the one hand, the administrator bears a heavy responsibility for the unceasing administrative demands of the school such as scheduling, programming, supplying, managing, and monitoring the activities of others. After all, it is largely up to the administrator to see that the school functions according to its plans and objectives.

On the other hand, however, it is desirable that the administrator provide leadership in the school. Some sort of balance is required to provide for the administration of the school much of the time and to provide for

---

[20] Herbert A. Thelen, "New Practices on the Firing Line," *Administrator's Notebook*, XII, No. 5 (January, 1964).

[21] Carl R. Steinhoff, *Organizational Climate in a Public School System* (USOE Cooperative Research Program Contract No. OE-4-10-225, Project No. S-083, Syracuse University, 1965), p. 104.

[22] Archie R. Dykes, "The Emergent Role of Administrators and the Implications for Teacher-Administrator Relationships," in Roy B. Allen and John Schmid, eds., *Collective Negotiations and Educational Administration* (Columbus, O.: College of Education, University of Arkansas and University Council for Educational Administration, 1966), p. 30.

leadership when necessary. Hemphill has given us some clues on this from his research, by identifying three categories of leadership efforts:

1. *Attempted leadership:* acts which are intended to effect leadership
2. *Successful leadership:* acts which have effected change in the process of solving a problem
3. *Effective leadership:* acts that have effected change which has *itself* solved a problem [23]

In his leadership efforts, then, the administrator can operate with regard to a range of possible effectiveness, and some of his efforts will "pay off" better than others. This leads us to the problem of frequency: How often should one attempt to exert leadership? Too frequent efforts to initiate change can result in confusion and disorganization, but too infrequent efforts can cause the school to become static, rigid, and unmoving.

Lipham [24] links the notion of *potency* to the idea of frequency in leadership, using the word in reference to the "magnitude of an initiated change" that results from a leadership act. He refers to low potency leadership as "tinkering," and compares this to powerful leadership such as Dewey's—which changed the entire nature of public elementary education.

In planning to exercise leadership, then, the school administrator should consider the variables that will affect the total impact of his behavior. Research encourages him to consider the following factors for exercising leadership:

1. *Strategy.* Reserve leadership efforts for major, significant changes which will make an important difference in the school's goals or in the way these goals are achieved. The administrator should be cautious about exerting leadership on behalf of minor changes.
2. *Timing.* Plan leadership acts frequently enough so that the school does not stagnate or merely drift, but not so frequently as to cause undue confusion or disintegration of the organization.
3. *Tactics.* Plan and carry out leadership acts thoughtfully and carefully, so as to secure the intended results for making change.

Harris has suggested a useful pattern for differentiating between change-oriented behavior and maintenance-oriented behavior. He describes a continuum with "tractive" behavior falling on one side and "dynamic" behavior on the other. Tractive behavior would tend to resist,

---

[23] John K. Hemphill, "Administration as Problem Solving," in Andrew W. Halpin, ed., *Administrative Theory in Education* (Chicago: Midwest Administration Center, University of Chicago, 1958), pp. 105–6.

[24] Lipham, *op. cit.*, pp. 124–25.

to enforce, or to codify; dynamic behavior would tend to up-grade, to restructure, or to innovate. The behavior patterns would arrange themselves on a continuum like that in Figure 6–1. In practice, the behavior

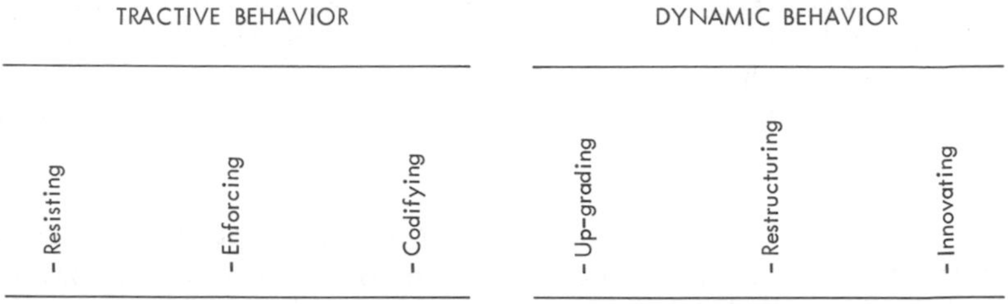

TRACTIVE BEHAVIOR   DYNAMIC BEHAVIOR

– Resisting   – Enforcing   – Codifying   – Up-grading   – Restructuring   – Innovating

FIGURE 6–1.   Tractive-dynamic continuum. Adapted from Ben M. Harris, *Supervisory Behavior in Education* (Englewood Cliffs, N. J.: Prentice-Hall, Inc., © 1963), p. 21.

of administrators can be interpreted on the tractive-dynamic continuum as shown in the chart in Figure 6–2.

The Leadership Role of Principals

Historically, the role of the principal in the school has been a developing one. Today, just what the role and functions of a school principal should be are far from clearly defined or universally accepted. The pressure for greater professional autonomy for teachers—or, as it may be expressed, the increasing militancy of teachers—has necessitated a clearer definition of the principal's legitimate professional role: Should he be an administrator or a leader? This is not an academic question.

As early as 1951, Moehlman called for a change in the principalship wherein, "Ideally, the faculty would select one or more of its own members to fill the principalship for a term and act as coordinator." [25] Those selected would take the responsibility without extra monetary compensation and would be able to return to the teaching ranks after a relatively brief term in office. Similarly, Lieberman has advocated a narrowing of the scope of the principal's role,[26] according to which the principal would be restricted to administrative responsibilities—in effect, to implementing the educational decisions undertaken by teachers. The above points of view are being expressed with increasing frequency by teacher groups.

---

[25] Arthur B. Moehlman, *School Administration: Its Development, Principles and Function in the United States* (Boston: Houghton Mifflin Company, 1951), pp. 274–75.
[26] Myron Lieberman, *Education as a Profession* (Englewood Cliffs, N. J.: Prentice-Hall, Inc., 1956), Chap. 15.

Tractive ⟷   Dynamic ⟶

CHARACTERISTIC	Resisting	Enforcing	Codifying	Up-Grading	Restructuring	Innovating
AIM	Actively preventing changes by resisting forces for change	Seeking substantial uniformity in practices	Formalizing practices	Minor changes in practices	Major changes in practices employing known elements	Radical departures from existing practice with unknown elements
BEHAVIOR	Lobbying Petitioning	Rating Inspecting	Writing regulations	Study groups Orientation Policy statements	Pilot programs Action research	Experimentation

FIGURE 6-2. Characteristics and examples of behavior on the tractive-dynamic continuum. Adapted from Ben M. Harris, *Supervisory Behavior in Education* (Englewood Cliffs, N. J.: Prentice-Hall, Inc., © 1963), p. 21.

However, in actual practice the administrator still has great power to lead and teachers are in a relatively weak position to effect basic and powerful change. Teachers, Brickell contends, can make three kinds of instructional changes without participation of the administrator:

1. Change in classroom practice
2. Relocation of existing curriculum content
3. Introduction of single special courses at the high school level [27]

Brickell's study of educational change in New York has convinced him that "Rearrangements of the structural elements of the institution depend *almost exclusively* upon administrative initiative. Teachers are not change-agents. . . ." [28] Although speakers at conventions attended by principals still exhort them to be educational leaders, as do journal articles, a trend toward changes in the responsibilities of the principalship is growing. One may speculate as to whether these changes might not constitute a *decline* in the principalship [29]; there thus seems to be reason to be concerned about the place of leadership in the principal's future.

It is evident that much of the current interest in this problem stems from a feeling that the school principalship is not providing the leadership demanded under present conditions. Very few of the significant educational developments of recent decades can be credited to the leadership of school principals. The general pattern of change in schools has been to adopt—with modifications—programs already being undertaken by others. National curriculum groups, foundations, rebellious parents, unwilling taxpayers—all have frequently been more clearly the causes of change in schools than the leadership of principals. At the present time forces such as corporate mergers of publishing, communications, and electronic firms are establishing new procedures in education more effectively than school principals. It is possible that principals have become identified with the status quo through emphasis on their administrative concerns rather than their leadership concerns. Certainly, the increasing complexity and diversity of the school curriculum has weakened the principal's ability to supervise instruction in the traditional sense. But there are, clearly, other factors which are challenging the principal's leadership position in the school.

---

[27] Brickell, *op. cit.*, p. 24.

[28] Henry M. Brickell, "State Organization for Educational Change: A Case Study and a Proposal," in Matthew B. Miles, ed., *Innovation in Education* (New York: Teachers College Press, 1964), p. 503. © 1964 by Teachers College, Columbia University. Reprinted by permission of the publisher.

[29] Donald A. Erickson, "Changes in the Principalship," *The National Elementary Principal*, XLIV, No. 5 (April, 1965), 16–20.

One of the most sought-after characteristics which are frequently thought to be assets to principals is experience; unfortunately, this assumption is presently very much open to question. The young, newly appointed principal is emotionally close to teachers; he has a place in their informal communications networks; he tends to be less formal and more adaptable than he will be later.[30] However, as time passes, he will be *perceived by teachers* as conforming more and more to the bureaucratic mold. He seems to be oriented to the expectations of his superiors and expects rewards for conforming to the rules, regulations, and behavior patterns expected by the bureaucracy. Moreover, once he becomes a principal, he orients his career aspirations not to teachers and teaching but to the values and norms of the central office. His rewards are often contingent upon the impersonal, dependable, predictable attitudes and behaviors that will identify him with the bureaucratic hierarchy. Looked at from this point of view, the probability that the experienced principal will be an able and effective leader is not very great.

A part of the National Principalship Study investigated the Executive Professional Leadership (EPL) of elementary school principals.[31] EPL was defined as "the effort of an executive of a professionally staffed organization to conform to a definition of his role that stresses his obligation to improve the quality of staff performance." [32] This study found, first of all, a definite connection between the EPL of principals and three criteria that seem useful in judging the principal's effectiveness: (1) staff morale, (2) the professional performance of teachers, and (3) pupil learning. In other words, in those schools with principals high in EPL there will be high morale, a high level of teaching, and relatively good pupil achievement.

If, as this study seems to indicate, the leadership behavior of principals does affect what occurs in the school, the next question is, "How can a principal increase his EPL?" Definite answers are not immediately available, of course, but the *Staff Leadership* study gives some interesting leads:

1. Principals who participated in the selection of their teachers had higher EPL.
2. Principals whose superiors had high EPL tended also to exhibit high EPL.

---

[30] Edwin M. Bridges, "Bureaucratic Role and Socialization: The Influence of Experience on the Elementary Principal," *Educational Administration Quarterly*, I, No. 2 (Spring, 1965), 19–28.

[31] Neal Gross and Robert E. Herriott, *Staff Leadership in Public Schools: A Sociological Inquiry* (New York: John Wiley & Sons, Inc., 1965).

[32] *Ibid.*, p. 8.

3. Principals whose superiors strongly endorsed their efforts to improve conditions had high EPL.
4. The smaller the school enrollment, the higher the principal's EPL.

Whether these factors are prior conditions of high EPL is not specifically clear. But it does appear clear, from this nationwide study of large school districts, that there are specific circumstances and situations which are associated with the Executive Professional Leadership of school principals. Gross and Herriott speculate from their study that several behavioral patterns may affect the extent to which a principal serves as the leader of his staff:

1. His willingness to allow teachers to particiate in *central* school problems
2. The extent to which he stresses status and bureaucratic impersonality
3. The degree to which he offers social support to teachers
4. The extent of managerial support he offers them
5. The extent to which he supports his teachers when their authority over pupils is challenged [33]

Who tends to exhibit this kind of behavior? What guides can we use in selecting people who will be high in EPL? Will mature, seasoned persons of long experience with extensive university preparation be highest in EPL? Unfortunately, Gross and Herriott were not able to find a relationship between these characteristics and high EPL. Rather, younger, highly committed people—unhampered by too much experience or too much professional education—tended to rate higher in leadership. Now, we must not believe that we can solve all our school leadership problems by replacing experienced principals with "greenhorns"; the subtleties and complexities of the problem indicate further study is needed. However, research on this subject necessitates more than an emotional response; the principal has genuine cause to question just how much leadership behavior he actually exhibits.

Leadership Style

There are five main leadership styles: (1) authoritarian, (2) democratic, (3) laissez-faire,[34] (4) bureaucratic, and (5) charismatic.[35] In each

---

[33] Adapted from *ibid.*, p. 155.
[34] The first three styles mentioned were suggested by Ralph White and Ronald Lippitt, "Leader Behavior and Member Reaction in Three 'Social Climates,'" in Dorwin Cartwright and Alvin Zander, eds., *Group Dynamics* (New York: Harper & Row, Publishers, 1960).
[35] The last two styles were proposed by Hubert Bonner, *Group Dynamics* (New York: The Ronald Press Company, 1959).

style, the leader can select from a repertoire of four key methods to influence or direct the group:

1. *Force.* The force available to the leader can come from various sources. The administrator's official status and position with the school's bureaucracy is in itself often powerful enough to assure compliance by teachers.
2. *Paternalism.* This method tends to reduce the visibility of the leader's power. Influence tends to center around the expectation that teachers will be loyal to and show respect for the administrator by complying with his wishes.
3. *Bargaining.* This type of leadership suggests a reciprocity arrangement whereby teachers will gain certain satisfactions in return for deference to the administrator's leadership.
4. *Mutual means.* This leadership method is one in which both the group and the leader have identical objectives; this congruence, of course, obviates the need for the use of force or power to influence the group.[36]

Practically speaking, leadership style is complex and can embrace many less easily definable methods than the oversimplified listings suggest. However, style is of great importance to the administrator, and the extent to which he can vary his leadership style—both deliberately and consistently—to suit (1) the situation, (2) the faculty group, and (3) his own personality will determine his success. In the extreme autocratic situation, of course, all policy determinations are made by the administrator; few administrators today would want to be identified with this end of the leadership style continuum for long. Laissez-faire, at the other end of the continuum, allows individuals of the group complete freedom; again, most administrators feel the need to exert greater influence most of the time. The democratic style of leadership features group discussion and decision making with bargaining the essence. Paternalistic methods are not necessarily tied to any style, for paternalistic leaders can favor almost any style from authoritarian to laissez-faire because influence depends upon personal loyalty to the leader. Few administrators can claim to be charismatic leaders like Ghandi or Joan of Arc. School administrators are rarely endowed with the personal charm and inner spiritualness that is usually associated with charismatic leadership.

An administrator is, rather, a bureaucratic leader, which presents him with leadership style problems. A bureaucratic leader is one who is the incumbent in a bureaucratic office and who exercises leadership. His style is, typically, a combination of autocratic, democratic, and laissez-

---

[36] This list of four leadership methods is adapted from Irving Knickerbocker, "Leadership: A Conception and Some Implications," *The Journal of Social Issues*, IV, No. 3 (Summer, 1948), 39.

faire. How well he integrates, blends, balances, and adjusts the components of his style in harmony with the situation, the group, and his personal being will largely determine his impact as a leader in the school.

Focusing on *behavior* offers more promise to the administrator than attempting to conform to some abstract image of *style*. Further, seeking to develop an appropriate "mix" of *consideration* and *initiating structure* behaviors for his particular subordinate group and his particular situation has powerful implications for the practice of leadership by school administrators.

Theory into Practice

The following specific suggestions may be helpful to administrators who are interested in developing their leadership in harmony with current research findings.

1. *Plan to exercise leadership.* Not infrequently, school administrators oversee administrative responsibilities almost exclusively, to the detriment of their effectiveness as leaders. Administering the affairs of a public school today is an important job, and the ever-mounting administrative chores that must be faced cannot be regarded as mere "adminis-trivia." However, if an administrator is not involved in leadership, then he will almost certainly be busy with administrative matters. Therefore, until the exercise of leadership has become a habit—almost an instinct—the administrator who wishes to be an effective leader must plan ahead with regard to at least three elements:

   a. *Strategy.* This is the "map" of what one plans to do, how is it to be done, and the approximate sequence for proceeding. This "map" should be planned in some detail, yet be flexible enough to allow for various contingencies and changes.
   b. *Timing.* With an eye to scheduled and probable events, one must carefully consider the timing for each step so that the strategy will unfold in an orderly manner.
   c. *Power.* "No man is an island, entire of itself," wrote John Donne. "Every man is a piece of the continent." And a school administrator exercises leadership within an organization; his power to lead is bounded by the realities of organizational life. Power to act is conferred partially by the status of the administrator's official position and, to no small degree, by the authority conferred upon him by the faculty members, in return for what they regard as expertise. Successful leadership is a sign of expertise—it begets more power. In the beginning stages of developing his leadership, then, the administrator may want to engage in projects which he is almost certain he can

"put across." And he must soon decide how much of his plan he should reveal to others. It may well be that the administrator will find it useful to reveal only limited portions of his overall plan to selected people as it becomes necessary to gain their cooperation.

In developing a leadership plan, it is useful to remember the essential functions that a leader performs: (1) to set goals for the group, (2) to develop plans for achieving these goals, and (3) to rally support for the goals and the plans for achieving them. Each of these functions requires certain abilities; those who are able to perform these functions will have much leadership ability.

In reality, many staff members may also contribute to the three functions of leadership; but it is almost always necessary for a leader to grasp and express those things the group is willing and able to do. The sensitive administrator who is in close communication with the people in his organization is in a unique position to sense the needs of the group, to devise ways of meeting these needs, and to stimulate enthusiasm in support of the job to be done.

2. *Devote less time to administration and more time to leadership.* The pressures of school administration today are often so great that it is difficult to find time to do more than the most pressing things. As the size of administrative staffs increases, Parkinson's Law seems increasingly to be taking effect. The larger the central-office staffs, the more reports, meetings, and time will be required. As the administrator is assigned assistants, he often finds that they seem to keep him busy rather than free him. Let us keep in mind, however, that finding time for leadership in the school is probably related in part to the desire one has to be an effective leader. It is reasonable to assume that administrators with a strong desire to be leaders will thus find more time to do so than those administrators whose interests are primarily administrative.

Utilizing the *exception principle* of management can be helpful. Stated generally, this principle holds that frequently recurring decisions should be reduced to a routine and should be delegated, if possible, to others. Such decisions can be reduced to routine by the establishment and application of decision making criteria. For example, if it is decided that after a pupil has been absent for three consecutive days some action should be taken by the school, this is routine: the criterion is three consecutive days of absence. Another criterion decision could be made about the *kind* of action that should be taken after three consecutive days of absence; it could well be that this action could be delegated to a subordinate, and thus not handled by the administrator at all.

Some administrators take pride and satisfaction in dealing personally with many repetitive and routine problems of this kind. It is often believed that this intimate contact with problems gives administrators a "feel" for the school that is of great value to them. However, application of the exception principle can free the administrator and give him time to sense and work on larger, more important problems; can permit him to work personally on the criteria for making decisions and on the procedures for applying the criteria; can free him from much of the routine, repetitious work which can tie him down for hours; and can bring non-routine matters—the exceptions—to his attention at once.

One of the contributions electronic data processing has made in business and other fields is facilitating the application of the exception principle. In their early experiences with electronic data processing, administrators in many kinds of organizations have found that although computers cannot actually "think" for them—as was once supposed possible—computers do establish criteria for handling routine decisions, which eventually results in freeing the administrators to handle the exceptions or unforeseen problems.

3. *Obtain an objective assessment of leadership behavior.* A new Jersey elementary school principal had initiated a carefully planned project with his teachers which he hoped would improve their level of participation in democratic curriculum decision making. Progress was slow; the teachers seemed suspicious of attempts to involve them and did not seem able to work together as a decision making group. A professor was employed by the principal as a consultant and was invited to meet with the group. Finally, the principal began to see that the group really was accomplishing something; the meeting went harmoniously, decisions were made, and the principal was convinced things were "clicking." As the teachers emerged from the meeting, the principal was elated that his leadership was finally producing results; the professor suggested that he and the principal go out for a glass of beer.

A bit later the consultant examined his glass carefully, looked at the principal levelly, and said, "Boy! That sure was a classic display of autocratic control you put on in that meeting today!" Of course, the principal was crestfallen and a bit hurt. But it soon became evident that the things he did and said—his behavior—were not seen by others as being in harmony with his own ideas of leadership. In his anxiety to register progress—to see his leadership succeed—the principal had resorted to insistence on *compliance*, which is a far different thing than *involvement*.

Summary

In this chapter we have discussed the traditional conflicting approaches to studying leadership—both psychological and sociological—as background to the more current behavioral approaches. *Initiating structure* and *consideration* were described as dimensions of leader behavior. The concept of democratic leadership was discussed in relationship to recent research and newer behavioral concepts, which emphasize the basic differences between administrator behavior and leader behavior. Leadership problems of school principals were discussed with particular reference to the concept of Executive Professional Leadership. Leadership styles were discussed with particular reference to methods of implementing them. The chapter concluded with three suggestions for putting theory into practice.

❦ 7 ❧

change in an
organizational setting

*Among the most conspicuous values in American culture of the twen-
tieth century are progress, efficiency, science and rationality, achievement and success. These values have helped to produce a highly
dynamic society—a society in which the predominant characteristic
is change.*
                                    —*Floyd C. Mann and Franklin W. Neff* [1]

Sooner or later, discussions of change in the public schools seem always
to turn to the observations of Paul Mort. "Educational change proceeds
very slowly," he commented.

> After an invention which is destined to spread throughout the school
> appears, fifteen years typically elapse before it is found in 3 per cent of
> the school systems. . . . After practices have reached the 3 per cent point
> of diffusion their rate of spread accelerates. An additional 20 years usually
> suffices for an almost complete diffusion in an area the size of an average
> state. There are indications that the rate of spread throughout the nation
> is not much slower.[2]

---

[1] Floyd C. Mann and Franklin W. Neff, *Managing Major Change in Organizations* (Ann Arbor, Mich.: The Foundation for Research on Human Behavior, 1961),
p. 1.
[2] Paul R. Mort, "Educational Adaptability," in Donald H. Ross, ed., *Administration for Adaptability* (New York: Metropolitan School Study Council, 1958), pp.
32–33.

The result, he added, was that it took about 50 years for a newly invented practice or improvement to be generally diffused and accepted in schools throughout the country and ". . . the average school . . . lags 25 years behind the best practice." [3] Mort was not alone in his concern about the slow pace at which schools change. It is a commonplace observation that actual change in schools—significant, meaningful, effective change—is even now proceeding in desultory fashion, even after years of heavily financed plans backed by private foundations and federal programs such as the National Science Foundation and a myriad of Office of Education-supported projects. Although the "winds of change" are apparently freshening in public education, many wonder why things cannot move faster and surer.

As a gauge by which to judge what a desirable rate of change *might* be in education, many people have looked to American medicine and agriculture for comparisons. In the medical profession, once a new drug or procedure has been introduced and tested to the satisfaction of federal medical examiners, the innovation is usually put to use widely and quickly. Among the more dramatic public illustrations of this process was the rapid, worldwide spread of heart-transplant surgery in the late 1960's following the pioneer effort of Dr. Christian Barnard in the Union of South Africa. This may be compared with the introduction and spread of kindergarten education. In 1873—nearly 20 years after the introduction of private kindergartens in America from Germany—the city of St. Louis established kindergartens in its public schools. By the mid-1950's there was little doubt that kindergarten education had been firmly established in the profession as a desirable educational practice and, indeed, such federally funded projects as Head Start have provided strong stimuli for spurring its development. However, as late as the 1967–68 school year (94 years after the introduction of the kindergarten in St. Louis), only 46 per cent of the nation's 21,159 public school districts provided kindergarten education for their children. [4]

A medical treatment or procedure that is still in use fifteen years after its introduction is considered to be standard—if not classic—whereas a parallel innovation in education would be used by only about 3 per cent of the schools after the same length of time. Is the explanation for such a discrepancy to be found in the life-and-death urgency of medical progress? Perhaps, but let us consider the situation in agriculture. The relative

---

[3] Paul R. Mort and Donald H. Ross, *Principles of School Administration* (New York: McGraw-Hill Book Company, 1957), p. 181.

[4] "Kindergarten Education, 1967–68," *NEA Research Bulletin*, XLVII, No. 1 (March, 1969), 10.

resistance of education to change is even more apparent when it is compared to the recent history of diffusion and adoption of innovative techniques in American agriculture.

The Tradition of Change in American Education

The patterns by which innovations are diffused from their inventor to the ultimate adoptors has been the subject of considerable research. Although more study of these patterns is continually being undertaken in public education, the research tradition in agriculture—heavily influenced, as it is, by rural sociology—has contributed considerably to an understanding of change in education. During the era of American history which was so deeply concerned with improving the lot of the farmer, rural sociologists became highly sophisticated about overcoming *barriers* to change and about speeding up the *diffusion* process. There is at the present time considerable interest in adapting the insights of rural sociology to education.

For many years Paul Mort was considered the leading student of educational change in this country. The main thesis of his work was that adequacy of financial support is the key factor in determining how much lag a school system exhibits in adopting innovative practices. Vigorously active in his many years as a teacher and researcher at Teachers College, Columbia University, Mort left a storehouse of knowledge and a large number of devoted students who have heavily influenced the thinking of school administrators with regard to the factors that enhance change and innovation in schools. Largely because of this influence, per-pupil expenditure has long been considered the most reliable predictor of a school's chances of adopting educational innovations.

The systematic underpinnings of the cost-quality relationship in education are generally felt to have been established by Paul Mort and Francis Cornell's study of Pennsylvania schools in 1936.[5] Numerous studies dealing with the relationship between expenditure and measures of school output have followed, which generally support the not-too-surprising notion that high expenditure is *generally* associated with various indicators of superior school output. A troublesome fact was noted rather early in this research, however: it is possible for school districts to have high

---

[5] Paul R. Mort and Francis G. Cornell, *American Schools in Transition* (New York: Teachers College, Columbia University, 1941).

per-pupil costs and still have inferior schools.[6] Considerable research has been undertaken since 1938 to explain this fact. The most recent approach of Mort's followers has been to explore the *nature* of the cost-quality relationship itself. Mort tended to think of this relationship as linear: more money would tend to assure higher educational quality, and there was no point of diminishing returns. Since 1965, however, increasing attention has been paid to the possibility that cost-quality relationships in education are actually curvilinear, and have an optimum point beyond which additional expenditure fails to yield increased school output.[7]

Although it would be absurd to say that the schools' efforts to reduce the lag in change will be enhanced by penurious circumstances, more recent research tends to emphasize the influences of social structure on the amount and rate of change. For example, Richard O. Carlson studied the rate and pattern of the adoption of "new math" in a West Virginia county.[8] Carlson reported that the position which the superintendent of schools held in the power structure of the other school superintendents of the county made it possible to make reasonable predictions about the amount and rate of innovation in that superintendent's school district.[9] When the superintendent was looked upon as a leader by his peers, influential among other superintendents and in communication with many of them, his district tended to adopt innovations early and thoroughly. Contrary to the bulk of existing research on cost-quality relationships, Carlson did not find a parallel between innovation and the financial support level of the school district. If nothing else, such studies—and Carlson's study represents only one of *many* sociological studies of organizational change and innovation—indicate that money spent is only one factor in the adaptability of schools, to use Mort's term; within limits which are not yet clear, it is probably not even the major factor.

The *strategy* by which money is spent may have greater impact on change in schools than conventional indices such as per-pupil expenditure may indicate. One of the more spectacular and better-known attempts to significantly alter the pattern of change in the public schools in the post-Sputnik era was undertaken by the Physical Science Study Com-

---

[6] A. G. Grace and G. A. Moe, *State Aid and School Costs* (New York: McGraw-Hill Book Company, 1938), p. 324.

[7] Austin D. Swanson, "The Cost-Quality Relationship," in *The Challenge of Change in School Finance*, Proceedings of the Tenth Annual Conference on School Finance (Washington, D. C.: Committee on Educational Finance, National Education Association, 1967), pp. 151–65.

[8] Richard O. Carlson, *Adoption of Educational Innovations* (Eugene, Ore.: The Center for the Advanced Study of Educational Administration, University of Oregon, 1965).

[9] *Ibid.*, p. 63.

mittee (PSSC) in 1956 under the leadership of Professor J. R. Zacharias of the Massachusetts Institute of Technology.[10] Briefly, the PSSC group wanted to improve the teaching of physical science in American high schools. The job of retraining thousands of teachers, developing new curricula for all sizes of school districts, and persuading all the local school boards to buy the needed materials and equipment—all of this by traditional methods might well have taken half a century to accomplish. Instead, within ten years after the project was inaugurated high schools were considered to be behind the times if they did not offer a PSSC course.

This incredibly swift mass adoption was achieved by a strategy which involved three phases: (1) inventing the new curriculum, (2) diffusing knowledge of the new curriculum widely and rapidly among high school science teachers, (3) and getting the new curriculum adopted in local schools, a strategy which involved the use of a number of new ideas. In addition to by-passing local school districts wherever possible, the PSSC group invested its money in novel and powerful ways. First, by spending $4.5 million in two and one half years to hire a full-time professional "team," a portable self-contained curriculum "package" was developed and tested in practice. This "package" included filmed lessons, textbooks, teachers' guides, tests, and laboratory guides and apparatus—a completely unified, integrated unit that could be moved *in toto* into almost any high school. Second, physics teachers were introduced to the new techniques by attending institutes, for which they received financial grants and stipends. Some 40 institutes were made available each year throughout the country for this purpose. Third, by providing funds to be matched by the federal government (largely through the National Defense Education Act), local school boards were persuaded to buy the PSSC package for their schools. As school principals are well aware, the strategy and tactics of PSSC have raised a good many questions ranging from those concerned with learning theory to questions about broader social and political implications of what was accomplished.

Although the PSSC experience has not been replicated, variations of many of its strategies have been utilized by other groups such as the Biological Sciences Curriculum Study (BSCS), the Chemical Bond Approach Project (Chem Bond or CBA), and the School Mathematics Study Group (SMSG). The National Science Foundation, which financed PSSC, SMSG, and others, appears to have demonstrated that new strategies of expenditure can have profound effect on the rate and pattern of change in education.

---

[10] See Paul E. Marsh, *The Physical Science Study Committee: A Case History of Nationwide Curriculum Development* (unpublished doctoral thesis, Graduate School of Education, Harvard University, 1963), for a full description of PSSC.

Comparison with the Agricultural Pattern

A good many people both in this country and in others have observed the rise of the American farmer with great interest. Throughout the world farmers are noted for their traditional attitudes; yet a highly productive American agriculture was built with the help of scientific and technological developments. Few parallels exist to the American farmer's acceptance of change and exploitation of opportunities for utilizing both new and proven knowledge in the practical business of boosting production and lowering costs. When agriculture is compared to the public schools in terms of the speed with which new knowledge and improved techniques are put into widespread use, it is seen to adopt innovations with far less lag than the schools. However, comparisons between the situations in agriculture and education must be made with some caution. An agricultural adoptor of change is usually an individual—the farmer. For education, however, the adoptor is an organization—the school, rather than the individual teacher. Keeping this distinction in mind, we can make at least four generalizations that help to explain the differences in rate of change between agriculture and education.

INADEQUATE SCIENTIFIC KNOWLEDGE BASE

The development of agricultural experiment stations and the land-grant colleges has done much to provide an extensive, reliable scientific background for agricultural innovations, including not only discovery and invention, but also development and precise field-tests for utilizing new knowledge. In part, the foregoing is accounted for by the fact that farming is based largely on the physical sciences, which are amenable to relatively precise control and measurement. Medicine, and other professions based on the physical sciences, enjoy a similar advantage. Education, however, is largely allied to the behavioral sciences such as psychology and sociology; it is concerned with people, how they learn, and how they react to their environment. The bushel-per-acre production of a new strain of seed can be seen and measured, but educators still do not know how to precisely measure how much a child learns in a given situation.

It is encouraging that education is now acquiring a scientific tradition, albeit more slowly than agriculture, for many farmers have a better understanding of the role of research, and are more committed to it, than some school administrators. Unfortunately, however, today the label "experiment" is often attached to projects in schools which fail to meet fundamental criteria of serious scientific inquiry. More significant, perhaps, is the fact that education does not have a knowledge base that is comparable to the network of agricultural experiment stations which have contributed so much "pure" and "applied" research to farming. Until the knowledge base of education becomes more orderly, precise, and extensive, ways to achieve desirable educational change will remain ambiguous and confusing.

EDUCATION DOES NOT HAVE AGRICULTURE'S "CHANGE AGENTS"

There are significant "middlemen" in agriculture who link scientists and farmers, such as the county agent of the Agricultural Extension Service. Through a network of county agents, who can be thought of as "change agents," new scientific knowledge and its technological and procedural implications are quickly communicated to individual farmers. Generally, in the school situation, it is the administrator who must play the role of change agent—if there is to be one. However, the administrator is largely concerned with keeping the organization running smoothly and not with changing it. Observers have frequently commented on the influence of administrators in maintaining the status quo, rather than acting as change agents.[11]

There has been some progress in overcoming this problem of change agents in recent years. The establishment of federally financed educational research and development centers in education has been a promising start. The Center for the Advanced Study of Educational Administration (CASEA) at the University of Oregon has, for example, tried to incorporate existing knowledge in the behavioral sciences in educational administration. The aim of the CASEA—as it was for each of the eight R&D centers that were in operation by 1968—was to carry out activities in (1) research, (2) development, and (3) dissemination. Partly due to a lack of vigorous leadership in Washington, it is not yet clear whether the funds for these centers—and proposed satellite centers—will be continuous and/or adequate enough to insure success that parallels the Agricultural Extension Service experience.

THERE IS LITTLE INCENTIVE FOR SCHOOLS TO ADOPT NEW WAYS

Unlike business or industry, there is virtually no profit motive for being an innovator in American public education.[12] Existing salary plans

---

[11] An excellent example of research on this topic is Gerhard Eichholz, *Development of a Rejection Classification for Newer Educational Media* (unpublished doctoral dissertation, The Ohio State University, 1961).

[12] For a discussion of the motivations of educational innovators, see J. H. Pelley, *Invention in Education* (unpublished doctoral dissertation, Teachers College, Columbia University, 1948), pp. 170–71.

generally reward long preparation and long years of service so that the innovative educator—whether administrator or teacher—stands to gain nothing in the way of economic incentive for being innovative. Moreover, although it is (1) easy to ascertain how much a new educational practice *costs*, it is (2) very difficult to assess the extent of the results. A farmer who invests a large sum in irrigation equipment—pumps, pipes, fittings, extra trucks, a dam—can measure the wisdom of his investment in increased yield. Physicians who utilize new drugs and techniques can easily see that patients are receiving improved treatment. But schools, which invest in team teaching facilities, or a FLES program, or a kindergarten program cannot point to unassailable evidence that their investment of time and money has really paid off. In an era when businesses utilize computers to hold down costs and remain competitive, schools have barely reached the stage when the costs of data processing are accepted as "justified" by the results, which illustrates the difficulty of having incentive to adopt even proven desirable practices from other fields.

THE SCHOOL IS A "DOMESTICATED" ORGANIZATION

Students of organizations have identified a number of types and, in turn, have classified these types according to elements such as production organizations vs. service organizations; the school, obviously, belongs to the latter classification. Service organizations can be further classified according to whether (1) the organization selects its clients and (2) participation in the organization is voluntary or involuntary.

Organizations which select their clients from among volunteers have been colorfully labeled "wild" organizations,[13] a term which comes from a comparison of the environments of animals and organizations. "Wild" organizations must struggle to survive; success depends largely on their own performance. An example of such an organization is a private summer camp which must pick its campers (clients) from among those whose parents choose to allow them to attend; the campers are not required by law or circumstances to attend. The continued existence of the camp—its income and its flow of clients—is directly tied to the success it achieves in doing its job. "Domesticated" organizations, however, are protected and secure in many ways. Their clients *must* participate—whether they want to or not—and the organization will be perpetuated

---

[13] Richard O. Carlson has described the terms "wild" and "domesticated" as they apply to schools. See "Environmental Constraints and Organizational Consequences: The Public School and Its Clients," in Daniel E. Griffiths ed., *Behavioral Science and Educational Administration*, The Sixty-third Yearbook of the National Society for the Study of Education, Part II (Chicago: The University of Chicago Press, 1964), pp. 264–67.

almost regardless of its performance. The implication is that "domesticated" organizations—of which public schools are an example—are assured of vital protection which permits them to overlook some of the needs which "wild" organizations find essential.

Although public schools must compete for money from the public treasury, they are virtually assured by law that they will not be literally forced to go out of business. Even school districts which suffer what amounts to bankruptcy somehow continue to exist and are assured of eventually obtaining operating funds to reopen their doors. In 1968, for example, the Inkster school district in Michigan and the Youngstown schools in Ohio made headlines for having "gone under." However, after an appropriate hiatus these districts, and others in similar straits, received fresh infusions of cash and resumed operations.

In contrast, an educator who operates a summer camp with a steadily dwindling enrollment and/or increasing operating expenses knows that he must improve conditions or be forced to go out of business and, quite probably, suffer serious losses in the process. There are indications that "domesticated" organizations are generally slower to change and adapt to new situations than "wild" organizations. Although the terms "domestic" and "wild" may seem inappropriate when applied to educational organizations the descriptive nature of these terms is useful to administrators for considering organizational factors involved in processes of change.

Sources of Pressure for Change

The stages for utilizing an innovation have been described in a manner roughly similar to the stages for solving a problem:

1. *Awareness.* Someone must first realize that there is need for change and that some innovation for facilitating this change does exist.
2. *Interest.* In this stage more information is sought and implications are explored.
3. *Evaluation.* This stage is still a planning process; the proposed idea is thought through in terms of how it might work in the particular situation.
4. *Trial.* Not an experiment, the trial stage is, rather, a small-scale application of the idea.
5. *Adoption.* If the trial is promising, the innovation will probably be adopted.[14]

---

[14] This listing is adapted from Special Report 15 of the North Central Rural Sociology Subcommittee on the Diffusion of Farm Practices, *How Farm People Accept New Ideas* (Ames, Ia.: Cooperative Extension Service, Iowa State University, 1962).

It would be advantageous if awareness of educational needs and of new ways to meet these needs would come from within the school; there is little evidence that this occurs very often, nor is it likely to occur on a significant scale in the near future. Schools generally become *really* aware of innovative practices and *really* aware of the need to adopt these practices largely as a result of external pressure. Significant change in American schools—both past and present—has seldom occurred as a result of the initiative of public school educators. A Sputnik is orbited in space and rising public indignation and fear dictates to schoolmen that things must change. What, specifically, must be done to remedy this situation? Schoolmen soon learn of innovative ideas from English professors, admirals, professional writers—virtually everyone except public school educators. When many young men fail their physical examinations for the draft, patriotic citizens soon besiege principals about the need to overhaul the schools' physical education program—and how to do it. Minority groups protest, rebel, and riot, and as a consequence the schools are told their programs are inadequate. Senators, federal bureaucrats, military administrators—all feel that they must offer innovative ideas to a profession which is perceived as preserving the *status quo*, making only feeble efforts to invent bold new plans to meet the deepening crisis.

However, the awareness stage of innovation is not always accompanied by public clamor. Mergers between large publishing corporations and electronics and "software" [15] producers, which began to occur in the mid-1960's, signaled the beginning of a powerful trend that may do much to change fundamental public educational processes. Although this trend is, in part, merely one recent example of how business exploits a newly profitable market, it also represents the creation of a potentially powerful distribution network by which the fruits of recent scientific research—in fields such as learning theory—can be made available to schools in usable form. As a parallel, let us consider the recent history of soil-testing.

A few years ago one needed a Ph.D. in soil chemistry with access to a laboratory to be able to test a soil sample; today a high school student with an inexpensive, factory produced kit can do it just as well. The result: more soil is tested at lower cost, and Ph.D.'s are freed to work on newer, more powerful ideas. A similar process which made the knowledge of research available to schools in industry developed and tested teaching-

---

[15] "Software" refers to the detailed instructions that must be prepared so that data-processing equipment and computers will perform the tasks we want with the data we supply. A self-teaching "program" is an example. "Hardware" refers to the equipment itself (sometimes called "black boxes," regardless of color). In order to utilize electronic computers any user must have "software" that will enable the computer to do the job that the user wants done.

centered products began to expand rapidly in the late 1960's. This new source of educational change, with the drive, skill, and resources so characteristic of American industry, will undoubtedly be increasingly influential in initiating change in schools for some years to come.

The chief school administrator of the district, the school superintendent, is in a unique position to block or facilitate the initiation of change. He is a powerful figure in a typically hierarchical structure and is also the most exposed professional in the hierarchy. Interposed between the community which protects and supports the school organization and the professional staff of the organization, the superintendent can take an authoritative, powerful stance on emerging needs and new ideas. Although the superintendent must exercise professional leadership of the staff, his tenure is more directly related to the confidence the community has that the schools are meeting its needs adequately.

Many individuals and organizations communicate with and seek to influence the superintendent: the press, community leaders and groups, the board, private foundations, commercial interests, university professors, state and federal agencies, professional and union organizations—to name a few. Consequently, studies of change processes have tended to emphasize the role of the superintendent. An extensive survey of how educational change occurs in New York State concluded that the superintendent of schools is generally the key figure.[16] The more the superintendent investigates a situation, finds out what other people are doing, senses needs, and facilitates changes, the greater the likelihood that change will occur. Superintendents who are out of touch with current conditions, do not keep alert to emerging needs and ways of meeting them, and do not facilitate change have great power to keep change in the schools to a minimum.

Let us emphasize that we are referring to genuine *change*, not mere *organizational drift*. It is almost impossible today to maintain a school in *status quo;* forces for change in our society are so powerful and so pervasive that remaining static is nearly impossible. For example, a principal in a wealthy suburban school district needed some new arithmetic books; when he discovered that "good old-fashioned" arithmetic books were no longer available, he purchased a currently well-known brand of textbooks—which dutifully claimed to be based on "modern math." Thus, simply because the "old" books were no longer available, the principal, by signing a purchase requisition, introduced a "change" in the school which he promptly labeled in his annual P.T.A. address as "an innovation." Actually, the change in instructional methods and content which the pupils experienced in the classroom was relatively minor.

---

[16] Henry M. Brickell, *Organizing New York State for Educational Change* (Albany, N. Y.: State Education Department, 1961), p. 22.

The fact that some organizations seem to drift along, virtually unaware of the need to adapt to changing conditions in their environment or seemingly unable to change in an adequate way, has been the subject of much comment and some research. In the midst of the tumultuous inner-city "rebellions" of the summer of 1967, a number of American leaders pointed to education as *the* basic place where change was needed. But, as the late Senator Robert F. Kennedy once exclaimed,

> We pass bills and appropriate money and assuage our consciences, and local school systems keep right on doing things the way they've done them for decades. The kids in the ghettos will never recover unless we do something right now. We can't wait ten years.[17]

The term "organizational health" has been used to describe the tendency of organizations either to take the lead in adapting to significant changes in their environment or to hesitate, being buffeted about and rendered ineffectual by changes in external demands and conditions.

Organizational Health

In Chapter 3 we described the school organization as an open social system. A definition of "open social system" might be useful at this point; Matthew Miles has given us a simple, concise one:

> [An open social system is] a bounded collection of interdependent parts, devoted to the accomplishment of some goal or goals, with the parts maintained in a steady state in relation to each other and the environment by means of (1) the standard modes of operation, and (2) feedback from the environment about the consequences of system actions.[18]

This is a general definition of a system, and it describes the organizations that educators deal with. But all organizations—whether businesses, hospitals, or armies—have two additional characteristics:

1. They are social systems that are larger and more complex than *primary* or face-to-face groups.
2. Their goals are rather clearly defined and limited.

---

[17] *The New York Times* (July 25, 1967), p. 14. © 1967 by The New York Times Company. Reprinted by permission.

[18] Matthew B. Miles, "Educational Innovation: The Nature of the Problem," in Matthew B. Miles, ed., *Innovation in Education* (New York: Teachers College Press, 1964), p. 13. © 1964 by Teachers College, Columbia University. Reprinted by permission.

Much has been done and said in the last decade to emphasize the simple truth—long denied by educators—that schools and school systems are organizations which have much in common with other kinds of organizations. This new emphasis has had many desirable results, one of which is the increased attention that educational administrators have been giving to the way other organizations have tried to solve similar problems. Although it is true that educational organizations have some unique characteristics which they do not universally share with organizations in general, we will now focus on some organizational characteristics which seem to be universal.

An organization exists in a setting or environment from which it receives inputs. These inputs may be varied and numerous, but for schools they must include children and money. The organization also produces outputs, which for schools may be goal attainment and attitudes and learning of the schools' clients—the children. Presumably, between the inputs and the outputs of an organization something occurs to induce the goal achievement that is noted and the changes that appear. In order for the maximum goal achievement to be attained, the members of the organization must have a reasonably accurate idea of the organization's goals. Further, the accuracy of their perception of these goals will affect the way in which these members carry out their roles. Standards, or norms, of interpersonal behavior must be established. The organization must have a system of rewards and penalties for regulating the role-behavior of its personnel, as well as methods of obtaining information at certain points in the on-going processes so that it can react so as to regulate and adjust whatever is occurring. The latter is a form of feedback.

This entire procedure of inputs, process, and outputs is a dynamic whole; changes must be balanced by other changes and unforeseen circumstances must be adapted to, yet the organization must be durable and on-going at the same time. Different organizations are not equally adaptable or durable. In other words, they exhibit different degrees of *organizational health*. Briefly, a healthy organization has the following characteristics:

> [It] not only survives in its environment, but continues to cope adequately over the long haul, and continuously develops and extends its surviving and coping abilities. Short-run operations on any particular day may be effective or ineffective, but continued survival, adequate coping, and growth are taking place.[19]

---

19 Matthew B. Miles, "Planned Change and Organizational Health: Figure and Ground," in Richard O. Carlson, *et al.*, *Change Processes in the Public Schools* (Eugene, Ore.: The Center for the Advanced Study of Educational Administration, University of Oregon, 1965), p. 17.

This condition, of course, indicates only a relative position on a continuum, at the other end of which we find *unhealthy* organizations. The unhealthy organization is steadily ineffective. It may cope with its environment effectively on a short-term basis such as a "crash program" or a concentrated drive to meet a particularly threatening situation, but in the long run, the unhealthy organization becomes less and less able to cope with its environment; rather than gaining in its ability to cope with a situation, it declines over a period of time in this capacity.

Chris Argyris uses the concept of *organization effectiveness* similarly to Miles and Bennis' use of *organizational health*. Argyris contends that organization effectiveness hinges on an organization's ability to accomplish three essentials:

1. Achieve its goals
2. Maintain itself internally
3. Adapt to its environment

In addition, Argyris contends, the effective organization will accomplish these three "core activities" at an increasing—or, at least, steady—rate of effectiveness over a period of time.[20] Some of the more specific dimensions which Miles uses to describe organization health are:

1. *Goal focus.* This is the extent to which people in the organization understand and accept the achievable and appropriate goals of the organization.
2. *Communication adequacy.* This is vertical and horizontal internal communication and external communication with the environment, or the amount of "noise" and distortion and the ease and facility of communication.
3. *Optimal power equalization.* An important element of this dimension is the action of collaboration versus coercion.
4. *Resources utilization.* This is effective use of personnel so that they —as persons—feel "self-actualized," feel that they are growing and developing in their jobs.
5. *Cohesiveness.* This is the extent to which participants like the organization and want to remain in it in order to influence the collaborative style.
6. *Morale.* This is exhibited as feelings of well-being and satisfaction.
7. *Innovativeness.* This is the tendency to devise new procedures and goals, to grow, to develop, and to become more differentiated over a period of time.
8. *Autonomy.* Rather than being merely a "tool of the environment"

---

[20] Chris Argyris, *Integrating the Individual and the Organization* (New York: John Wiley & Sons, Inc., 1964), p. 123.

which responds passively to outside stimuli, the autonomous organization tends to determine its own behavior in harmony with external
demands.

9. *Adaptation.* Healthy organizations should be able to change, correct,
   and adapt faster than the environment.
10. *Problem-solving adequacy.* This includes mechanisms for sensing
    and perceiving problems as well as those for solving problems per-
    manently and with minimum strain.[21]

Organizational health, then, is a broadly descriptive term which refers
to the processes through which the organization approaches problems.
No single output measure or time-slice of organizational performance
can provide a reliable, accurate measure of organizational health, a central concern of which is the organization's continuing ability to cope
with change, to adapt to the future. This ability is best viewed in the
perspective of time. "The measure of health," Kubie tells us,

> is flexibility, the freedom to learn through experience, the freedom to
> change with changing internal and external circumstances, to be influ-
> enced by reasonable argument, admonitions, exhortation, and the appeal
> to emotions; the freedom to respond appropriately to the stimulus of
> reward and punishment, and especially the freedom to cease when sated.
> The essence of normality is flexibility in all of these vital ways.[22]

The concept of organizational health suggests the existence of a continuum, with some organizations on the "healthy" end, some on the
"unhealthy" end, and many organizations between these extremes. Over
a period of time, organizational health includes, among other things, the
ability of the organization to achieve goals, maintain itself, and adapt to
environmental changes. "Spot" appraisals of organizational health are
inadequate because we must expect that, over a period of time, the state
of health will alternately improve and worsen. In appraising organizational health, the administrator must consider (1) the present state of
organizational health and (2) the trend over time with particular reference to the organization's probable health in the future.

Survey Feedback

If a school administrator takes the notion of organizational health at
all seriously he begins to ask practical questions such as: "What is the
status of my school?" Since most organizations, like most individuals,

---

[21] Adapted from Miles, "Planned Change," *op. cit.,* pp. 18–21.
[22] Lawrence S. Kubie, *Neurotic Distortion of the Creative Process* (Lawrence,
Kan.: University of Kansas Press, Porter Lectures, Series 22, 1958), pp. 20–21.

will want to maintain good health, the next question might be "What can be done to improve things?" Fortunately, the very process of assessing organizational health can have a salutory effect on organizational health.

Much of what schoolmen now know about organizational health comes from the experience of business and industry, for which the need of the organization to survive and develop in rapidly changing and highly competitive conditions has been a matter of high priority for some years. This experience has shown that the traditional ways of measuring the effectiveness of an organization do not suffice under present conditions of change. Static, discrete, time-slice measurements "do not provide viable measures of health, for they tell us nothing about the processes by which the organization copes with its problems." [23] A number of techniques for measuring the effectiveness of an organization have been developed, which are characterized by some kind of self-study approach. We will now consider a technique that is generally known as *survey feedback*.

In practice, survey feedback can take many specific forms; however, essentially two steps must be taken:

1. *The survey.* In this step information data are obtained from people in the organization and its environment, data which concern how participants perceive the organization functioning. Survey data can be obtained through questionnaires to which organizational participants respond or through other means and can include information about perceptions and reactions to how the school is functioning, how well the school is achieving its goals, and what the roadblocks to progress are.

2. *The feedback.* Once useful data on the organization's processes have been gathered, they are fed back into the organization by being given to the participants. *How* this is accomplished is very important in terms of the effect it has; for example, a principal could include the essential data in a few lines of a routine bulletin to teachers, which would probably evoke very little further response. Or a principal could arrange to make the detailed data for the school available for study and discussion at a meeting of the faculty. In the latter situation there would probably be greater discussion, more questioning, and more involvement and interaction than in the former. With regard to organizational health, it thus is important how this phase of survey feedback is handled.

A rudimentary form of feedback is the frequent practice of "following-up" students after they graduate from public school. If some students do poorly in college, this information is fed back to the faculty so that the

---

[23] Warren G. Bennis, *Changing Organizations* (New York: McGraw-Hill Book Company, 1966), p. 44.

curriculum and teaching procedures can be improved, a good illustration of the "loop," in which part of the organization's output is fed back into the organization as a new input. The feedback from the follow-up of students in college becomes a new input into the organization; presumably, the result is a better way of doing things. But it is not sufficient to determine that some of a school's graduates are doing poorly in college and that others are doing well; as soon as this is known, new questions arise, for example, what kind of trouble is being experienced? Why aren't some students doing well? Is the cause a weakness in English? What can be done in high school to improve preparation for college? What, specifically, are the problems? How can they be solved? When answers to these questions begin to come back to the faculty, changes can occur to improve the school's performance.

When we use survey feedback to improve organizational health, we must feed a different kind of survey data into our study. Following are listed some of the *kinds* of survey data that would be meaningful to the organizational health of schools:

1. How decisions *are* made and how they *should* be made
2. Morale
3. The relationships between teachers and principals
4. How the school relates to the community
5. Communication—its adequacy and clarity
6. Organizational climate
7. How satisfied people are with their roles in the school and why
8. Goals of the school and how to interpret them

The survey feedback serves an important function in that it enables a school staff to examine and analyze their own operations: it provides objective data which can be discussed, questioned, and challenged with little of the emotion that accompanies similar discussions that might be based solely on subjective opinions. And if it is found, during the analysis of feedback data by the faculty, that more information is needed to complete the analysis, this information can be obtained. If operational decisions are based on present information, then data about future operations can be gathered in order to determine the direction and extent of the effect of such decisions. The analysis process itself, involving the give and take of discussion, can do more than simply develop cognitive awareness of various social and psychological variables involved in organizational behavior; this process provides for attitudes, behavior norms, and the interactions between people in the organization to be reshaped by the participants in a nonthreatening way. Information such as the organizational climate data of a school, or perceptions that teachers have of morale in the school, can become a fascinating source of discussion and challenge for a school faculty. The participants of an analysis of such data for their school would most likely wish to continue their analysis in order to understand their school and perhaps change it. If the process is skillfully guided, a new awareness of problems, a new interest in solving these problems adequately, and a new desire to improve the overall situation could well begin the process of change for improved organizational health.

Survey Feedback in Practice

School administrators who wish to appraise and/or improve the organizational health of their schools through the use of survey feedback techniques should be aware that at least three requirements are involved:

1. *The project should be an on-going one.* For reasons mentioned earlier, organizational health cannot be assessed on only one occasion. Success will depend, at least in part, on an extended opportunity to obtain adequate data; nor will trends and changes occur very quickly. Just as one must observe the "Big Board" over a period of time to obtain an adequate idea of American stock market conditions, so will a school's organizational health improve and decline at intervals and require continuous appraisal.
2. *It will take time.* The feedback data must be studied, questioned, and discussed. Meetings must be held—both large and small. People must interact, test, express, challenge, and solve problems. A valuable part of this process occurs *after* the data is collected, when it is subject to analysis by the staff. Some administrators may confuse survey feedback with the traditional business technique of furnishing "management" with facts on which to base decisions. The organizational health of a school requires wide participation in the analyzing of information and in decision making. Encouraging communication and interaction and testing ideas and values is central to this technique, since the development of more effective problem solving behavior, openness, collaboration, and trust is what is being sought. This takes time, patience, and many attempts to accomplish much that is lasting and meaningful.
3. *An "outside" consultant should be employed.* The experience of business and industrial organizations, as well as educational organizations, indicates that a knowledgeable, semi-detached person in a consultant role is virtually necessary to the success of the kind of effort we are proposing. The consultant is a facilitator—not an expert who tells everyone what is wrong and what to do about it. He helps the faculty group ask questions and get answers; he prods; he supports and en-

courages; he suggests ways to break impasses. Finally, he is a temporary figure in the picture; he is hired to help the organization analyze and attack its own problems. When he is no longer needed, he leaves and the organization must continue on its new and better course which resulted from his efforts to improve organizational health.

Schools need to increase their ability to cope with changing environments. Although the crises in the schools may seem to be deepening in urban areas in particular, the need for adequate, appropriate change is pressing in schools everywhere. Indeed, schools should strengthen their ability to do more than *survive* the changes and pressures to which they are being subjected by their environment; to be more adequate, schools must increase their effectiveness in anticipating change and even in *creating* change. We have noted that one way to keep an organization strong and harmonious is to stress standard operating procedures. Emphasis on rules and regulations and adherence to traditional, orderly procedures can be powerful tools in the administrator's hands for maintaining a strong organization. One effect of this approach is to insulate the school organization from much of the environment's insistence on change. For, by the time a fresh idea has been negotiated past all the rules and through the committees, and has been formally made a part of the standard operating procedure it is all too frequently no longer fresh and it includes so many compromises that it actually results in little change.

A second way to maintain an adequate organization is to provide for feedback. When it is fed back into the organization, some part of the organization's output can serve as the basis for more adaptive behavior by the organization. If, for example, a school faces mounting criticism from the community, there are two general ways it can meet the crisis: (1) it can clamp down on the staff to be sure that everyone is following all policies and rules or (2) it can try to find out just what the criticism really means and what is needed to overcome the problems pointed out by this criticism. In practice, of course, most schools use both techniques. However, schools which emphasize standard operating procedures tend to be rigid, nonadaptive organizations, whereas those which emphasize skillful use of feedback processes tend to be more flexible, adaptive, enduring, and effective.

One illustration of failure to use feedback processes sensitively and with profit occurred in a meeting held in the summer of 1967. The meeting brought 150 inner-city teachers face to face with a group of ten students from their schools to explore the causes and cures of classroom discipline problems. The students frankly expressed their feelings that teachers did not really want to communicate with them and that white teachers simply did not like or respect their Negro ghetto students. As the students described their reactions to school in greater detail, many of the teachers became incensed—and expressed their feelings by shouting rejoinders or walking out of the meeting in anger. Here teachers had available one form of feedback about the impact of the schools; rather than listen carefully to this message—whether they liked it or not—they sought to ignore it. This behavior resulted in further isolation of the schools' social systems from their external environments and reduced the possibility that the schools would take the lead in adapting to external pressures for change. Although the illustration given here is more clear-cut than most, and somewhat dramatic as well, it is typical of the way that feedback is handled in many school situations. In school districts that are "nicer" than the ghetto district mentioned above—such as wealthy suburban communities—the same effect can often be obtained by quietly ignoring feedback; in some cases this has succeeded for a long period of time before an "explosion" occurred.

Functions of the Administrator in Change

The characteristics of innovators differ greatly from the qualifications that are usually required for principals:

1. Innovators generally are young.
2. Innovators have relatively high social status in terms of amount of education, prestige ratings, and income.
3. Impersonal and cosmopolite sources of information are important to innovators.
4. Innovators are cosmopolite.
5. Innovators exert opinion leadership.
6. Innovators are likely to be viewed as deviants by their peers and by themselves.[24]

Innovators—those who are among the first 2.5 per cent to adopt a new idea—are young and venturesome, like risks, and are viewed as successful. They are members of cliques and groups, where they meet and talk with other innovators; they have cosmopolitan tendencies and travel frequently, getting to know many people outside their own local reference groups. They attend out-of-town meetings and read widely, including cosmopolitan press and journals. In sum, they have ideas, look for ideas,

---

[24] Everett M. Rogers, "What Are Innovators Like?" in Richard O. Carlson, *et al.*, *Change Processes in the Public Schools* (Eugene, Ore.: The Center for the Advanced Study of Educational Administration, University of Oregon, 1965), pp. 58–59.

and travel among people with ideas. Those who are not innovators—laggards—are localistic in their outlook, traditional, and somewhat wary of change. By the time laggards adopt a new idea, innovators are already concerned about new ones.

School administrators, in contrast, are not particularly young; often, longevity in service is important when they are seeking an appointment. Emphasis on local attitudes is usually also considered an asset in school administration: "knowing" the community, having roots and friends there.[25] Many administrators reflect in great part the need structure of their respective school cultures, and thus, to a great extent, help maintain the *status quo*.[26] And yet:

> School principals are key figures in the process [of innovation]. Where they are both aware of and sympathetic to an innovation, it tends to prosper. Where they are ignorant of its existence, or apathetic if not hostile, it tends to remain outside the blood stream of the school.[27]

Thus, the great authority and influence of the principal have an impact on innovation in the schools that parallel those of the superintendent in the school district. However, the behavior of administrators with regard to change and innovation generally seems to be influenced by their local orientation and their interest in mandates which have originated in the hierarchy. The school administrator tends to be upwardly mobile; even if he does not have immediate expectations of moving up in the hierarchy, he generally identifies with the values, beliefs, and expectations held by his superiors in the organization.[28] Thus, the administrator behaves in the way he believes the hierarchy expects him to behave and will therefore approve of. Naturally, the administrator's immediate superior's support and reinforcement will influence his behavior most of all. If this support reinforces *status quo* behavior by the administrator, he will then be expected to maintain the *status quo*, and similarly, if the support favors his efforts to encourage change, the administrator will probably take on

---

[25] For a study of the career patterns of school principals that bears on this point, see Alan F. Hillier and Frank Farner, "An Experience Profile of Elementary School Principals," *The Oregon School Study Council Bulletin*, VII, No. 9 (Eugene, Ore.: School of Education, University of Oregon, March, 1964).

[26] Carl F. Steinhoff, *Organizational Climate in a Public School System*, USOE Cooperative Research Program Contract No. OE-4-10-225, Project No. 5-083 (Syracuse University, 1965), p. 108.

[27] Lee H. Demeter, *Accelerating the Local Use of Improved Educational Practices in School Systems* (unpublished doctoral thesis, Teachers College, Columbia University, 1951), p. 23.

[28] Edwin M. Bridges, "Bureaucratic Role and Socialization: The Influence of Experience on the Elementary Principal," *Educational Administration Quarterly*, I, No. 2 (Spring, 1965), 25.

the role of change agent. It is significant that support and encouragement are more effective when they come from the administrator's immediate superior than when the originator is the more-distant superintendent of schools.[29] In sum, the administrator is largely influenced by a combination of two factors as he deals with change processes in his school:

1. His personal characteristics, which "naturally" influence his attitudes toward and interests in change
2. Organizational constraints which may limit his tendency *either* to foster change or to hinder it

Change Strategy in the School

The administrator must either leave change in his organization pretty much to chance or deliberately map out a strategy to foster change. Assuming that the latter is preferable, a practical, proven strategy will be suggested here which can be adapted in the school. Before we discuss the details of a possible change strategy, however, let us emphasize two chief characteristics:

1. *Education or situational induction.* There are two primary bases on which to develop a strategy of change: one emphasizes altering a situation with secondary emphasis on re-education of people in the organization, and the other emphasizes re-education of participants as a prior condition for change, which follows. For practical reasons, since most administrators are unable to significantly reorganize their schools by themselves to induce meaningful change in them, the strategy suggested here is based on fostering the personal growth of people in the organization to facilitate change.
2. *Change agent.* Various change strategists have differed on the role of the change agent; the chief issue is whether to use a consultant from within the organization or one from outside it. And, of course, the administrator who wishes to play the role of change agent must remember that he is already a part of the living social system of the school; he cannot step in and out of it at will. The strategy suggested here calls for an outside consultant, who can be considered a change agent.

Thus, if we decide (1) that the school's change strategy will be aimed at re-education of the organization's participants and (2) that an outside consultant will be used, it becomes evident that our strategy will be an

---

[29] Neal Gross and Robert E. Herriott, *Staff Leadership in Public Schools* (New York: John Wiley & Sons, Inc., 1965), p. 108.

action-research type.[30] Although such a plan can include a number of steps, which may be repeated in a cyclical fashion, they will fall into two main phases: *diagnosis* followed by *re-education.*

DIAGNOSIS

The consultant facilitates the diagnosis by talking with members of the organization; usually he asks each member to give his own diagnosis of what the problems are in the school. This not only gives the consultant insight into what some of the problems are but also enables him to develop rapport with a number of people in the school and find out who is most concerned and ready to work on the school's problems. From these staff members the consultant can form a planning group with which he can meet, preferably for a two- or three-day period—hopefully to accomplish the following:

1. The diagnostic information can be "fed back" and pondered.
2. The group can be encouraged to develop free communication, openness, and trust.
3. The consultant can help the group learn concepts about organizations and change that can help to facilitate change.
4. The group can plan just how to proceed from that point; such plans usually include (a) plans for involving other people, (b) plans to learn more about problems, and (c) plans to "feed back" some of the diagnostic information to more people.

This group is a *temporary* social system within the organization which would be created for the express purpose of facilitating change in the organization.[31] In effect, the consultant develops a group of change agents *within* the organization. The feeding back of the diagnostic information is an attempt to give these change agents objective insights into the assumptions and conventions which are often so firmly embedded in their environment that they are accepted as true and immutable. Frequently, in order for significant change to occur, it is these very assumptions and traditions that must be questioned.

RE-EDUCATION

The diagnostic phase of the change strategy is intended to help the organization's participants discover for themselves—and perhaps see in

---

[30] *An Action Research Program for Organization Improvement* (Ann Arbor, Mich.: Foundation for Research on Human Behavior, 1960).

[31] For a comprehensive discussion of this topic, see Matthew B. Miles, "On Temporary Systems," in Matthew B. Miles, ed., *Innovation in Education* (New York: Teachers College Press, 1964).

a new light—some of the dynamics of organizational life in the school: the power relationships between people and groups, problems of communication within the social system, the nature of conflict, and other dynamic aspects of the "living social system." These discoveries can pave the way for acquiring new skills: this is the re-education phase of the change strategy. As an illustration of the way this procedure might work in a school, let us look at how the faculty deals with conflict.

Often, faculty members assume that conflict is "bad" and should be avoided; consequently, stratagems for avoiding conflict become so firmly embedded in the conventions of acceptable organizational behavior that they seem "real." Punctilious attention to politeness, emphasis on "being cooperative" and "getting along," and scrupulous avoidance of controversy are seen as desirable. Faculty meetings may deal at such great length with trivia that discussion of vital issues cannot occur; many problems may be considered too sensitive for open discussion; and even in informal moments such as a coffee break an attempt to discuss problems involving conflict may cause participants to drift away to attend to pressing clerical matters. If the diagnostic feedback in a school reveals this kind of situation, the group, working with the outside consultant, can discuss it for the purpose of understanding that *dealing effectively* with conflict in the school may be more productive than avoidance.

It is at this point that re-education can produce rewards for the organization. The participants—those in the temporary system—need opportunities to experiment with new ways of dealing effectively with intergroup and interpersonal relations, to deal openly and trustingly with one another, and to talk and think about their situation. These opportunities are educational and, if well handled, should give the participants new skills for effectiveness in the organization and therefore make the organization itself more effective. These learning opportunities should first be provided away from the job; many consultants favor some sort of "laboratory" arrangement for a time in a low-pressure setting. Later, as the participants return to their classrooms, they will need continuing consultant support and help for a time as they attempt to use their new-found skills to solve practical problems in the school.

Of course, we are suggesting that one practical way to change relationships between people in the organization—as a first step in making the organization itself more flexible and change-oriented—is to use training designed to develop the sensitivity and interpersonal skills of the faculty, both as individual persons and as a group. This requires skill-building and encouragement of individual decision making, more open interpersonal communication, and techniques for effective participation in the organization's operations. To provide this kind of training for the faculty, once they have indicated a willingness to participate, the following are needed: (1) time (at least a few days, perhaps a long weekend), (2) facilities (a quiet, contemplative atmosphere, preferably away from "home"), and (3) a highly skilled leader, specifically trained and experienced in T-group training work.

The term "T-group training" commonly denotes a kind of human relations training that has been widely used since the 1940's by business and industry as a basic tool for effecting organizational change.[32] Although "T-group" is a common designation for such training, a number of other terms are widely used: "sensitivity group training" and "laboratory group training" are two of the more popular. A rather comprehensive set of T-group programs is now available through the National Training Laboratories,[33] and many behavioral scientists have developed other specific programs tailored to the needs of client organizations. Portions of sensitivity training have been included in other programs from time to time, such as conferences, in-service seminars, and university courses. The term T-group merely means "training group," and although the technique is clearly an invented one, no one seems quite sure just where and when it got its start in the 1940's.

Among T-group leaders there are many opinions as to purposes and techniques, but there is substantial overall agreement. The T-group leader generally takes on a nonauthoritarian and permissive role—perhaps even a passive role. He attempts to establish a "helping relationship" [34] with the group, serving as a resource person concerned with how the group operates. His particular skill is as a facilitator with specialized knowledge of group processes. The group then proceeds to define its own problems, talk about them, and seek solutions to them. This process, when properly handled, soon leads to discussion and consideration of human relationships in the organization, processes which cannot take place within the organization itself, with its power structure and its conventional emphasis on coercion and compromise for achieving goal-oriented behavior. Such a training process is sometimes referred to as "power equalizing" because the T-group does not use a power structure; it is egalitarian and, therefore, a participant is concerned with such things as group goals and the power of the group to get things accomplished. In contrast, in the typical

---

[32] For one description of T-group training in the field of business management, see Alfred J. Marrow, *Behind the Executive Mask* (New York: American Management Association, 1965).

[33] National Training Laboratories, *Explorations in Human Relations Training* (Washington, D. C.: National Training Laboratories, 1953).

[34] Carl R. Rogers, although primarily concerned with the techniques of counseling individuals, has described the nuances of the relationship by which a counselor can help the individual to grow and develop in his ability to be self-actualizing. See "The Characteristics of a Helping Relationship," *Personnel and Guidance Journal,* XXXVII (September, 1958), 11–16.

school organization, "Rebelliousness, submissiveness or withdrawal [is] the characteristic response to authority figures." [35] T-group training has been called a "people approach" [36] to improving organizational effectiveness because it capitalizes on developing the power of the people in the organization for improving the organization's performance; the results will be increased and more effective participation in communication, decision making, and other elements of change processes.

Participants in the strategy suggested here usually find it stimulating and exciting. Upon their return to the school, they will very likely attempt to put their newly acquired insights and skills to work, during which time it is desirable that as much consultant help as possible be provided to insure the greatest possible success. It is highly likely that the nonparticipating faculty members will develop an interest in what is occurring because of the enthusiasm and optimism of those who have had the T-group training, which can result in more people being drawn into the diagnostic and training processes of the change strategy. This cycle can be repeated and extended.

Essentially, this change strategy has as its purpose the improvement of the organization's health to make it more adaptable, more sensitive to the need for change, and more able to effect change. The strategy assumes that the faculty can develop its full potential to create, express, and act on a professionally responsible level only in a climate of openness and trust. It therefore stresses behavioral imperatives such as genuineness, authenticity, and open communication, as well as training in how to achieve these imperatives in organizational life. This strategy seeks to establish in the school the dynamics of collaboration and consensus as working relationships rather than as a system based on coercion and compromise. And it recognizes that teachers, being at the bottom of the school's professional hierarchy, are the people through whom the school's goals will be realized and, yet, who will be most likely to resist change forced on them by their superiors. Finally, this strategy inevitably calls for a consideration of the administrator's behavior.

In a system based on coercion and compromise, typical of schools, the administrator must employ strong controlling—even authoritarian—behavior; if he does not, he will be weak and ineffective. In a system based on collaboration, the principal must be able to resolve conflicts and influence decisions largely on the basis of openness and cooperation with teachers. In effect, behavior which may be highly appropriate in the

---

[35] Warren G. Bennis and Herbert A. Shepard, "A Theory of Group Development," *Human Relations*, IX, No. 4 (1956), 415–57.

[36] Harold J. Leavitt, "Applied Organizational Change in Industry: Structural, Technological and Humanistic Approaches," in James G. March, ed., *Handbook of Organizations* (Skokie, Ill.: Rand McNally & Co., 1965), p. 1155.

collaboration and consensus system can be the very behavior that is interpreted as weak and inadequate in the dynamics of a system that is based on the power of coercion and compromise. In embarking on a planned strategy for change in the school, the administrator should carefully consider the implications for his role and function in any arrangement that is essentially designed to facilitate change in the organization.

Summary

Although earlier studies of change in American schools emphasized the importance of fiscal adequacy, as expressed in such terms as per-pupil expenditures, it now appears that the connection of fiscal adequacy with a school's inclination to adopt change is far from clear. More recent attempts to understand the nature of change processes in schools have drawn heavily on the discoveries of behavioral scientists who have been studying similar problems in fields such as American agriculture for some decades. The chief barriers to change in schools which were not present in the agricultural experience are: (1) an inadequate base of scientific knowledge, (2) a lack of "change agents," (3) the absence of a profit motive, and (4) the "domesticated" status of the school organization. Change in the school can be expected, by and large, to result from external pressures rather than from internally generated forces. The organizational health of the school is an indicator of how well the organization copes with the continuing need to change, adapt, and—at the same time—maintain itself internally. A strategy for increasing the school's ability to facilitate change has been suggested which is based on the concept of organizational health; this strategy calls for an outside consultant to facilitate the feedback of diagnostic information as a basis for human relations training of the faculty.

❦ 8 ❦

organizational climate

*As any teacher or school executive moves from one school to another
he is inexorably struck by the differences he encounters in Organizational Climates. He voices his reaction with such remarks as, "You
don't have to be in a school very long before you feel the atmosphere
of a place."*

—Andrew W. Halpin[1]

Recognizing that schools differ markedly—and not merely in their
architecture or in such obvious characteristics as the ethnic composi-
tion of their student populations—experienced principals are quick to
sense, or to "feel," the individuality of a school. Sometimes this individuality is called the *atmosphere* of a school; other popular labels include
the *tone* of the school, the school's *climate*, or the school's *personality*.
This "feeling" which lets us know that one school is different from another is relatively intangible, as every practitioner knows. What evidence
do we actually have that the atmosphere of one school differs from that
of another?

Much of this evidence comes from observations of the behavior of
people in the schools. In one school faculty members appear to be relaxed
and at ease with each other; somehow they seem competent and generate
within us a sense of confidence in them. In another school, we find greater
tension and the teachers show it in their faces, the manner of their speech,

---

[1] Andrew W. Halpin and Don B. Croft, *The Organizational Climate of Schools*
(Chicago: Midwest Administration Center, The University of Chicago, 1963), p. 4.

and how they teach and supervise students. Some schools seem to be very noisy and "on edge," and often the teachers in these schools shout a great deal. In some schools the principal appears to emphasize his authority and status, often stressing formality and correctness in dealing with others, and in others the principal gives the impression of being much too busy to give much personal attention to any individual. Yet, in many schools the principal seems to accommodate an appropriate, easy informality without undercutting his important role in the scheme of things. The subtle differences—and sometimes they are not so subtle— which characterize the psychological environment (which Argyris calls the "living system" of organizations) are the domain of organizational climate. "Analogously," Halpin states, "personality is to the individual what Organizational Climate is to the organization." [2]

The significance of that analogy can be rather important for anyone who is concerned with organizational behavior in schools. As educators, it makes sense to accept the fact that individual persons—each possessing his own individual personality characteristics—"behave" in their own uniquely idiosyncratic manner. Some are able to cope with the challenges in their lives rather easily and move on to new challenges with confidence. Some are fearful and feel that they are manipulated by forces with which they cannot cope adequately. Some are easy to meet, outgoing, and have a knack for generating trust, confidence, and liking among their colleagues. And others may evidence an almost unlimited range of behavior characteristics; we tend to label people with terms such as "he's reserved," or "she's very bright," etc.

But as educators, we find such classifications insufficient; we want to know why people behave as they do in the hope that insights of this sort will make us more effective in our educative efforts. And we must not stretch the analogy between organizational climate and personality too far, for our interest is in schools and organizational behavior in them. One useful way of viewing organizational behavior in schools—perhaps to understand it better and possibly to direct and control it more effectively—is through the concept of organizational climate.

For a long time the term *climate* has been rather generally and imprecisely used to describe the "feeling" or "atmosphere" of organizations. The term *organizational climate* has been given somewhat more precise meaning in recent years through the contributions of a number of researchers. Chris Argyris is generally credited with the first attempt to describe systematically the factors which comprise organizational climate in a study of organizational relationships in a bank.

---

[2] Andrew W. Halpin, *Theory and Research in Administration* (New York: The Macmillan Company, 1966), p. 131.

As usually happens, the newer term—organizational climate—has already been seized upon by a few writers to identify the kind of "feeling" that has been discussed here. It will not be used in that generalized sense in this chapter or elsewhere in this book. To develop some perspective against which we may more adequately understand organizational climate, its broadest theoretical connection to the general field of organizational behavior will be described in this chapter. Then we will discuss some ways of defining and describing organizational climate. Next, we will describe two techniques for systematically assessing the organizational climate of schools. And finally, implications that research in organizational climate has for the professional practice of school administration will be highlighted.

Social Systems Theory and Organizational Climate

The main emphasis of recent research supports the view that organizational behavior, in a general way, can be seen as a function of a dynamic interrelationship between the needs of the individual person and the needs of the organization as they are expressed by demands on the individual. As discussed previously, the precise nature of this interrelationship is not fully understood; at our present "state of the art" a number of theoretical and conceptual models have been developed, tested, and put before us. The popular "Getzels-Guba Model," which describes the interconnection between the nomothetic, or organizational, dimension and the idiographic, or personal, dimension, has proven to be a useful framework for expressing one way of viewing this concept.[3] A good deal of attention has been paid—by practitioners, as well as researchers—to the desirability and, indeed, the possibility of attaining congruence of the personal needs of individuals and the demands that organizations make on them. Some administrators, for example, have given high priority to efforts to create the kind of school situation in which teachers would find the organizational demands on them to be just exactly what they—as individuals—actually desired.

Although he does not deprecate the desirability of achieving as close a needs-demands congruence as possible, Chris Argyris—who has an

---

[3] The "idiographic-nomothetic" model, which has been discussed in earlier chapters of this book, was first proposed as a collaborative effort of Getzels and Guba and was apparently based on earlier concepts of the interactive relationship between organization and man that had been posited by Kurt Lewin. See Jacob W. Getzels and Egon G. Guba, "Social Behavior and the Administrative Process," *School Review*, LXV (Winter, 1957), 423-41.

impressive background of research and practical experience in organizational facets of business, industry, and government—has posited that the needs of the individual cannot be totally congruent with the demands of the organization. The title of one of his better-known books, *Personality and Organization: The Conflict Between the System and the Individual*, clearly suggests the essence of his viewpoint.[4] Argyris suggests that it is important to find ways to *manage* this inevitable conflict and keep it within tolerable bounds. Among the techniques for doing so that Argyris has successfully explored are those that develop an interpersonal atmosphere in the organization which permits people to admit that conflict even exists, to talk about it, and to work toward reducing the causes of conflict. This, Argyris, contends, requires, first, that an interpersonal atmosphere of trust, openness, and low threat be created, without which people feel they must attempt to hide conflict, which makes the problem that much more difficult to identify and deal with. For example, if teachers feel that it is "disloyal" or "unprofessional" to discuss shortcomings in the school, it is likely that they will indeed avoid discussing these shortcomings or dealing openly with them.

Four years after the publication of Argyris' book, Amitai Etzioni pointed out that the situation may not be quite so simple.[5] Describing what he calls "compliance theory," Etzioni contends that the "fit" between individual needs and organizational demands will depend to a considerable extent upon how the organization attracts participants and keeps them involved. Etzioni labels as *coercive* those organizations which can force the individual to join and then compel him to remain a participant, such as a prison. Other organizations are largely *utilitarian*, that is, people join and remain as members in return for remuneration. Factories and business organizations readily fit this category. There are also *normative* organizations which attract and hold participants largely on the basis of their high commitment to certain ideals and goals. Some— and we do not say *all*—religious groups, voluntary associations, and educational organizations would fit this description.

In those organizations which rely on normative modes of obtaining compliance of its participants to organizational demands one would expect to find lower conflict between the individual and the demands of his role than in an organization that relies primarily on coercion. We usually expect that volunteer workers in, say, a church find greater congruence

[4] Chris Argyris, *Personality and Organization: The Conflict Between the System and the Individual* (New York: Harper & Row, Publishers, 1957).

[5] Amitai Etzioni, *A Comparative Analysis of Complex Organizations* (New York: The Fress Press, 1961).

of their personal needs and the demands of the organization than we would expect to find among the inmates of a prison. The ill-fated campaign of Senator Eugene McCarthy to obtain the Democratic nomination for President in 1968 was an excellent illustration of normative organization. Veterans of "regular" political organizations—accustomed to the rewards and punishments of patronage—found it difficult to comprehend why McCarthy's idealistic, youthful backers worked so hard and effectively when there was such a slight chance of obtaining material reward. The answer, at least in part, lay in the very fact that many of the participants were interested in promoting certain ideals and philosophy and would not otherwise have participated.

Of course, Etzioni does not state that every kind of organization fits neatly into his categories: some must be classified as *dual*. We might find, for example, an organization which has great attraction, in terms of its goals and ideology, for a professional person, but which must still pay him well to keep him.

These representative efforts of Argyris, Getzels, and Etzioni provide us with generalities about the social environment of organizational life. They utilize structures such as role theory, social systems theory, and compliance theory which are helpful for conceptualizing the dynamics of organizational behavior.

Ways of Studying Climate in Organizations

It would be misleading, however, to devote all our attention to the congruence problems between the individual and the organization in its formal sense. Somewhat similar relationships exist in the participant's relationships with informal aspects of the social system.

If the concept of formal organization is only part of the management story, what is the rest? How can we learn about the operations of the informal organization and the human factors of individuals in it? How can we utilize this knowledge to improve the functioning of our organizations? Some of these questions are quite similar to the ones that the Western Electric studies tried to answer. But that situation was industrial: the organization studied was a factory, a setting in which workers were grouped as production teams in a room to turn out tangible, manufactured products every day. We must exercise some care—and perhaps, even some skepticism—in applying the findings from that situation to other, dissimilar types of organizations. How can we find out more about the "human side" of these organizations? One way is to apply appropriate knowledge and research techniques of the behavioral sciences.

In the late 1940's, for example, William Foote Whyte took up such a problem in a fourteen-month study of twelve restaurants in Chicago.[6] The research was done under the auspices of the National Restaurant Association, which, we may safely suppose, anticipated that the practical management "know-how" it obtained from such a study would be worth the investment. Whyte and three assistants spent a period of from one to four months in each restaurant as observers, noting especially the behavior of people as they interacted with one another in the course of their work. Whyte reports on the relationships between customers, waitresses, supervisors, pantry-help, countermen, kitchen help, and others who worked in the restaurants. His systematic observations are reported in sufficient detail to show clearly the emotional involvements and the conflicts and tensions between the participants. For example, Whyte found that countermen balked and stalled when waitresses called out their orders and urged the men to turn out the food faster. Service was faster and conflict much reduced when the waitresses wrote their orders and left them on spindles for the men to pick up, for this added some needed dignity to the role of the men who did not appreciate being ordered around in public by women. Service at the bar was faster when the bartender was permitted to mix drinks in batches—all the martinis at one time, then all the whiskey sours, and so on—rather than drink-by-drink as the waitresses ordered them. Here, again, Whyte pointed out, women were giving orders to men; by permitting the men to reorganize the task so as to satisfy some of their own needs for what they perceive to be respect and status, they completed orders for drinks faster and with less fuss—to everyone's greater satisfaction.

The body of this kind of research literature is very extensive and represents a wide range of types of organizations. The focus is generally on the interpersonal relationships between members of the organization. Such research deals with complexities of behavior arising from essential facts of organizational life: that the individual finds himself in an interlocking, dynamic set of relationships involving formal *and* informal organizations, as well as the dynamic interplay between his own needs and the demands of the organization. More and more, such studies are being done in schools, where they are helpful in developing more penetrating insights into effective administrative practice.

For example, when a research team wanted to create a simulated school situation in which principals could confront "real" problems in a laboratory setting, it soon became evident that information about the school's faculty would have to be made available as part of the simulated environ-

---

6 William Foote Whyte, "The Social Structure of the Restaurant," *American Journal of Sociology*, LIV (January, 1949), 302–8.

ment. The simulation would be unrealistic if the principal did not have some information about the teachers in the school, including how they get along with each other and who is able to influence whom. In order to get such information, Iannacconne [7] conducted a study of an elementary school by using social systems theory as a frame of reference; he found that norms and expectations of the informal organization can be most frustrating to goals and purposes of individual teachers.

Willower and Jones [8] later reported a study of a junior high school which was carried out in a manner roughly similar to Whyte's restaurant study; one of their favorite observation posts in the school was the faculty lounge. They observed and reported what every seasoned administrator knows: new teachers are quickly apprised by older teachers "how things are done around here." The informal group norms, in the case of the school studied, soon indicated to young, idealistic teachers that if they wanted to be "accepted" by their colleagues they had to abandon their "permissive" attitudes toward discipline in favor of a "tough" attitude. Many of the ideas the younger teachers had brought from college—which they had thought were worthwhile—soon gave way to the "established" way of doing things if the teacher wanted to fit in at all comfortably with the faculty. What alternatives, then, does the young teacher have? Willower and Jones say he has three: "He may go along, submerge his ideals and not act on them; he may engage in conflict with his colleagues; or he may leave the organization." [9] Many would agree with Argyris' position that the first and third alternatives, which are forms of avoidance, are too frequently selected because the nature of an organization's social environment renders conflicts too painful to handle.

The above kinds of descriptions and analyses can be helpful in understanding the climate one senses in a school. However, they are only descriptions, lacking any normative base which enables us to compare one school's description with another. They tend to be generalized, rather than dealing with comparative data from which we might develop norms for judging whether a school is "high" or "low" in the quality of its organizational environment. The unique contribution of research on organizational climate has been to provide us with (1) *dimensions* along which we may take measurements of certain factors which make up the climate of an organization's environment and (2) *normative data* from many schools which enable us to determine more accurately where a

---

[7] Daniel E. Griffiths, David L. Clark, Richard D. Wynn, and Laurence Iannacconne, *Organizing Schools for Effective Education* (Danville, Ill.: The Interstate Printers and Publishers, Inc., 1962), p. 240.

[8] Donald J. Willower and Ronald G. Jones, "When Pupil Control Becomes an Institutional Theme," *Phi Delta Kappan*, XLV (November, 1963), 107-9.

[9] *Ibid.*, p. 109.

given school stands in comparison with others. By the late 1960's, two general techniques for assessing and describing the organizational climate of schools had been developed: one was largely credited to Andrew Halpin and the other to George Stern.

Organizational Climate Description Questionnaire

By far the most popular and widely used technique for assessing the organizational climate of schools has been the Organizational Climate Description Questionnaire (OCDQ), partly because of the clarity with which Halpin described his concept of organizational climate, and partly because of the relative simplicity with which the OCDQ assessment technique can be used in the practical school situation. This technique has been employed repeatedly by researchers, many of whom wished to determine whether certain kinds of organizational climate were found in schools with principals having certain characteristics.

For instance, if a principal is socially distant and emphasizes the "no-mothetic" aspect of his role—if he "goes by the book"—can we expect to find a distinctive "personality" or organizational climate in his school? Conversely, if a principal is highly idiographic—if he is more concerned with the personal dimension of organizational life—can we predict that the organizational climate in his school will be distinctively different from that of the nomothetic principal? Such speculation reveals a tendency to view the principal as a leader who has significant impact on the shaping and maintaining of the organizational climate in his school. In fact, the concepts underlying the OCDQ originate in Halpin's earlier research work on leadership, first, among Air Force flight crews, and later, with the Ohio State Personnel Board where Halpin was involved in the development of the Leader Behavior Description Questionnaire.

The rationale underlying the OCDQ assumes, first, that something actually exists which can properly be called organizational climate. Further, it is assumed that organizational climate is closely related to the perceived behaviors of teachers and principals.

The term *perceived behaviors* is important. Suppose that teachers are asked questions which are designed to elicit information about the school's principal, such as "How considerate is he?" "How energetic and effective is he?" "How approachable and how 'genuine' is his manner?" One may object that the principal may actually evidence behavior quite different than that which the teacher "perceives." The principal, for instance, may be attempting to emphasize "consideration" in his role-behavior because he associates "consideration" with leader behavior, and he wishes to be a leader. However, if a teacher does not "see" this behavior as evidencing consideration, then to him it is *not* consideration. Consider the school principal who thinks of himself as genial, easy-going, and thoughtful, whereas teachers—in private—refer to him as "old iron-pants." We enter here the sensitive territory of selective perception, in which people "see," in the psychological sense, what they are prepared to see (or hear). In dealing with the interpersonal relationships which are inextricably bound up in organizational behavior, we are constantly confronted with the truism that much of behavior is, like beauty, in the eye of the beholder.

Also, much is subtly communicated to our referents by what Edward T. Hall has so brilliantly described as "the silent language." [10] Halpin has commented lucidly on "the eloquence of behavior," [11] and we earlier commented on his caution regarding "spray-gun consideration" which, for school principals, can take the form of "the P.T.A. smile and . . . oily affability dispensed at faculty picnics and office parties." [12] In the popular vein, Eric Berne's best-seller of 1967–68, *Games People Play*,[13] has emphasized the fact that we communicate not through words alone but through our actions as well.

It may be that in dealing with the delicate fabric of the "atmosphere" of a school, what is *not* said frequently speaks louder than what *is*. A principal may say—and *mean*—"my door is always open." But a teacher may be unable to find him in his office; an open door to an empty office may say something to that teacher that is quite different from the principal's intentions. "Come and see me," another principal may urge. "Let's talk about your ideas for improving things here." Yet, when a teacher would sit down with such a principal in his office, he might notice his furtive glance at the clock, the urgent incoming telephone calls which interrupt frequently, and other evidences of pressure on the principal that may clearly tell him "He's not listening. He hasn't time for me and my ideas. We're both wasting time!"

Working under a grant from the United States Office of Education, Halpin and Croft carried out what they called an exploratory inquiry.[14] Because this was a pioneer study, the investigators felt it desirable to carve out an area of research from virtually uncharted territory and leave the rest to others who would follow. They chose, first, to concentrate on the impact of the behavior of teachers and the principal on the orga-

---

[10] Edward T. Hall, *The Silent Language* (Garden City, N. Y.: Doubleday & Company, Inc., 1959).

[11] Andrew W. Halpin, "The Eloquence of Behavior," in *Theory and Research in Administration* (New York: The Macmillan Company, 1966).

[12] *Ibid.*, p. 86.

[13] Eric Berne, *Games People Play* (New York: Grove Press, 1964).

[14] Halpin and Croft, *op. cit.*

nizational climate of schools, leaving a host of other possible factors, such as the environment in which the school happens to exist, for others to examine later. Second, they elected to try to develop an instrument which could be used to identify and describe the organizational climate of elementary schools. The result was a 64-item questionnaire called the Organizational Climate Description Questionnaire. In many ways this highly popular instrument resembles the Leader Behavior Description Questionnaire which we described in Chapter 6.

The OCDQ is easy to use. All teachers and the principal are asked to indicate their responses to each of 64 items on a four-point scale as follows:

1. Rarely occurs
2. Sometimes occurs
3. Often occurs
4. Very frequently occurs

Typical items from the OCDQ are shown in Figure 8–1. This questionnaire can be administered to the school faculty in less than hour or, if desired, the questionnaires can be completed individually by teachers and

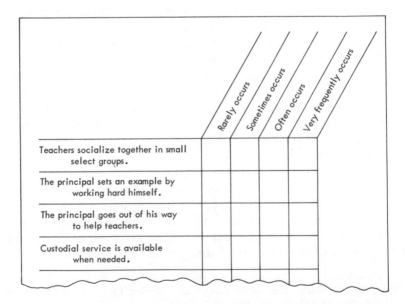

FIGURE 8–1. Sample items from the Organizational Climate Description Questionnaire. From Andrew W. Halpin and Don B. Croft, *The Organizational Climate of Schools* (Chicago: Midwest Administration Center, The University of Chicago, 1963), pp. 122–24.

handed in at their convenience; there is no time requirement, as one might expect for a "test." However, scoring is complex and requires rather sophisticated computer procedures, which fortunately can be easily handled at low cost through a scoring service.[15] Interpretation for a particular school requires some care. Principals who wish to use the OCDQ in their schools should inquire at a nearby university to ascertain if there is a professor of educational administration on the faculty who is familiar with Halpin's technique.

The OCDQ comprises eight subtests,[16] four of which describe selected facets of the teacher behavior—*as it is perceived by the teachers*—and four of which deal with the principal's behavior—again, *as it is perceived by the teachers*. The eight subtests are labeled and described as follows:

Teachers' Behavior
1. *Disengagement* refers to the teacher's tendency to be "not with it." This dimension describes a group which is "going through the motions," a group that is "not in gear" with respect to the task at hand. . . . In short, this subtest focuses upon the teachers' behavior in a task oriented situation.
2. *Hindrance* refers to the teachers' feeling that the principal burdens them with routine duties, committee demands, and other requirements which the teachers construe as unnecessary busy-work. The teachers perceive that the principal is hindering rather than facilitating their work.
3. *Esprit* refers to "morale." The teachers feel that their social needs are being satisfied, and that they are, at the same time, enjoying a sense of accomplishment in their job.
4. *Intimacy* refers to the teachers' enjoyment of friendly social relations with each other. This dimension describes a social-needs satisfaction which is not necessarily associated with task-accomplishment.

Principal's Behavior
5. *Aloofness* refers to behavior by the principal which is characterized as formal and impersonal. He "goes by the book" and prefers to be guided by rules and policies rather than deal with the teachers in an informal, face-to-face situation. His behavior, in brief, is universalistic rather than particularistic; nomothetic rather than idiosyncratic. To maintain this style, he keeps himself—at least, "emotionally"—at a distance from his staff.
6. *Production emphasis* refers to behavior by the principal which is char-

---

[15] Information on scoring the OCDQ may be obtained from Professor Andrew W. Halpin, School of Education, The University of Georgia, Athens, Georgia.

[16] The term *subtest* as used here is unfortunate. We use it in lieu of a more accurately descriptive term. Let us note that the OCDQ—and, indeed, *any* such instrument—is not a *test* which a school passes or fails, but is, rather, an assessment of what *is*.

acterized by close supervision of the staff. He is highly directive, and plays the role of a "straw boss." His communication tends to go in only one direction, and he is not sensitive to feedback from the staff.

7. *Thrust* refers to behavior by the principal which is characterized by his evident effort in trying to "move the organization." "Thrust" behavior is marked not by close supervision, but by the principal's attempt to motivate the teachers through the example which he personally sets. Apparently, because he does not ask the teachers to give of themselves any more than he willingly gives of himself, his behavior, though starkly task-oriented, is nonetheless viewed favorably by the teachers.

8. *Consideration* refers to behavior by the principal which is characterized by an inclination to treat the teachers "humanly," to try to do a little something extra for them in human terms.[17]

In their orginal study, Halpin and Croft administered the OCDQ in 71 elementary schools in various parts of the country, and, predictably, the schools varied in their climate profiles. In some schools, teachers thought morale was high, whereas in others, teachers thought morale in their organizations was somewhat lower. In some schools, the principal was rated high in consideration, whereas in others, the teachers thought their principal evidenced less consideration. Teachers in some schools thought their colleagues were fairly well "disengaged," whereas other school faculty groups thought their members were quite involved. And so on.

In their nationwide sample of schools, Halpin and Croft were able to identify "school profiles" which tended to cluster; they arbitrarily identified six such school climate profiles and called them *climate types:*

1. Open climate
2. Autonomous climate
3. Controlled climate
4. Familiar climate
5. Paternal climate
6. Closed climate

The characteristics of each of these climate types may be described after the Halpin and Croft research as follows:

1. *Open climate*
   a. *Characteristics of climate*
      High esprit
      Low disengagement

---

[17] Halpin and Croft, *op. cit.,* pp. 29 and 32.

Low hindrance
Average intimacy
Average aloofness
High consideration
Average thrust
Low production emphasis

b. *Behavioral description.* The behavior of the principal will represent an appropriate integration between his own personality and the role he is required to play as a principal. In this respect, his behavior can be viewed as genuine. Not only will he set an example by working hard himself (thrust), but, depending upon the situation, he will either criticize the actions of teachers or will make a special effort to help a teacher (high consideration). He will possess a personal ability to be "genuine," whether he is required to control and direct the activities of others or show compassion in satisfying the social needs of individual teachers. He will possess integrity, in that he is "all of a piece" and therefore can function well in either situation. He will not be aloof, nor will the rules and procedures he sets up be inflexible or impersonal. Nonetheless, he will feel that regulations must be adhered to, for it is through these regulations that he provides subtle direction and control for the teachers. The principal need not emphasize production; nor must he monitor teachers' activities closely (low production emphasis). Nor will he do all the work himself, for he has the ability to let appropriate leadership acts emerge from the teachers. In sum, such a principal will be in full control of the situation and he will provide clear leadership for the staff. Under his leadership teachers will obtain considerable job satisfaction and will be sufficiently motivated to overcome difficulties and frustrations. They will develop the incentive to solve their own problems and keep the organization moving. Such teachers are proud to be associated with the school and do not feel burdened by busy-work or routine reports.

2. *Autonomous climate*

   a. *Characteristics of climate*
   High esprit
   High intimacy
   Low disengagement
   Low hindrance
   High aloofness
   Low production emphasis
   Average consideration
   Average thrust

   b. *Behavioral description.* The principal will give teachers complete freedom to provide their own structures for interaction, as well as find ways within the group for satisfying their social needs. The scores in such climates will lean slightly more toward social needs satisfaction than toward task achievement (high esprit and intimacy). Teachers in these climates will be able to achieve goals quickly and easily (low disengagement), will work well together, and will accomplish the tasks of the organization. Such teachers will not be hindered by administrative paperwork, and will not complain about reports they must submit. Their principal will have set up procedures and regulations to facilitate the teachers' tasks (low hindrance) and will establish controls that enable teachers to by-pass the principal about matters concerning school supplies. Teacher morale will be high, but not as high as in an open climate. Esprit would probably be higher if greater task accomplishment also occurred within the organization. High aloofness will be evident, for such a principal will run the organization in an impersonal, businesslike manner. His leadership style will favor the establishment of procedures and regulations which provide guidelines that the teacher can follow; he will not personally check to see that things are being done and he will not force people to produce, nor say that "we should be working harder." Instead, he will appear satisfied to let the teachers work at their own speed and will monitor their activities very little (low production emphasis). On the whole, the principal will be considerate, and he will attempt to satisfy the social needs of the teachers as well as most principals (average consideration). He will provide incentive for the organization by setting an example of hard work himself. He is genuine and flexible, although not to the extent of principals in an open climate.

3. *Controlled climate*
   a. *Characteristics of climate*
      High esprit
      Low disengagement
      High production emphasis
      Low consideration
      High thrust
      Average aloofness
      High hindrance
      Low intimacy
   b. *Behavioral description.* The principal will press for achievement at the expense of social needs satisfaction. Everyone will "work hard" and there will be little time for friendly relations with others or deviation from established controls and directives. Such a climate stresses task achievement to the detriment of social needs satisfaction. Nevertheless, since morale will be high (esprit), this climate can be classified as more open than closed. The teachers will be completely "engaged" in the task and will not bicker, complain, or differ with the principal's directives. They know they are in the school to do a job, and they will expect to be told individually

just how to do it (low disengagement). There will be an excessive amount of paper-work, routine reports, busy-work, and other obstacles which will hinder the teachers' task accomplishment. Few procedures will have been set up to facilitate their work; in fact, paper-work will be used merely to keep them busy (high hindrance). Accordingly, teachers will have little time to establish very friendly social relations with each other, and there will be very little feeling of camaraderie (low intimacy). Teachers will ordinarily work alone and be impersonal with each other. Social isolation will be common and there will be almost no genuinely warm relationships among teachers. The principal will dominate and direct, having little flexibility and insisting that everything must be done his way (high production emphasis). He will also be somewhat aloof and will have distributed impersonal, mimeographed directives about procedures for teachers to follow in accomplishing tasks. Means and ends will be predetermined by the principal, who will become dogmatic when his procedures are not followed. He will care little for the feelings of teachers, but will do whatever is necessary to get the job done his way. He will evidence low consideration, and will not seek to meet teachers' social needs. He will attempt to motivate the teachers by his personal example of hard work (high thrust) and personally ascertain that nothing goes wrong. He will delegate few responsibilities and will initiate leadership acts rather than allow them to come from the group.

4. *Familiar climate*
   a. *Characteristics of climate*
      High disengagement
      Low hindrance
      High intimacy
      Average esprit
      High consideration
      Low aloofness
      Low production emphasis
      Average thrust
   b. *Behavioral description.* The principal and teachers will be conspicuously friendly. Social needs satisfaction will be extremely high and little will be done to direct or control a group's activities toward goal achievement. The principal will exert little control in directing teachers' acts, resulting in disengagement and few task-oriented accomplishments (high disengagement). Too many people will attempt to tell others how things should be done, but low hindrance will make paper-work as easy as possible. Socially, the teachers will be all part of a big, happy family (high intimacy). Morale or job satisfaction will be average and will stem from social needs satisfaction. The principal will be afraid to make changes lest he disrupt his "big, happy family" (high consideration), and

will want everyone to know he is part of the group, is in no way
different from anybody else, and is neither impersonal nor aloof.
He will insist on few regulations and will not emphasize production,
nor check to see whether teachers are performing their tasks correctly. Under such a principal's guidance, no one will work to capacity, and no one will ever be wrong. Tasks accomplished by
teachers will rarely be criticized (low production emphasis). In
short, little will be done by either direct or indirect means to evaluate or direct the activities of teachers. However, teachers will
attribute *thrust* to the principal—he is a "good guy."

5. *Paternal climate*
   a. *Characteristics of climate*
      High production emphasis
      High disengagement
      Low hindrance
      Low intimacy
      Low esprit
      Average thrust
      Low aloofness
      High consideration
   b. *Behavioral description.* The principal will be so *non*aloof that he
      becomes intrusive. He *must* know everything that occurs. He will
      continually emphasize what should be done (production emphasis),
      but nothing will, in fact, seem to get done. The principal will set
      up schedules, class changes, and the like personally. The school and
      his duties within it will be the principal's main interest in life. Such
      a principal will be considerate, but his consideration will be a form
      of seductive oversolicitousness, rather than a genuine concern for
      the social needs of others, and he will use this consideration be-
      havior to satisfy his own social needs. He will demonstrate average
      thrust in his attempts to motivate the organization; nonetheless, he
      will fail to motivate teachers primarily because he will not provide
      an example or an ideal which teachers can emulate. He will be in-
      effective in controlling teachers and in satisfying their social needs,
      and will evidence nongenuine behavior that will be viewed by
      teachers as nonmotivating. Teachers in his school will not work
      well together, but will split into factions. There will be high dis-
      engagement because of the principal's inability to control activities
      of teachers, low hindrance because he will insist on doing most of
      the busy-work himself, and low intimacy and low esprit among
      teachers: they will neither enjoy friendly relations with each other
      nor obtain adequate satisfaction with regard to tasks accomplished
      or social needs. The principal will appear to be everywhere at
      once, scurrying, checking, and monitoring.

6. *Closed climate*
   a. *Characteristics of climate*

High disengagement
High hindrance
Average intimacy
Low esprit
Low thrust
High aloofness
High production emphasis
Low consideration

b. *Behavioral description.* Group members will obtain little satisfaction with respect to task achievement or social needs. The principal will be ineffective in directing the activities of the teachers and will not be inclined to look out for teachers' personal welfare. Teachers will be disengaged and will not work well together; their group achievement will be minimal. High hindrance will be caused by the principal's inadequate facilitation of teacher task accomplishment. Esprit will be low, in fact, as low as possible, reflecting low job and social need satisfaction. There will be average intimacy: teachers will feel that they must obtain job satisfaction from friendly relations with the other teachers. There will also be a very high turnover rate among teachers. The principal will be highly aloof and impersonal in controlling and directing teacher activities. High production emphasis will reflect the principal's feeling that "We should work harder." He will set up rules which are usually arbitrary. Such a principal will not get too involved personally with his teachers and their problems, for he will "go by the book." He will frequently feel that external forces are directing the course of events in his school and will thus put little personal drive into his own work, demonstrating little thrust to the teaching staff. He will keep perfect records and turn out all necessary paperwork (high hindrance), and will usually urge people to work harder. He will tend to be either philosophical about high teacher turnover or blame it on conditions over which he has no control. He will not be inventive or ingenious in reducing obstacles and annoyances that teachers encounter in their work.[18]

Much about the OCDQ may raise questions. For example, its six "climate types" are arbitrary; other researchers have identified both fewer and more "types." Later research has shown that principals' perceptions expressed through the OCDQ tend to be significantly different than the perceptions of teachers in the same schools.[19] The use of the OCDQ is apparently not well suited to large, urban, or secondary schools, and

---

[18] Adapted from *ibid.*, pp. 60–66.
[19] J. Foster Watkins, "The OCDQ: An Application and Some Implications," *Educational Administration Quarterly*, IV, No. 2 (Spring, 1968), 57–58.

whether it can appropriately be used for evaluating a school's effectiveness—a possibility which Halpin has raised—remains very much in question. Some may challenge Halpin's readiness to assume that openness of organizational climate is, necessarily, good. And Halpin himself has questioned whether "open" climates can be attained in very large city schools.

However, the OCDQ has been used many times since the original study, and, until better instruments are subsequently developed, it will provide useful feedback information to the administrator with a grasp of its limitations. Let us consider the research of Anderson, in which the characteristics of principals in schools of certain climate-types were recorded.[20] Anderson's findings, as summarized in Figure 8–2, can be of help to school principals who wish to re-examine their own organizational behavior with regard to its effect on the organizational climate of their schools.

Organizational Climate Index

Working independently of Halpin, George Stern and Carl Steinhoff have developed a different approach to the description and measurement of organizational climate in organizations. Stern's early interest was in human personality; dealing with college students, as both a teacher and researcher, he became interested in the fact that colleges are distinctively dissimilar in many significant ways [21]: the kinds of students they attract, the values and goals of students and faculty, the make-up of the faculty, and so forth. Stern, like Halpin, a psychologist, tended to see an analogy between human personality and the personality of the institution, and he drew on the much earlier work of Henry A. Murray, who had developed the concept of *need-press* as it shaped human personality.

Murray postulated that personality is the product of dynamic interplay between *need*, both internal and external, and *press*, which is roughly equivalent to environmental pressures that lead to adaptive behavior.[22] Stern and others evolved two questionnaire instruments to determine the need-press factors they felt influenced development of climate in colleges: the Activities Index (AI), which dealt with the needs of individuals, and

---

[20] Donald P. Anderson, *Organizational Climate of Elementary Schools* (Minneapolis: Educational Research and Development Council of the Five Cities Metropolitan Area, Inc., 1964).

[21] For a detailed description of Stern's extensive work in this field, see George G. Stern, *People in Context: Measuring Person-Environment Congruence in Education and Industry* (New York: John Wiley & Sons, Inc., *in press*).

[22] Henry A. Murray, *et al.*, *Explorations in Personality* (New York: Oxford University Press, Inc., 1938), p. 124.

Climate Dimension	Characterization of Principal in High Scoring School	Characterization of Principal in Low Scoring School
Teachers' Behavior		
Disengagement	Submissive, dependent Shy, withdrawn, cold Practical, conventional	Dominant, assertive Adventurous, genial Imaginative, creative
Hindrance	Cool, aloof, obstructive Practical, conventional Group dependent	Trustful, adaptable Imaginative, creative Self-sufficient
Esprit	Mature, calm, stable Assertive, aggressive Persistent, conscientious Confident, self-secure Controlled, exacting High social values	Worrying, emotional Mild, submissive Undependable, frivolous Timid, insecure Uncontrolled, lax Low social values
Intimacy	Of less intelligence Aggressive, competitive High social values	Brighter Mild, dependent Low social values
Principal's Behavior		
Aloofness	Cool, suspicious, rigid Mild, noncompetitive Calculating, exacting Low social values	Kindly, trustful Assertive, self-assured Simple, unpretentious High social values
Production emphasis	Brighter Persistent, consistent Anxious, demanding High economic values	Of less intelligence Relaxed, frivolous Realistic, self-reliant Low economic values
Thrust	Dominant, assertive Responsible, persistent High theoretical values High esthetic values	Submissive, "milk-toast" Casual, undependable Low theoretical values Low esthetic values
Consideration	Of lesser intelligence Enthusiastic, cheerful Controlled, exacting	Brighter Silent, depressed Uncontrolled, lax

FIGURE 8–2. Significant relationships between climate dimensions and personality-value factors. From Donald P. Anderson, *Organization Climate of Elementary Schools* (Minneapolis: Educational Research and Development Council of the Twin Cities Metropolitan Area, Inc., 1964), p. 5.

the College Characteristics Index (CCI), which probed the organizational press as experienced by persons in the organization.[23] Over the years, these two questionnaires have been used on a number of campuses where

---

[23] George G. Stern, "Characteristics of the Intellectual Climate in College Environments," *Harvard Educational Review*, XXXI (Winter, 1963), 5–41.

they have helped researchers assess organizational climate in colleges. Differences among various institutions of higher learning—denominational colleges, state universities, liberal arts colleges, and teachers colleges, among others—are observable for measurable factors such as staff and facilities, achievement standards, aspirations of students, extent of student freedom and responsibility, academic climate, and social life on the campus. The level of intellectual press seems to be particularly valuable in explaining the differences among collegiate institutions.

Stern and Steinhoff developed an adaptation of the CCI, applicable to schools and other organizations, called the Organizational Climate Index (OCI), which was first used in a study of the public schools in Syracuse, New York in 1965.[24] The OCI presents teachers with 300 statements which could apply to their schools; the teachers are then asked to mark these statements true or false, as applicable to their schools. Typical statements presented in the OCI are shown in Figure 8–3. After compilation,

T   F

☐   ☐   Administrators are sometimes given uncomplimentary nicknames.

☐   ☐   People here mind their own business.

☐   ☐   People here are usually quick to help each other out.

FIGURE 8–3.   Sample items from the Organizational Climate Index Form 1163. Copyright © 1963 by George G. Stern.

the items on the OCI provide data from organizational participants on 30 of Murray's need-press scales. Analysis of these data from Syracuse schools have led to the formulation of the six OCI Climate Index Factors, shown in Figure 8–4, which are called first-order factors. The first five first-order factors together describe a second-order factor called *development press*, which is the capacity of the organizational environment to support, satisfy, or reward self-actualizing behavior. Another second-order factor, *control press*, refers to those characteristics of environmental press which inhibit or restrict personal expressiveness. Control press is also derived from a combination of the six first-order factors and reflections of factors 1 and 2. The definitions of the scale items which comprise development press and control press are shown in Figure 8–5.

In sum, the two key dimensions which describe the organizational climate of a school, using the Stern-Steinhoff Organizational Climate Index, are development press and control press. By representing these dimensions along intersecting axes, as shown in Figure 8–6, we can pinpoint the OCI score of a school and describe its organizational climate

---

[24] Carl R. Steinhoff, *Organizational Climate in a Public School System* (USOE Cooperative Research Program Contract No. OE-4-225, Project No. S-083, Syracuse University, 1965).

I. Development press

1. Intellectual climate. This factor describes a concern with intellectual activity, social action, and personal effectiveness. It is based on the scales for humanities–social sciences, science, reflectiveness, understanding, fantasied achievement, sensuality, ego achievement, exhibitionism, and change.

2. Achievement standards. This factor reflects a press for achievement. Schools high on this factor stress hard work, perseverance, and a total day-by-day commitment of institutional purposes. It is defined by counteraction, energy, achievement, emotionality, and ego achievement.

3. Practicalness. This factor suggests an environmental dimension of practicality tempered with friendliness. It is defined by practicalness and nurturance.

4. Supportiveness. This factor deals with aspects of the organizational environment that respect the integrity of the teacher as a person, but the implication is that dependency needs must be supported rather than personal autonomy emphasized. It might be considered a measure of democratic paternalism. The scales defining it are assurance, tolerance, objectivity, affiliation, conjunctivity, supplication, blame avoidance, harm avoidance, and nurturance.

5. Orderliness. The components of this factor are concerned with the press for organizational structure, procedure, orderliness, and a respect for authority. Conformity to community pressures and an effort to maintain a proper institutional image probably are also concomitants of a high score on this factor. It is based on order, narcissism, adaptability, conjunctivity, deference, and harm avoidance.

II. Control press

In addition to the reflection of factors 1 and 2 above, control press involves:

6. Impulse control. This factor implies a high level of constraint and organizational restrictiveness. There is little opportunity for personal expression or for any form of impulsive behavior. It is based on work, prudishness, blame avoidance, deliberation, placidity, and inferiority avoidance.

FIGURE 8–4. Organizational Climate Index factors and their definitions. From Robert G. Owens and Carl R. Steinhoff, "Strategies for Improving the Effectiveness of Inner-City Schools," *Phi Delta Kappan*, L, No. 5 (January, 1969), 260.

either in terms of the dimensions or with regard to the data from other schools. As the OCI is applied in more and more schools, we can develop normative data which is useful for interpreting the score of an individual school.[25] In 1968 Steinhoff administered the OCI to a number of New York City schools in an effort to obtain such normative data for that big-city situation in order to supplement the normative data which he had already obtained from medium-sized Syracuse.

The OCI data collected from a study of fourteen elementary schools by Owens and Steinhoff [26] illustrates one way that this assessment technique may be used. The schools studied were selected from a group of demonstration schools in a large-scale project for improving the education of socially disadvantaged pupils. The score for each school was calculated for both dimensions—development press and control press—and the distribution plotted as in Figure 8–7.

We can see that school 17 is very low in development press and high in control press. At the other extreme, in the upper-left-hand quadrant, school 4 is relatively high in development press and low in control press.

---

[25] For information on the Organizational Climate Index and scoring services for it, write Professor George G. Stern, Syracuse University, Syracuse, New York.

[26] Robert G. Owens and Carl R. Steinhoff, "Strategies for Improving Inner-City Schools," *Phi Delta Kappan*, L, No. 5 (January, 1969), 259–63.

1. <u>Abasement-assurance</u>: self-deprecation versus self-confidence

2. <u>Achievement</u>: striving for success through personal effort

3. <u>Adaptability-defensiveness</u>: acceptance of criticism versus resistance to suggestion

4. <u>Affiliation-rejection</u>: friendliness versus unfriendliness

5. <u>Aggression-blame avoidance</u>: hostility versus disorganization

6. <u>Change-sameness</u>: flexibility versus routine

7. <u>Conjunctivity-disjunctivity</u>: planfulness versus organization

8. <u>Counteraction-inferiority avoidance</u>: restriving after failure versus withdrawal

9. <u>Deference-restiveness</u>: respect for authority versus rebelliousness

10. <u>Dominance-tolerance</u>: ascendance versus forebearance

11. <u>Ego achievement</u>: striving for power through social action

12. <u>Emotionality-placidity</u>: expressiveness versus restraint

13. <u>Energy-passivity</u>: effort versus inertia

14. <u>Exhibitionism-inferiority avoidance</u>: attention-seeking versus shyness

15. <u>Fantasied achievement</u>: daydreams of extraordinary public recognition

16. <u>Harm avoidance-risk-taking</u>: fearfulness versus thrill seeking

17. <u>Humanities-social sciences</u>: interests in the humanities and the social sciences

18. <u>Impulsiveness-deliberation</u>: impetuosity versus reflection

19. <u>Narcissism</u>: vanity

20. <u>Nurturance-rejection</u>: helping others versus indifference

21. <u>Objectivity-projectivity</u>: detachment versus superstition (AI) or suspicion (EI)

22. <u>Order-disorder</u>: compulsive organization of details versus carelessness

23. <u>Play-work</u>: pleasure-seeking versus purposefulness

24. <u>Practicalness-impracticalness</u>: interest in practical activities versus indifference

25. <u>Reflectiveness</u>: introspective contemplation

26. <u>Science</u>: interest in the natural sciences

27. <u>Sensuality-puritanism</u>: interest in sensory and aesthetic experiences

28. <u>Sexuality-prudishness</u>: heterosexual interests versus inhibition of heterosexual interests

29. <u>Supplication-autonomy</u>: dependency versus self-reliance

30. <u>Understanding</u>: intellectuality

FIGURE 8–5. Definitions of scales from which development press and control press are derived in the Organizational Climate Index. From George G. Stern, *People in Context: Measuring Person-Environment Congruence in Education and Industry* (New York: John Wiley & Sons, Inc., *in press*).

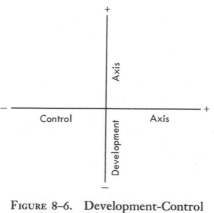
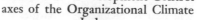

FIGURE 8–6. Development-Control axes of the Organizational Climate Index.

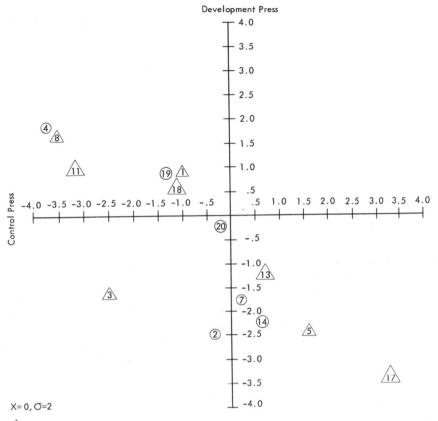

FIGURE 8–7. Distribution of fourteen elementary schools on Development-Control axes of the Organizational Climate Index. From Robert G. Owens and Carl R. Steinhoff, "Strategies for Improving the Effectiveness of Inner-City Schools," *Phi Delta Kappan*, L, No. 5 (January, 1969), 261.

These data—which represent the perceptions of teachers in the schools—includes data for one school in which there is obviously little chance to be self-actualizing or to exercise initiative, a situation in which freedom is quite inhibited. In contrast, another school offers participants a great deal of freedom to "be themselves," and there is little in the environment that is inhibiting. The sample of schools represented here is an especially interesting distribution because before the project it was generally felt by professionals in the educational community that the schools in the project were "all alike." Yet, as we can see, there is a relatively broad, even range along the two axes, which indicates that the schools were not only not alike—in terms of their organizational climates—but also that they exhibited a variety of climate types that are not clustered nor likely to have occurred merely by chance.

But, a principal may ask: How accurate is all this? Has the organizational climate of these schools *really* been measured? Or have a dozen factors which must be taken into consideration before judgment is pronounced been overlooked? The answer can be defensive: "Yes! We've measured the organizational climate of these schools well! The figures are accurate." However, for all practical purposes, this is irrelevant. What matters is just what is done with the assessment to make a difference in the school.

Why Assess the Organizational Climate of a School?

When they first become interested in the concept of organizational climate, many school administrators tend to look upon an assessment of their school's organizational climate as a "test." When the OCDQ or the OCI instrument is brought to the school, it may be described as a test that teachers are being asked to take. The implication is clear: a climate study is an evaluation of the school, and—more particularly—of the teachers and principal in it. This implication is highly unfortunate, for it emphasizes a sort of test syndrome with all the usual anxieties about not doing well. After all, what does it means if one finds that the organizational climate of one's school is "closed" or high in control press and low in development press? Today, amid all the criticism of schools, not every administrator is anxious to generate still more data to be used against him and his school; the reading scores are probably already low enough and the dropout rate too high. Who needs more?

Such an attitude is justified when one considers the viewpoint of Halpin, for example; he stoutly affirms that an open climate is *good* and a closed climate, *bad*. In his terminology, climate types represent arbitrary points along a continuum from open to closed (see Figure 8–8), and the principal should attempt to change a school from "closed" to "open." And yet, Halpin recognizes that not every school can do this:

> [I]t is possible that some schools in urban-core areas cannot afford to contend with an "open" organizational climate. The situation is similar to that of some neurotics who, despite their unhealthy symptoms, manage to cope with their world, even at a low and precarious level of effectiveness.[27]

[27] Andrew W. Halpin, "Change and Organizational Climate," *Ontario Journal of Educational Research*, VIII, No. 3 (Spring, 1966), 235.

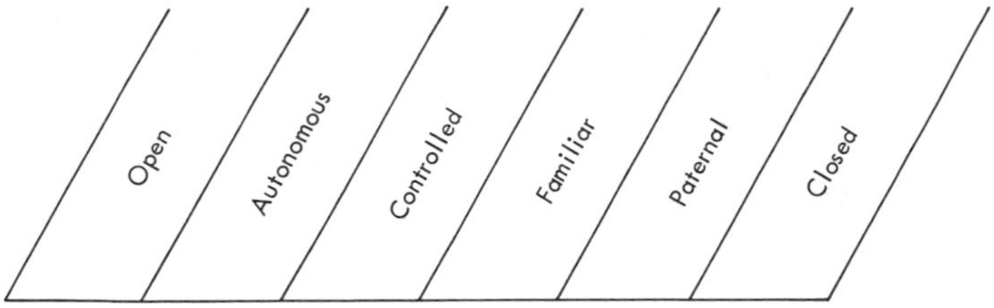

FIGURE 8–8. Continuum of organizational climate types based on Halpin's terminology.

In such cases, Halpin suggests, attempts to alter the school's organizational climate may do more harm than good. Moreover, he contends, some schools are in a hopeless condition:

> The conditions in some of our schools are so bad, and the physical and social environments in which these schools are located are so frightful, that we may have to cross off some of these schools as expendable. This is a shocking statement, I know, but I think that we had better face it.[28]

And, early in his work on organizational climate, Halpin raised "the possibility that the climate-profiles may indeed constitute a better criterion of a school's "effectiveness" than many measures that already have entered the field of educational administration. . . ."[29]

We see, then, that the OCDQ or, indeed, any assessment of organizational climate, may very readily be used as one measuring criterion. If this occurs, what happens when the results of such a test are known? Halpin has already pointed to the obvious: we do not improve the organizational climate of a school by saying to the principal, "Look, the test shows that you're low on *thrust*. Now, you've got to get on the ball and exhibit more thrust!" Certainly, we cannot hope to improve things by telling a principal that his efforts at more effective behavior must be *authentic*.

Organizational climate assessment data can be extremely useful in a practical way if, *first*, it is not construed to be a test or a criterion measure in the judgmental or evaluative sense and, *second*, if it is proffered to the school faculty as feedback for their analysis, evaluation, and discussion. If there is concern among teachers about the organizational effectiveness of the school, as was discussed in Chapter 7, then there is a need for more adequate feedback about the consequences of their actions. If a faculty is expressing concern about organizational ineffectiveness—communica-

---

[28] *Ibid.*
[29] Halpin and Croft, *op. cit.*, pp. 82–83.

tion failure, bickering, tension between factions, or confusion over goals and policies—it is showing some recognition of the fact that problems do exist and some interest in doing something about these problems. But how can a faculty examine its own actions without unbearable pain and undue threat? Many times avoidance has become such a fine art that problems simply cannot be discussed. This dilemma can be compared to a patient seeking therapy. If someone tries to push him into analysis he may balk defensively; but if he is ready to seek help, the task may be much easier. And few therapists would begin by telling a patient all of his faults and advising him to "get over them." So too, in a school, the discussion of organizational climate assessment data by teachers and administrators permits them to open up discussion of sensitive matters which could be very difficult to deal with from an objective point of view.

As an illustration, let us consider the profile (OCDQ) in Figure 8–9

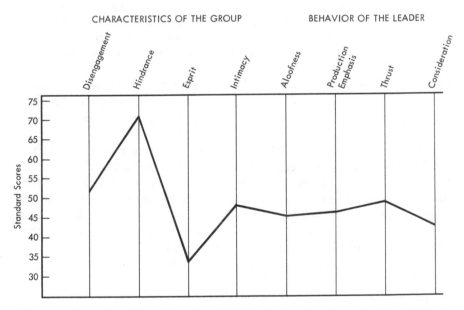

FIGURE 8–9. Climate profile of school A (using the Organizational Climate Description Questionnaire, Form IV).

of a small elementary school in a wealthy suburban community. We notice at once the high score for *hindrance* and the low score for *esprit* and for *consideration* by the principal. What does this mean? Because such a picture of teachers' perceptions is available, the faculty can discuss the significance of the profile, what it means to them, and what can be done about it. A somewhat different school profile, shown in Figure 8–10, is of a somewhat larger suburban school. What is the significance of this

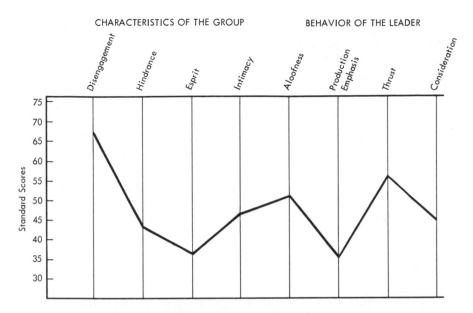

CHARACTERISTICS OF THE GROUP   BEHAVIOR OF THE LEADER

FIGURE 8–10.   Climate profile of school B (using the Organizational Climate
Description Questionnaire, Form IV).

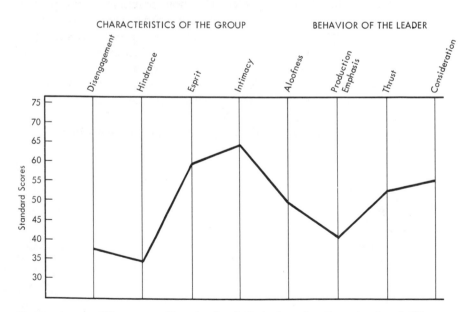

CHARACTERISTICS OF THE GROUP   BEHAVIOR OF THE LEADER

FIGURE 8–11.   Climate profile of school C (using the Organizational Climate
Description Questionnaire, Form IV).

high disengagement-low hindrance-low esprit combination? What caused
the teachers to look at their school's climate this way? Should anything
be done? What? Finally, as a contrast, let us examine the profile of a
third suburban school, as shown in Figure 8–11. Is this a "good" school
profile? Why? Should the staff try to change it?

In sum, it is quite important to determine *why* one assesses the organizational climate of a school. Although such an assessment could con-
ceivably be used as a measure of effectiveness, the consequences of
employing the concept of organizational climate this way must be
considered. Utilized as objective data which can be fed back to the
participants of the organization as a part of the process of maintaining
organizational health, the data from an organizational climate assessment
can be helpful to faculty-groups for perceiving and solving problems.

Summary

In this chapter, two concepts of organizational climate were presented:
one chiefly associated with the research of Andrew W. Halpin and the
second stemming from the work of George G. Stern. Halpin's OCDQ
and the Stern-Steinhoff OCI represent the most practical of the pioneer
techniques available for assessing the organizational climate of schools
in a systematic way. These techniques provide an overall assessment of
the interpersonal milieu of a school organization expressed in terms of
certain behavioral dimensions as perceived by teachers. The data from
such an assessment is valuable feedback information for the school staff
to be used as an aid for maintaining organizational health. And, since such
data is objective, teachers will be able to examine and discuss their implications more openly than would normally be the case with information
about such sensitive matters.

❧ 9 ❧

styles of
organizational behavior

*It is not too infrequently stated by members of organizations that re-
sults in behavioral science, specifically those in organizational behavior,
do not agree with their observations of the real world. Perhaps the
research studies . . . are limited and do not apply to all situations;
perhaps the people who object do not really understand the behavior
around them . . . .*

—*Philip B. Applewhite* [1]

Most of the research on schools as organizations that is available is
concerned with structural aspects: coordination of units, controlling
the sequence of organizational processes, efficient geographical distribution of physical facilities, optimum size of units, rearrangements of hierarchical arrangements, and so forth. Common examples are studies of
optimum school size, bus routes, desirable attendance areas, nongrading,
team-teaching, and "house plans" for large schools. However, this entire,
vitally important field has never been subjected to a comprehensive, systematic study. Our knowledge and concepts are based largely on folk
wisdom or scattered, narrow studies which have concentrated on some
subsystem or activity within the school or school district. As a consequence, the literature is fragmentary and largely discontinuous, and
requires that practitioners utilize common sense or hunches for much of
their decision making. A general description of the school as an organization has yet to be made.

---

[1] Philip B. Applewhite, *Organizational Behavior* (Englewood Cliffs, N. J.:
Prentice-Hall, Inc., © 1965), p. 3.

This book is concerned not so much with the *structure* of school organizations, but with a less well-explored domain: *organizational behavior*. Systematic efforts to study the organizational behavior in schools —the dynamics of human interpersonal behavior in its larger organizational setting—have occurred quite recently and consequently offer us far more knowledge—although this knowledge is fragmentary—than we possess even of the structural side. Again, the lack of extensive systematic research on behavioral aspects of school organizations is partly due to the unpopularity of education among behavioral scientists as a field of study. In 1965 Foskett commented:

> Even such a short time as twenty years ago only a few sociologists were carrying on inquiries that related to education, and these few individuals were somehow regarded by their colleagues as second-class citizens. . . . [Since 1945] a remarkable shift has taken place. Currently, many sociologists, and particularly those who are regarded as first-class citizens, are actively engaged in investigations that relate both directly and indirectly to public school affairs.[2]

A similar statement could be made about other behavioral scientists such as social psychologists and political scientists. The result has been a rapid enlargement of the body of concepts and knowledge available to the school administrator, which aid him in more clearly viewing organizational behavior. As these concepts become better known among administrators, their utility for predicting and understanding organizational behavior will be more clearly understood.

We can say that our conceptualization of the school as an organization—how it is structured, how it functions, and how people behave in it—is largely dependent upon three sources:

1. The knowledge of folk wisdom
2. Relatively scattered and narrowly focused researches which have largely been concerned with processes of activities of subsystems of the overall organization
3. Attempts to relate useful concepts from research in other kinds of organizations to the school

And, not surprisingly, the result is a body of research literature which is somewhat incomplete—if not fragmentary—lacking in precise coherence, and from which it is difficult to abstract the generic and unique attributes

---

2 John M. Foskett, *Sociology and Educational Administration: A Discussion* (Eugene, Ore.: Center for the Advanced Study of Educational Administration, University of Oregon, 1965), p. 1.

of schools as organizations. This situation, having undergone an almost dramatic change for the better since the end of World War II, has improved greatly in the past few years. This book deals with the practical problem of synthesizing and relating some of the research on organizational behavior which has been done in schools and some which has been done in other types of organizations and which can be related to school organizations.

In the present chapter we will discuss an aspect of organizational behavior which is particularly useful to the practicing school administrator: characteristics of organizational behavior style. We will relate some of the concepts now emerging from school-oriented studies and also draw upon research in non-school settings.

Style in Organizational Behavior

"What kind of guy is he?" a teacher may ask a colleague in reference to his school principal. A typical reply might be, "Well, he's OK—he keeps out of your way; you won't see much of him so long as you keep things quiet. He's tied down to the office pretty much, with all those reports and paperwork that principals have to fool with in this system." In another situation the principal might be described as, "really on the ball. He knows what's going on around here. But he's a real human being —you can talk to him and you can count on what he says." With even fragments of insights such as these, we can anticipate, at least to some degree, what the principal's behavior on the job will be like. And we can predict, however tentatively, the principal's "style" and how he might react to certain situations. This element of predictability is important to those who work with him: it enables them to initiate ideas and suggestions—or to modify them or withhold them—in such a way as to maximize the chances of success and minimize the chances of conflict from unanticipated consequences.

In Chapter 5 we discussed eight "administrative styles" which were identified in a study of the decision making behavior of the principalship. High compliance style of principals was characterized by the principal who generally tended to follow suggestions made by others. Principals with a high outside-orientation style are inclined to tailor their performance to pressures from outside the school. A principal might be described as utilizing a high-discussion style if he places unusual emphasis on the importance of face-to-face discussion. Other so-called "administrative styles" revolve around the tendency of principals to stress communication, careful analysis of problems, relationships with superordinates in the organization, the need to give directions to others, or the scheduling and organizing of their own work. If the staff of a school recognizes that school administrators differ in organizational behavior style and that these differences are somewhat systematic and subject to description, they will be able to understand the administrator's values and his attitude toward on-the-job situations and thus predict his organizational behavior in advance.

Compliance Style

We tend to place considerable emphasis on the influence of the work-group and other small-group social relationships on the organizational behavior of individuals. This was the chief finding of the Western Electric researches and has, quite properly, been the focal point for much research into organizational behavior since. Halpin's dimensions in organizational climate are a good illustration: he calls attention to *disengagement, hindrance, esprit,* and *intimacy* as meaningful dimensions for assessing the impact of the group on the personality of the organization. Similarly, the behavior of the leader can be seen in reference to the workgroup: the concepts of *aloofness, production emphasis, thrust,* and *consideration* all involve aspects of the principal's behavior in reference to the workgroup in the school. The entire field of group dynamics emphasizes the central importance of the dynamic interrelationships between individuals and their workgroups. Compliance with group norms undoubtedly plays a large part in shaping organizational behavior.

In the study of the pajama factory by Coch and French which was discussed in Chapter 7, it was noted that after some procedural changes had been introduced, one woman machine operator began to produce work much faster than the rest of her group. She was soon accused of being a "rate buster" by her fellow workers and her rate of production then fell to the average units-per-hour of the group. All the other girls were transferred out three weeks later; four days after that the woman began working at an even faster rate, and she continued to do so thereafter. This observation accords with similar observed relationships between the group and the individual which are frequently reported in the literature: events that occurred in the Bank Wiring Room of the Western Electric researches also clearly illustrated the influence of the workgroup in controlling behavior of individuals and thereby controlling goal achievement of the organization.

The influence of the group on individual behavior is not simple; there are many variables in the dynamic relationship between the group and the individual; one important variable is the unique personality of the individual involved. This was illustrated by an experiment in which a group of seven to nine people were assembled in a classroom; the group was told that they would be shown lines of different lengths and they were asked to match up the lines that were equal in length. As cards with lines of various lengths were held up, the participants would call out the matching pairs. Trial 1 and trial 2 would proceed without problems because this task was not difficult. However, in the third trial the experimenter introduced something new: he told all the members of the group *but one* to unanimously call out incorrect responses. Thus, in the third trial, one lonely individual found himself responding to what he thought he saw differently than anyone else. Actually, over a period of time it became evident that about one third of the dissenting individuals decided to agree with the judgment of the group. After careful study, it was determined that these "yielders" could be grouped into three categories:

1. Those who actually convinced themselves that they saw what the rest of the group had seen
2. Those who decided they were mistaken and that the others in the group must be correct in their judgments
3. Those who simply suppressed their own judgments and "went along" with the judgment of the group because they felt a need to conform

Illustrations such as these underscore the importance of the dynamic interplay between the workgroup—or the role-set comprised of one's colleagues—and the individual. The effect of such interplay on organizational behavior must not be underestimated.

We must also consider the influence of individual participants' personal characteristics in shaping this dynamic relationship. For schools, it is widely assumed that the formal organization is largely staffed by middle-class workers whose lives and very personalities have been shaped by the values, education, and life-style so often associated with the middle class. The stereotype of the teacher is therefore generally that of a submissive, nurturant-oriented, rather repressed person who puts much emphasis on group conformity and has a low tolerance for conflict in interpersonal relationships. Interestingly, this stereotype has been reinforced repeatedly by the observations of researchers.

However, such a stereotype is too glib and oversimplified to be very useful as a guide to the effective understanding and prediction of organizational behavior in specific circumstances. A significant study which explored the relationships between the organizational behavior of teachers and their personality characteristics was Ryans' *Characteristics of Teachers*.[3]

---

[3] David G. Ryans, *Characteristics of Teachers: Their Description, Comparison, and Appraisal* (Washington, D. C.: American Council on Education, 1960).

Behavioral Characteristics of Teachers

In one of the landmark research studies of teacher behavior, Ryans attempted to determine the relationships, if any, that existed between the characteristics of teachers and the behavior they exhibited in the classroom. Ryans' massive Teacher Characteristics Study, which involved 6,000 teachers in 1,700 schools of 450 school systems, made important use of the critical incidents technique. No attempt will be made here to summarize this complex study, but two aspects of the findings are pertinent.

In an application of the critical incidents technique, appropriate people were asked to report specific incidents of behavior by individual teachers they knew. The approach was "open ended"—allowing respondents to report on whatever behaviors they felt were significant. Interestingly enough—and, perhaps, significantly—most of the teaching incidents reported described the personal or social behaviors of teachers. When teachers were allowed to describe whatever they thought was relevant in another teacher's behavior, incidents which concerned scholarliness or unique teaching skills or academic subject matter were generally ignored; incidents which revealed personal and social characteristics of the teacher received most of the attention.

Another data-gathering technique of the Ryans study called for direct observation of in-classroom behavior of teachers. From the data collected, three behavioral patterns, which we can call *dimensions*, were noted:

1. TCS pattern X: warm, understanding, and friendly versus aloof, egocentric, and restricted teacher classroom behavior
2. TCS pattern Y: responsible, businesslike, and systematic versus evading, unplanned, and slipshod teacher classroom behavior
3. TCS pattern Z: stimulating and imaginative versus dull, routine teacher classroom behavior [4]

The description of a teacher's observed in-classroom behavior can be characterized in part in terms of the teacher's position in these patterns—either high or low. When these behavioral ratings were correlated with a complete range of personal characteristics, it was found that the "high"-rated teachers—the warm, understanding, responsive, and imaginative teachers—were also rated by their principals as superior. The "low"-

---

[4] David G. Ryans, "Research on Teacher Behavior in the Context of the Teacher Characteristics Study," in Bruce J. Biddle and William J. Ellena, eds., *Contemporary Research on Teacher Effectiveness* (New York: Holt, Rinehart & Winston, Inc., 1964), p. 76.

rated teachers—who tended to evidence restricted, dull, and unplanned classroom behavior—were (not surprisingly) looked upon as poorer teachers by their principals.

Thus, one significant part of Ryans' study seems to support the idea that organizational behavior style of a teacher is important and is relevant to the achievement of the school's goals. It is not sufficient that teachers have an adequate educational background, expertise, and knowledge of the subject matter: the dynamics of interpersonal behavior in the organization have much effect on the teacher's impact in the classroom.

Among the most useful concepts which behavioral scientists such as Ryans have made available to practicing school administrators are those which aid the practitioner to identify and describe distinctive types or styles of organizational behavior. For example, earlier in this book we described a concept so often associated with Guba and Getzels which stresses the interaction between the individual personality needs of the role-incumbent and the demands which the organization makes on him in his role. As we look about us in the schools we *do* find principals who "go by the book" and seem to stress the rules and the "oughts" outlined by bureaucratic procedure; such school administrators conform to a perception of their role as the *organization* views it. And they may frequently indicate that their behavior is not really what they would actually *want* to project but, "you know, we have no choice. The rules are laid down by the superintendent and the Board and—well—we have no choice. These things are required of us." Such an attitude can be identified as an emphasis on the nomothetic dimension of the principal's role; this identification provides us with some guidelines for predicting the individual's behavior in certain circumstances, well illustrated by the issue of time-clocks in the New York City schools in the mid-1960's.

One of the least-publicized focal points of frustration in the years of rising militancy among New York City's teachers was the time-clock in school offices which teachers were required to punch. In many instances this device and the requirement to punch *in* and *out* represented to teachers the restrictive, constraint-laden, unsympathetic attitude of the school's administration—specifically, that of the school principal—and it was resented. Teachers frequently protested the time-clock requirement, and in many cases, principals adamantly insisted that punching the clock was a requirement of "the Board" (meaning the whole central office administrative apparatus) and that the matter was out of their hands.

The terms *idiographic* and *nomothetic* apply here. It is evident that some principals were so intent on conforming to the nomothetic dimension of their role that they insisted on maintaining this much disliked procedure and felt compelled to force teachers to submit to the "necessary" requirements of an overwhelming bureaucracy. These principals stressed the nomothetic dimension of organizational behavior and urged others to do the same. Many such principals actually seemed to believe that some sort of rule—which could not be modified—required the time-clock procedure. Yet at the same time there were other school principals in New York City who quietly responded in a rather different manner; they replaced the punching of time-clocks with more acceptable procedures—and still met the administrative requirements of the system. These principals were tempering the demands of the organization with a more idiographic interpretation of their roles [5]—and of the roles of their teachers.

The foregoing discussion provides some insights into the practical usefulness of some of the concepts and their accompanying terminology which behavioral scientists have made available. One can speculate—however tentatively—that principals "with" the time-clock would tend to be similarly oriented to nomothetic pressures in making other decisions; we can associate these principals with an inclination for acquiring bureaucratic rigidity, being "sticklers to the rules," and tending toward depersonalization in their organizational behavior. These principals, as individuals outside the school, might well be charming, accomplished, warm people. But in the organization under consideration, their behavior must be viewed otherwise.

However, one can reasonably speculate that the "without time-clock" principals tended toward behavior which characterizes the idiographic approach in other aspects of their role. They can be seen as ranking somewhat higher in consideration and more concerned with human satisfaction in performing the organizational role well. How much the idiographic-nomothetic "mix" is caused by the personality make-up of the principal as an individual and how much is caused by the effects of training and experience is not understood well, but such a mix must be operative.

To summarize briefly, then, the normative dimension-personal dimension construct posited by Getzels and Guba has frequently been used in research literature as a model for analyzing leadership style; that is, one speaks of a principal who evidences a nomothetic *style* or an idiographic *style*. Ryans has described a group of commonly observed behavior patterns among teachers which in effect describe and identify certain behavioral styles. The administrative styles associated with the so-called

<hr/>

[5] The dichotomy "nomothetic-idiographic" has been stressed here for illustrative purposes. A third, infrequently discussed and called *transactional* style, should not be overlooked; it is a synthesis of the other two, balancing goal achievement emphasis against stress on individual need fulfillment as appropriate. See Jacob W. Getzels and Egon G. Guba, "Social Behavior and the Administrative Process," *The School Review*, LXV, No. 4 (Winter, 1957), 423–41.

DCS studies have emphasized normative percepts of behavior which help identify eight "administrative styles."

We have been concerned throughout this discussion with "real" human beings, not roles nor offices in a hierarchy, but individual persons whose behavior style in the school has a distinct bearing on organizational life in the school. No matter how crude our model may be, we will find it useful to conceptualize an individual's behavior pattern along the idiographic-nomothetic continuum. If the practicing administrator is careful to bear in mind the hazards of arbitrary categorization of people, he will find some of the dimensions which can be used to conceptualize and describe the behavior style of his referents in the organization very useful. We shall, therefore, suggest other patterns or dimensions of organizational behavior which have proven useful to students and which also have utility for practicing administrators.

Cosmopolitans and Locals

One of the more popular, useful characterizations of organizational behavior style, generally attributed to Alvin W. Gouldner, is the distinction between *cosmopolitans* and *locals*.[6] These terms refer to specific *latent roles*, as differentiated from the *manifest roles* of the individual in the organization.

For example, a teacher occupies the manifest role of teacher, but, as we have already seen, he simultaneously occupies several latent roles such as father, community leader, and social activist. If we may oversimplify for a moment, Gouldner has pointed out that individuals in organizations occupy certain latent roles which center around the personal loyalty or attachment one feels toward the organization. "Cosmopolitans" may be described as those whose commitment is essentially to their profession, whereas "locals" are those whose prime loyalty is to the organization; this orientation in the latent role is associated with organizational behaviors which we can easily observe. The organizational behavior of "locals" is quite different from that of "cosmopolitans."

Gouldner's definitions are:

1. *Cosmopolitans:* those low on loyalty to the employing organization, high on commitment to specialized role skills, and likely to use an outer reference group orientation

---

[6] Alvin W. Gouldner, "Cosmopolitans and Locals: Toward an Analysis of Latent Social Roles," *Administrative Science Quarterly*, II (December, 1957; March, 1958), 281–306 and 440–80.

2. *Locals:* those high on loyalty to the employing organization, low on
   commitment to specialized role skills, and likely to use an inner reference group orientation [7]

Locals generally join organizations, stay in them, and work toward
their goals because they wish to be a part of them. And a good many
school teachers and administrators are committed to their school system,
want to render long, faithful service to it, and tend to identify with it.
Even though school organizations emphasize the professional expertise
of their teachers, they also do reward them—through public statements,
if in no other way—for long, faithful "dedication" to the organization.

Cosmopolitans, however, participate in the organization in order to
pursue their commitment to their profession. Some teachers, who change
jobs more frequently than "locals," willingly transfer to another school
to obtain greater prestige in the eyes of other teachers. However, let us
note that the cosmopolitan-local dichotomy is *not* based on geography;
in our mobile country, locals do move from place to place and a cosmopolitan frequently can operate from a rather fixed base.

Gouldner's original study of these latent roles took place in a liberal
arts college which he called "Co-op College": it had 1,000 students and
130 faculty members and was located in a community with a population
of 5,000. Gouldner found that the labels "cosmopolitan" and "local"
were not fully descriptive of types of latent roles; rather, he found that
these terms identify clusters of types, within which clusters were four
kinds of locals and two kinds of cosmopolitans. His description may be
summarized as follows:

1. *Locals*
   a. *The dedicated.* These are the "true believers" who attach much
      importance to the goals and philosophy of a specific organization.
      They stress commitment to the institution, rather than to the
      technical competence of colleagues; they tend to see themselves
      primarily as members of the faculty and only secondarily as pro-
      fessional specialists; they stress consensus and internal harmony; and
      they comprise an inner reference group in the organization—the
      loyal and reliable group.
   b. *The true bureaucrats.* They resist "outside" control of the institu-
      tion, and their loyalty is not so much to the ideals of the school as
      it is to the idea of the school, or the place itself. Sensitive to external
      criticism, true bureaucrats are willing to make changes in traditional
      institutions in order to ameliorate it. They generally recommend
      their school to young teachers as a place to start their careers.

---

[7] *Ibid.*, p. 290.

They do not favor lighter work-loads to provide more time for research and writing. Finally, as "true bureaucrats," they tend to favor formal regulations.

c. *The homeguard.* In the college studied, these tended to be second-echelon administrators, mostly women. They have the least professional specialization and attend few professional conventions. They are not committed to the distinctive values of the organization, nor to its community; many of the "homeguard" in Gouldner's study were people who had graduated from the college they worked for.

d. *The elders.* These are the oldest locals and have been with the organization for the longest time. Generally in their fifties or sixties, elders are deeply rooted in the informal organization; they look forward to retirement and tend to evaluate the present situation in the organization in terms of past events they have experienced.

2. *Cosmopolitans*

a. *The outsiders.* They have very little involvement in either the formal or informal structure of the organization, little influence in the faculty—and do not want more—and are not likely to stay with the organization permanently. Such cosmopolitans are highly committed, not to the institution, but to their specialized professions. Their outer-reference orientation is expressed in their feelings that they do not get much intellectual stimulation from their colleagues: they read many journals and meet with fellow specialists at meetings and conventions which they often attend in various locations.

b. *The empire builders.* These cosmopolitans are similar to outsiders but are integrated into the formal structure of the organization (although not into its informal structure). Their affiliation to their department is strong, and they favor strong departmental autonomy. Like the outsiders, the empire builders feel they can easily find jobs outside the institution—they are economically and professionally quite independent. And they would quickly accept an appointment at an institution which would accord them higher professional prestige.[8]

The implications of this kind of analysis of behavioral style are clear. Locals and cosmopolitans view their organizations differently and interpret their relationship to them differently; moreover, their behavior style can be influenced by this differing orientation in both formal and informal relationships. In most public school organizations, locals will tend to exercise greater influence in the organization and will achieve greater acceptance in the social system than cosmopolitans. The local-cosmopolitan orientation of staff members can be a very real source of conflict

---

[8] This description is based on *ibid.,* pp. 446-50.

with regard to such issues as views held by teachers concerning the need for rules, the importance of loyalty to the organization, and the question of professional outer-reference orientation versus the value of local longevity of service.

Upward-Mobiles and Indifferents

The individual who participates in an organization is not merely an inanimate object being molded by forces and events, and he does not merely react to events around him which occur as a consequence of his being in the organization. His own values, goals, aspirations, and the needs he wishes to fulfill are important factors which cause him to shape not only his manifest role but his latent role as well.

Schools are largely staffed by people from so-called middle-class backgrounds; their home life and education have imbued them with a life-style which, for the most part, emphasizes success and/or security. We can say that cosmopolitans are generally success-oriented and locals are generally security-oriented. However, in schools both are likely to have middle-class backgrounds and to accept the behavioral standards implied by that fact: discipline, a certain amount of anxiety about their "image" (what will others think?), and avoidance of open aggression in interpersonal contacts. In their own organizational settings, both teachers and administrators tend to "stay in role," i.e., to look, act, and talk as they "should."

Conflict which is considered "bad" is camouflaged: fistfights and strong verbal language are rarities—and are virtually never condoned. Even ambition is restrained and carefully revealed only in forms which the individual thinks are acceptable to his role-referents. Over a period of years, the writer has asked many graduate students in educational administration what their goals were. The typical response usually was something like this: "Well, I hope that some day, if an opening occurs, maybe I will be considered for an assistant principalship in my district— or something." When asked, "Why do you want to become a school principal?" the typical response, accompanied by visible discomfiture, was, "Well, I think that I've been a good teacher—my supervisors have told me so—and maybe I can make a contribution as a leader. I believe in the importance of education and I want to do what I can to contribute to improving what we have." Although the trend today is toward greater openness and frankness, it is still rare to hear a teacher say, "I'd like to get to the top in this profession. I think I've got the stuff and I'm looking for opportunities to get ahead." Such an admission would generally not be well accepted by either a teacher's colleagues or his superordinates. In the social system of the school, laden with prohibitions and proscriptions imposed by its class structure, the administrator must look carefully at behavior through a variety of "lenses" if he wants to fully comprehend why individuals tend to mold their roles as they do—and how to deal with them effectively.

Robert Presthus has suggested that people view ambition in three different ways [9]; each type can be identified not necessarily by spoken declarations but by how organizational roles are shaped, particularly with regard to attitudes toward their superordinates in the hierarchy:

1. *Upward mobiles* generally accept "the system"—its goals and values, its authority and demands. This acceptance is genuine and, which is significant, the upward mobile sees his superordinates in a good light— as friendly and sympathetic.
2. *Indifferents*, however, largely ignore the organization and find their satisfactions away from the job. They work to "make a living" (or, often in the case of women, "to make a little extra money"), but they rarely are involved in the organization more than is necessary.
3. *Ambivalents* are tempted by the attraction of power, authority, and the prestige of success which accompany promotion; but they are not "organization men," for they value their own individuality and their friendships more than the rewards which the organization can offer. Presthus feels that there are relatively few ambivalents.

This additional set of dimensions, which can help us to understand the interpersonal behavior of people in the structured roles of an organization, is comprised of ideal types, of course, and will not necessarily be so easily identifiable in the "real" world of schools. But if we think of the ideal types as points on a continuum (see Figure 9–1) the concept is helpful for understanding and predicting organizational behavior. We

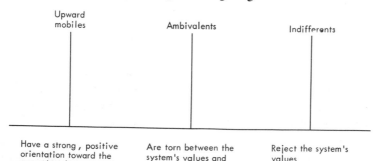

FIGURE 9–1. Upward-mobile—indifferent continuum of attitudes toward ambition.

[9] Robert Presthus, *The Organizational Society* (New York: Alfred A. Knopf, Inc., 1962), pp. 164–202.

have recently observed an increase in the number of teachers who are, organizationally speaking, ambivalent, and who have challenged well-established practices such as the primacy of administrators, the status traditionally associated with "promotion" from teaching to administration, and the rewards customarily reserved for administration. These teachers no longer see the foregoing organizational values as relevant to them or to their personal goals.

Such an attitude, which is bewildering to some administrators, is reflected in requests for election of principals by teachers, for removing or reducing pay differentials between administrators and teachers, and for increasing the emphasis on the central importance of the teacher as opposed to the conventional tendency to view him at the bottom of the hierarchy. In terms of administrative practice in the schools, the upward-mobile concept suggests the following especially appropriate ideas:

1. Administrators tend to show considerable drive for achievement, are strongly inclined toward mobility, are favorably inclined toward control from above, and tend to identify with their superordinates rather than with their subordinates. Even though the realities of organizational life may preclude further promotion for the principal, he still tends to associate himself with the central office and the values held there.[10]

2. Because of the sharply pyramidal structure of the school organization, there are many upward mobile-oriented persons in the organization who have been passed over and will never have their mobility needs met.[11] The behavioral effects resulting from this situation have not been fully explored in schools but it would appear that the sensitive administrator will find them worth considering in any study of the climate of interpersonal relationships in his school.

Career-Bound and Place-Bound Administrators

"An organization," Victor A. Thompson has pointed out, "is a structure made up of positions and roles that people move in and out of without destroying the organization." [12] But newly arrived role incumbents *do*, to some extent, shape their roles and, consequently, the orga-

---

[10] William E. Henry, "The Business Executive: The Psychodynamics of a Social Role," *American Journal of Sociology*, LIV, No. 4 (January, 1949), 286–91.

[11] For one approach to a solution to this problem, see Thomas E. Powers, "Administrative Behavior and Upward Mobility," *Administrators Notebook*, XV, No. 1 (September, 1966), 1–4.

[12] Victor A. Thompson, *Modern Organization* (New York: Alfred A. Knopf, Inc., 1961), p. 113.

nizations to fit their own behavioral style. Richard O. Carlson studied this problem at what is probably its most powerful level in school systems: the superintendency.[13] In so doing he has provided some useful insights into organizational behavior style that can, at least in general terms, be applied to other positions in the organization.

In studying the circumstances surrounding the employment of school superintendents, Carlson identified two distinct types of administrators:

1. One type is an insider who, having moved up through the school system's hierarchy, has waited for the superintendency to become vacant. If he eventually does become superintendent, he usually retires on the job and probably does not become superintendent in another district. He is described by Carlson as being *place-bound*.
2. Another type does not wait, but seeks the jobs he wants and does not hesitate to move from one district to another to advance his career. He is an outsider and may make a career of the superintendency, probably holding a position in more than one district before he retires. He is said to be *career-bound*.

The essential difference between these two types of men is the importance they attach to career and place. The insider stays in his organization by choice and attains the superintendency only if he can do so in that organization, but the outsider places great stress on his career objectives and is mobile in the course of his career development. The parallel between these career types and Gouldner's cosmopolitan-local typology is clear. For example, the place-bound man who longs for promotion—perhaps covertly—can be described as an upward mobile. It is significant that the data which Carlson used to develop his classifications were taken from actual career histories of a number of school superintendents, and were not responses to questionnaires or check-lists.

Not surprisingly, Carlson noted a systematic difference in the organizational behavior of place-bound and career-bound administrators. The latter, who had other job offers available, were in a stronger bargaining position with the board of education than were the former; thus, they had a freer hand and tended to make more and earlier changes in the system. However, these superintendents are not necessarily "steamroller" types. In a somewhat similar study, Seeman [14] found that the job-mobile superintendents were high on consideration; they probably relied

---

[13] See Richard O. Carlson, *Executive Succession and Organizational Change: Place-Bound and Career-Bound Superintendents of Schools* (Chicago: Midwest Administration Center, The University of Chicago, 1962).

[14] Melvin Seeman, "Social Mobility and Administrative Behavior," *American Sociological Review*, XXIII, No. 6 (December, 1958), 633–42.

heavily on a professional-collegial relationship to gain influence and get things accomplished, as differentiated from the place-bound man's emphasis on rules and the authority of his hierarchical position.

In this chapter we have discussed a number of typologies which are useful in thinking about the behavioral style of individuals in schools. If our concern is with role behavior in the schools, we must know more about the variables which influence different behavioral styles. It has been suggested that the school administrator will be better equipped to interpret —and therefore deal effectively with—organizational behavior he observes in his school if he has the necessary "lenses" for identifying some of the principal behavioral styles of his faculty. Essentially, these styles of organizational behavior express the belief systems of the individuals.

Participants in organizations have different feelings, values, perceptions. And they act accordingly. One of the more useful ways of describing the kinds of people who function in different kinds of belief systems has been Milton Rokeach's concept of the "open" and "closed" mind.

The Open Mind and the Closed Mind

As we have seen, the style of interpersonal behavior in an organizational setting is dependent upon many variable personality characteristics and drives. It has long been recognized that the quality of interpersonal behavior which one exhibits is not unrelated to how one expresses beliefs and values.

We have all seen principals and teachers who are intolerant of those with different viewpoints; they are generally people who can rarely accept an idea which would challenge their rigidly held belief pattern. Others, who may be in the same school, are more accepting of new ideas and more flexible in adapting them to their values and beliefs. The intolerant behavioral characteristic first described is sometimes called *authoritarianism;* one method of measuring it is to use the Adorno *F*-Scale.[15] This measures a particular concept which is, unfortunately, known as "fascism in the personality" (hence, "*F*"-Scale); the concept has gradually come to be interpreted as "authoritarianism in the personality." The *F*-Scale has been widely used in research concerning the effect that this particular personality characteristic has in the functioning of groups—the smoothness with which they operate, their ability to achieve goals, the effect of leadership on them, and so forth.

---

[15] T. W. Adorno, Else Frankel-Brunswick, D. J. Levinson, and R. N. Sanford, *The Authoritarian Personality* (New York: Harper & Row, Publishers, 1958), pp. 255–58.

Of course, one expects a highly authoritarian person to be somewhat assertive and inflexible, to "stick to the rules," and to favor a tight, controlling power structure. And this raises problems in group interpersonal behavior because, regardless of the *content* of different ideas that group members may hold, it is obvious that the effectiveness of the group is related to the members' compatibility. Unless members can get along reasonably well, open communication and the trust and confidence so necessary to adaptive, flexible, effective operations will not be attained.

William Schutz, working in this problem area, developed a measure to describe what he saw as the three ways that people relate to one another, which, taken together, he called FIRO: Fundamental Interpersonal Relations Orientation.[16] He has described the three elements of FIRO thus:

1. *Power orientation,* which deals with the tendency of the individual for "following rules, following the leader . . . and in general, conforming to, manipulating, and/or controlling the power structure"
2. *Personalness-counterpersonalness orientation,* which concerns an individual's tendency to form "close personal relations . . . [and to] treating people differently—not on the basis of status—but on the basis of personal liking"
3. *Assertiveness orientation,* which is a measure of the individual's tendency to express his beliefs in an open manner to others [17]

Especially pertinent to the discussion here is Schutz's conviction that high compatibility is essential to high goal-achievement of a group. "Compatibility," he noted, "is a relation between two or more persons, between an individual and a role, or between an individual and a task situation, that leads to mutual satisfaction of interpersonal needs and harmonious existence." [18] The question for the school administrator is: How can he foster the development of more highly compatible relationships in the school organization? The answer is not simple. A critical factor which is related to compatibility is the personality characteristic which has been called both *authoritarianism,* or the *F-factor,* a characteristic which is often associated with dogmatic people.

There are times when one tries to express an opinion to someone and—though he may be polite about it—he is simply unmoved. One may think, "He didn't even *hear* me!" The statement made to another person

---

[16] William C. Schutz, *FIRO: A Three-Dimensional Theory of Interpersonal Behavior* (New York: Holt, Rinehart & Winston, Inc., 1958).

[17] William C. Schutz, "What Makes Groups Productive?" *Human Relations,* VIII, No. 4 (1955), 431.

[18] Schutz, *FIRO, op. cit.,* p. 105.

may evoke an entirely different response. The second person may not have been entirely convinced, but it would be obvious that he understood what was said to him. The first individual might be said to have a *closed mind*, whereas the second individual has a somewhat more *open mind*.

The dimension *open mind-closed mind* is generally called degree of dogmatism; the authority in the literature on the subject is Milton Rokeach, who developed an instrument for measuring this characteristic: it is called the Dogmatism Scale.[19] A highly dogmatic person (with a closed mind) tends to distort his perceptions to conform to his previously internalized beliefs, values, and commitments; in truth, he actually does not perceive much that would threaten his preconceived notions. All closed-minded people do not necessarily cling to the *status quo*— although most probably do; it is quite possible for a closed-minded person to be so utterly opposed to "the establishment" that he cannot consider anything that would perpetuate or strengthen it.

Dogmatism may vary with intensity of values. For example, in the passion of racial tension or a military threat to the country, it sometimes appears that otherwise flexible, adaptable people develop a closed-minded attitude on that particular subject.

Closed-minded people present problems to decision making groups because of their tendency to be oriented towards rules, acceptance of authority, and the norms of the culture and the institution. One of the problems administrators and faculties face in deciding how to solve problems is how to take into consideration all of the *relevant* factors and to avoid making decisions on the basis of *irrelevant* factors. In the present era of rapid change, the relevant factors in a situation do not always coincide with orthodox practices. The open-minded individual is better able to receive—to "hear"—new ideas and information without much threat or discomfort. He tends to perceive ideas accurately, with a minimum of distortion, and to talk about them with some objectivity.

The closed-minded person who ranks high on the dogmatism scale does not tend to approach new experiences openly. He becomes defensive because he feels somewhat insecure in new situations, even threatened. He may project, or rationalize, or even ignore what he does not want to see; or he may look on a problem as a very narrow one, rather than recognizing its broader implications. Ambiguity and uncertainty are not his "cup of tea," and his world is largely a world of black and white.

The open-minded person, however, is much more at ease in sorting out facts and ideas; he can see many alternatives along a continuum,

---

[19] Milton Rokeach, *The Open and Closed Mind* (New York: Basic Books, Inc., 1960).

rather than a simple dichotomy. New ideas, flexibility, examination of feelings and emotions in the challenges of life—all come more readily to the open-minded person than they do to the closed-minded individual.

A somewhat similar dimension is concreteness and abstractness.[20] The open-minded individual is relatively capable of abstracting from his inputs —his knowledge and his experiences—and relating them together in an organized pattern. But the closed-minded person views life in more concrete terms, tending to think of his experiences in isolation, rather than relating them into a new pattern. Behaviorally, the "abstract" person seeks additional informaton when he encounters an ambiguous situation, although he is not generally concerned about uncovering information which does not support his beliefs. The concrete person tends to accept the facts he "sees" and to respond to these facts as he believes his behavior "ought" to be.

Summary

In the absence of a comprehensive theory or model of organizational behavior in schools we must draw upon an incomplete and somewhat discontinuous body of research literature; to make the fragments of knowledge and insight useful, we attempt to relate them to each other. In this chapter five styles of organizational behavior which have been widely used by researchers in attempts to understand organizational behavior in schools have been discussed:

1. Idiographic-transactional-nomothetic
2. Upward mobile-indifferent-ambivalent
3. Career oriented-place oriented
4. Cosmopolitan-local
5. Open mind-closed mind (dogmatism)

Knowledge of the concepts underlying these dimensions, together with their concomitant organizational behavior styles, provides the school administrator with a set of "lenses" which facilitate his perception of organizational behavior and what this behavior signifies. It has been emphasized that personality orientations such as these may be as meaningful for shaping organizational behavior style in the school as the frequently stressed relationship between the workgroup and the individual.

---

[20] O. J. Harvey, ed., *Motivation and Social Interaction: Cognitive Determinants* (New York: The Ronald Press, 1963).

Administrators who are contemplating the most efficacious course of action to take on some proposed venture may find it useful to assess—informally or otherwise—the individual members of their school faculties in terms of one or more of these characteristics with a view to predicting the likely reception awaiting alternative actions which might be taken. For example, if a teaching innovation is about to be introduced, how will the teachers receive it? Will they accept it or will they "kill" it—however subtly? Who in the faculty is most reliable in terms of listening to the new idea and giving it encouragement? Who, indeed, can be expected to have new ideas to suggest? And who could be expected to block a new proposal? The answers to these and countless other questions of practical importance to the administrator depend to a great extent on the administrator's possession of enough skill to assess his teachers—*and their perception of him.*

❧ 10 ❧

putting concepts of
organizational behavior to work
in school administration

It is my hypothesis that the present organizational strategies developed and used by administrators . . . lead to human and organizational decay. It is also my hypothesis that this need not be so.
—*Chris Argyris* [1]

The present emphasis on behavioral aspects of organization could be misinterpreted as suggesting that a "new" kind of administrative practice has appeared which should supplant the "old." In practice, however, behavioral concepts are actually supplementary to the more established conventional concepts of formal organization. Whereas formerly, administrators had virtually nothing but theories of formal organization and their own intuition to guide them, newer theories of organizational behavior offer them a greater choice of alternatives for managing an enterprise. These alternatives are highly apposite in that they suggest ways to meet some of the threatening organizational crises of our time: the need for greater creativity, the need for more flexible organizations, and the need for increased involvement and participation.

Much organizational behavior deals with (1) human relationships in the organization and (2) the antagonism between the life-style of the individual and the demands and constraints of the organization. Both

[1] Reprinted with permission from Chris Argyris, *Interpersonal Competence and Organizational Effectiveness* (Homewood, Ill.: Richard D. Irwin, Inc., and The Dorsey Press, 1962), p. 1.

these problems involve values which today are looked upon by teachers as necessary to their status as members of an organization; the most important of those values are the importance of the individual in the organization and his dignity as a professional person.

The challenge to the school administrator, therefore, is to incorporate the concepts of organizational behavior into his administrative style. This chapter offers some suggestions for meeting this challenge more adequately.

Much progress in recent years has been made in applying organizational behavior concepts to practice. We contend that:

1. The use of behavioral concepts is not a onetime affair: it has no beginning and no end, any more than the use of structural concepts such as line-and-staff. Rather, these concepts suggest a continual, on-going process of diagnosis, learning, and growing.
2. Applying behavioral theory and research to organizational problems should be a cooperative venture, with the scientist and the administrator working together in a collegial relationship, and employing a heuristic approach.

In this chapter we will first comment very briefly on the need to put behavioral research findings to work in the schools, second, discuss the four major problems that must be dealt with and, third, describe a heuristic plan of action.

The Need for Putting Behavioral Concepts to Work

As we are all painfully aware, schools are no longer quiet refuges away from the mainstream of life. The historic, century-long shift of schools from a sort of nice, genteel "frill" to their present status of central importance in our society has had a profound effect on the job of the school administrator. Today the administrator deals with pressures and problems the nature and dimensions of which plagued only management executives in business and industry a few years ago. Strikes, street demonstrations, boycotts, and violence hinge on what happens in a school. More important, as is more clearly understood than ever before, the purposes and goals of the school are among the most urgent priorities of our time.

Everywhere is evidence of seething discontent with the status quo, much of which is attributable to the daily routine of organizational existence. The situation becomes more obvious with each new survey, each feature piece in a magazine, each TV "special" on the topic: individuals are caught in faceless, dehumanizing organizational juggernauts which relentlessly apply bureaucratic rules and demand that individuals yield to the needs of the organization. *Anomie*—that free-floating anxiety so characteristically experienced by people who feel powerless in the organization—is increasingly evident as important decisions which affect individual participants are made in high places in the organization in unknown ways. School administrators who want more effective, efficient organizations (in the Barnardian sense) must, as McGregor would say, emphasize *the human side of enterprise.*

Administrators—and school administrators as a group are not exempt—have too often overemphasized organizational structure at the expense of proper utilization of people. Much has been said among school administrators about introducing non-gradedness, team-teaching, demand scheduling, "house plans," or other structural reorganization plans. But little consideration has been given to the development of lower-profile, less-pyramidal organizations in which teachers set standards and exercise control. Few school principals give serious thought to proposals which emphasize more effective involvement of teachers in *significant* problems or the *central* decisions of the school, partly because they view teachers as ill-equipped or unwilling to take on such serious responsibilities.

Yet, if we take Argyris' thesis seriously, we must admit that our present school organizations reward the dependent, submissive person at the expense of the more creative, independent individuals. Brickell is one of very few professionals who have had the audacity to say publicly what is widely accepted by teachers: teachers *are*, generally, powerless to innovate; they *are*, generally, involved in programs of change only after administrators have set goals and generally have made other critical decisions about proposed changes; and teachers *do*, too often, feel that their involvement is mere "window dressing"—they sit on useless committees where their proposals are subject to the veto of budget-wielding, powerful administrators. Is it any wonder that the organizational behavior of teachers is so frequently marked by withdrawal, apathy, and "disengagement."

So the vicious circle goes, with administrators deploring apathy and high staff turnover and calling for better teachers who will stay on the job longer, yet holding tight to the reins of organizational power and shoring up the traditional concepts of supervision. Research in organizational behavior makes it clear that these ends are mutually exclusive.

Our purpose is not to indict either schools or school administrators. It is precisely because administrators are sensitive to the need for greater organization effectiveness and efficiency, and are searching for solutions to this need, that this book was written. Concepts stemming from recent research in organizational behavior can offer guidelines to solutions, although we must bear in mind that translating the findings of research—or, more correctly, the concepts developed from research findings—in organizational behavior into directly usable form is, at the present time, often impossible. The practical usefulness of much behavioral science research in schools is limited by four major problems:

1. *The problem of role relationships*
2. *The problem of communication*
3. *The problem of internalizing*
4. *The problem of generalizing*

The Problem of Role Relationships

Administrators tend to think of academic people in "ivory tower" terms, and often for good reason. A noted behavioral scientist, speaking about organizational climate to a conference of elementary school principals, was asked about the nature and extent of his first-hand experience in school administration. Since he had never actually been an administrator, the scientist was somewhat flustered by the implication of the question, and responded that since he was a scientist it was not necessary for him to "get down in the muck and mire" of the schools to carry out his studies; his research data could be gathered by others and then brought to him for analysis. Actually, he was probably right in the limited sense he intended. But his unfortunate choice of words conveyed to the principals the traditional antagonisms which have long existed between researchers and practitioners in administration. Needless to say, the administrative behavior of those school principals was not greatly influenced by that conference.

The literature on management and organization has many such allusions to the traditional antagonisms between researcher and practitioner. In every field, whether it be business, industry, the military, or education, researchers are constantly being criticized by practicing administrators. Those who are "on the firing line" demand that researchers formulate something "useful" and that they discuss it without resorting to jargon. The researcher, however, is inclined to feel that the administrator is actually looking for gimmicks and is primarily concerned with temporary aids rather than genuinely searching for meaningful solutions.

However, since organizational research is conducted with the cooperation of administrators—or, at least, at their sufferance—the administrator's demands tend to carry much weight. The researcher who is concerned with producing "useful" output that can be applied in the school situation faces a new hazard when he leaves academe to venture into the schools for this purpose: he can seem to be condescending and judgmental —neither of which attitudes helps in his work with the practicing administrator.

This conflict is a problem of role relationships, and it certainly does not expedite the development of school organizations. The need of schools for fresh approaches to their critical problems requires relationships between administrators and researchers that are more productive. Indeed, it hardly seems necessary to argue that we can ill afford to perpetuate this traditionally antagonistic relationship; the problems of the day call for a change, a new relationship between professor and practitioner that gives greater promise of productivity. Researcher and administrator can more profitably be viewed as professional specialists who are partners in a team relationship. Each has his role to play—and they are complementary roles —and each has his contribution to make. If this kind of relationship can be established, one of the difficult roadblocks to putting research findings to work in the schools will be removed.

The Problem of Communication

In order to put new concepts to work in the schools, these concepts must be communicated to the school administrator. Language is a problem; the researcher is constantly striving for precision in his use of terms and he seeks new terms which are, for him, descriptive of new insights. And he hedges, perhaps appropriately, with qualifying terms, is inclined to use technical statistical terms, and often tends to avoid advocating a course of action which might exceed the limitations of his data. There is a genuine need for more "digestible" nontechnical research reporting to the administrator. Yet, it is difficult to adequately communicate much that is really new or complex in the compressed form that many administrators desire. And this difficulty is compounded if—as is often the case— the administrator has been so caught up in his administrative duties that he has not been able to keep pace with the general trend of organizational behavior research in recent years.

Generally speaking, however—and this may be declining over time— school administrators have little formal training in research design and methods. To the extent that this is true, the communication problem is considerably more difficult to overcome. Many administrators, particularly those with elementary school backgrounds, took heavy concentrations of education courses in both undergraduate and graduate programs of study. Moreover, not only was training in research often lacking, but little attention was devoted to courses in the behavioral sciences, particularly courses offered outside a school or department of education. Thus, the rapid communication of new knowledge and concepts made so urgent by changing conditions is further handicapped.

School administrators are not alone, however, in the presentday need to keep up with developments that were not anticipated in their undergraduate days. Their counterparts in business, industry, and other organizations are under similar pressure.

The Problem of Internalizing

As educators are well aware, "knowing about" organizational behavior does not necessarily have much observable effect on that behavior. Many of us are aware of the implications of human relations and group dynamics—we have read the books and can discuss the topics knowledgeably —but few can use this knowledge fully. This is illustrated by the case of a professor who thought he was an authority on human relations and taught the values of group decision making and participative supervision for many years. Yet, among his faculty colleagues he was often spoken of as being irascible, unpredictable, and hard to get along with. Frequently, we have not internalized what we know—we have not made it a part of the way we live.

Sometimes, perhaps due to long years of what might be viewed as miseducation as well as the pressures of social norms, we find it difficult to decide just how to handle interpersonal relationships. Argyris, working with a group of high-level corporation executives on this problem, found that "[i]n all cases they quickly and unequivocally emphasized that for them the human decisions were much more difficult" than big multi-million-dollar corporate decisions.[2] They disliked the interpersonal variety of decisions and avoided them if they could; moreover, the norms of the corporate system sanctioned and permitted such avoidance, presumably by allowing the executives to "forget" or overlook the need for such a decision, or to quietly exercise power to eliminate the problem in some way.

Argyris points out that the reasons for the executives' preferences are not so strange; million-dollar decisions are "studied by teams of men, spending countless hours, aided by computers, consultants, research, and any other help that is available."[3] Thus, the organization supports and encourages executives in technical decision making; they feel confident—

---

[2] *Ibid.*, p. 276.
[3] *Ibid.*

even if decisions ultimately are poor ones—that every effort was made to assure the best decisions under the circumstances. But, in matters dealing with behavior—matters of interpersonal relationships—we have learned to be less open, less cooperative. For emotions are involved in these kinds of decisions and we have learned to conceal or shy away from free and open consideration of emotional issues in organizational life: everyone is supposed to be mature and able to get along with others. Yet, it frequently happens that the individual is not fully aware of the effect of his own behavior on others when he is dealing with matters concerning behavior. The commonly observed discrepancy between what a person "knows" and the way his behavior affects others is a phenomenon often observed in the behavioral sciences.

The Problem of Generalizing

This book has emphasized that (1) although recent contributions of the behavioral sciences have much to contribute to the improved practice of school administration, (2) the knowledge domain of organizational behavior is far from fully explored or understood. Accordingly, we must be careful about jumping to unwarranted conclusions. Earlier, we illustrated this by recounting the misplaced zeal with which educators seized upon the concept of "democratic leadership"—which has since proven to be a source of so much disappointment. The earnest advocacy of this concept, and its resulting popularity in educational circles for many years, was a classic case of overgeneralizing from excellent behavioral research.

Overgeneralizing is at least partly the result of the administrator's constant search for solutions, for something "useful"—by which he frequently means something that can be "taken off the shelf" and, when "plugged into" his organization, will "work." When we deal with organizational behavior, however, we deal with an incredibly complex set of variables and relationships involving emotions, values, personality makeup, and the dynamics of interpersonal relationships. Overgeneralizing by applying the same prescription to all schools ignores unique factors in each school situation. Harvey Sherman contends that the only realistic approach—in view of the present state of the art—is "pragmatism," which he defines as "doing what works in a particular situation." [4] This, he says, "does not mean throwing out theory. It means, rather, knowing

---

[4] Harvey Sherman, *It All Depends: A Pragmatic Approach to Organization* (University, Ala.: University of Alabama Press, 1966), p. 55.

and using theory to the extent that it works, but not using it when it doesn't. Otherwise, pragmatism degenerates into nothing more than trial and error." [5]

Every school is a unique situation. Every school, being an organization, also has much in common with other schools and other organizations. Each administrator must work out for himself how and to what extent theory and research in organizational behavior should be applied in his situation. Overzealous generalizing from specific research can lead to irrational applications. Overemphasis on the uniqueness of one's situation can result in a virtual denial of the contributions that theory and research can make, and the result can be administration by crisis.

These, then, are some of the major problems which administrators must be aware of when they put theory and research-based concepts of organizational behavior to work in their schools. But, how *can* we make use of what is being discovered and made available? It must be evident to the reader that, at the present stage of the game, he cannot expect much in the way of prescriptions. He can, however, find guidelines which can be used to help him make his own decisions.

These guidelines can be used as a sort of check-list of considerations to be borne in mind as the administrator searches for the one alternative among many conflicting alternatives that are always available, which promises the most satisfactory results with the least unhappy side-effects. If it accomplishes nothing else, the domain of organizational behavior can broaden the search behavior for practitioners who seek better ways to organize and administer schools.

Behavioral Approach

There are essentially two opposing ways of perceiving an organization: *rationalistic* and *behavioralistic*. Traditional concepts of organizations tend to emphasize the holistic: they see the organization as an entity or organism which—as a collective—"acts" or "behaves." Such views, as represented by Weber or Taylor, are inclined to be highly rationalistic. They emphasize the prescriptions or rules which supposedly direct and control the behavior of individuals within the collective toward the goals of the organization.

The behavioral approach takes a fundamentally different point of view and departs from different premises. The behavioral approach emphasizes not the wholeness of the collective organism, but the role of individuals in the organism. The behavior of individuals who have been

---

[5] *Ibid.*

molded by their personality characteristics, by environmental circumstances, and by the behavior of others is at the heart of organizational behavior. The interrelatedness of the behaviors of individuals is of central importance because it is the total of these interpersonal behaviors which describes the organization. The organizational chart that is so vital to rationalistic approaches is seen somewhat differently in the behavioral view. For the latter, the organizational chart presumes to diagram and prescribe human interactions in the organization which, in fact, may never really exist, because the organizational chart ignores the informal organization which is of such practical importance in determining what gets done and how.

Rationalist adherents tend to think of improving the effectiveness and efficiency of the organization largely in structural terms: communication (cybernetics), input-output relationship (such as in classical economics), and the win-or-lose concepts of game theory. Although, in this enlightened age, people in the organization are seen in a humane way, the emphasis is on organizational relationships and on controlling behavior in accordance with the organization's goal-achievement. Behavioral approaches stress concepts such as role theory and take into account the perceptions, beliefs, and values of individual participants.

But behavioral concepts of organization are not atomistic; rather, the view is a molecular one, wherein individual participants are seen as bound together in a dynamic interrelationship. It is this mutual interrelationship which gives the organization its distinctive form and character. This dynamic whole, which we call an organization, is best described and understood as a social system; there exists not only an internal system (the school), but a larger system as well, of which the school is a dynamic part—the school district organization, the social-civic-economic community in which the school is located, and so forth.

Rationalist-oriented administrators think of the organization primarily as an entity, a complete organism, and tend to analyze it (i.e., try to understand it) in terms of structural subdivisions and their component parts. Organizational changes are generally perceived as a process of reorganizing, redefining, and realigning these parts of the structural whole so that they will perform more satisfactorily. "Human relations" becomes an important appendage to the central concern and must be reckoned with because it is clear that the informal organization—if too badly violated—can ruin the best-laid plans of administrators. Thus, new work processes that should be more productive turn out to be less productive than their predecessors; reorganization produces further confusion.

Behavior-oriented administrators tend to view (i.e., try to understand) their organizations primarily as open social systems. They feel that organizational changes are best accomplished by changing the behavior in the organization—the behavior both of individuals and of the group which comprises the social system.

What direction should this change in behavior take? Toward ready submissiveness, suppression of personal needs and desires, or acceptance of a position of powerlessness? If so, behavioral approaches can be powerful instruments for the aggrandizement of administrative power and the reduction of organizational effectiveness. Should behavioral change be directed toward increasing the happiness of participants or, negatively, reducing the alienation of the workgroup? This is the concern of morale and it is generally accepted that we cannot reliably demonstrate a causal relationship between morale and organizational effectiveness: "happy, happy, happy" does not necessarily lead to better performance of the organization. The change-direction most frequently sought by behaviorists is toward the development of highly motivated, self-fulfilling individuals who make the greatest possible use of their talents and capacities and at the same time are skilled contributors to the dynamic interpersonal relationships of the social system which comprises the organization.

Administration is concerned with the relationships among internal and external variables of the social system, which are primarily behavioral. The social system may be analyzed (i.e., understood) by, first, studying individuals in it along with the bases of their behavior, and second, by examining the behavior of the group in order to productively develop dynamic relationships. This involves problems such as meeting higher motivational needs (à la Maslow or Herzberg); developing authentic open relationships in which problems such as conflict, communication difficulties, and interpersonal friction can be faced and attended to; and adapting supervisory style to the realities of the situation.

The administrator's concern with the human relationships in the social system which we call a school is not merely to integrate the role-performance of teachers into an efficiently functioning organization, but also *to foster innovative and spontaneous behavior which goes beyond the usual role expectation of "teacher."* The response to demands from the external system—governmental, economic, and social—for greater effectiveness does not lie in merely seeing that adequate numbers of "warm bodies" stand before our classes. The challenge which traditional rationalist-structuralist concepts of the school have failed to meet is relatively new to public education; it deals not with mere satisfactory performance in role, but, rather, with *excellence.*

Saying this is another way of underscoring the fact that no single general theory of organization—rationalistic or behavioral—can adequately explain the organization. We are far from being able to seriously consider abandoning concepts of structure and organismic behavior of the organization. But, for the present, administrators must select from a number of theories which are available and utilize these theories in as judicious a manner as possible in the particular circumstances. The emphasis here is on utilizing behavioral approaches to organizational and administrative problems.

A Heuristic Approach

The domain of organizational behavior is well-adapted to a heuristic approach that is centered on a program of staff development. By *heuristic* we mean a process of inquiry, study, and learning with the following characteristics:

1. It can be acquired through practice and experience.
2. It stimulates further investigation and discovery.
3. It encourages the individual to continue learning on his own.

Since they are teachers and former teachers, public school staff members tend to expect their lifelong education and development to continue much as they experienced it during their years as students. This involved classes in which teachers were in charge and did the planning: the teacher decided what was to be taught, by what procedures, and the nature and extent of the participants' involvement. When new ideas are offered, or the pressures for change mount, a common response is to send for a speaker—an "expert"—who can help by performing a role similar to that of a teacher. It is also common for administrators and teachers to enroll in courses or organize one to "bring us up to date." Frequently, the principal or another administrator is expected to play the role of the teacher: he must lecture, lead discussions, suggest reading and field experiences, and guide learning. This classroom-type of learning experience has three effects which we should note:

1. It maintains the learner in a dependency relationship to the teacher.
2. It places little emphasis on behavioral interaction between learners.
3. It emphasizes the concepts of hierarchy and control which also underlie the conventional structural view of organizations.

Moreover, classroom-type of learning does little to stimulate or encourage continued efforts at discovery at the initiative of the individual. This is, perhaps, a good method for learning "about" organizational behavior, but it does not facilitate internalizing what is studied. The value of the typical teachers' convention—and, indeed, a good many professional meetings—is often questioned by administrators and teachers alike because so little is gained that can be applied in the school.

Organizational behavior is change-oriented. Few who become interested in the phenomena connected with decision making, or organizational climate, or leadership—to name a few examples—do not attempt to look at their own organizations through the "lenses" of these concepts. And, having done so, few would claim that some changes for the better are not possible. Therefore, when we put concepts of organizational behavior to work, we can appositely employ some of the techniques of change-agents. Four that will be discussed here are:

1. Team training
2. Temporary systems
3. Data feedback
4. The outside consultant

What follows is an attempt to guide the principal in the selection of heuristic techniques that will be useful in applying concepts from the research in organizational behavior to his school. Strategically, the decision to use an outside consultant is probably the most powerful idea we suggest. Therefore, following a general description of some of the key aspects of the heuristic approach being suggested, we will offer guidelines for locating and working with a consultant.

Team Training

If we look on the school as a social system, then a strategy of change must aim at changing the entire system—not merely part of it. In virtually every school, some faculty members have gone on sabbatical for specialized training at one time or another. But, as so often happens, upon the return of these faculty members to the school—with the same old problems—they are unable to get many new ideas introduced. The behavioral explanation for this is that the system itself has not been changed. The people and their problems are still there: the same communication blockage, the same clinging to traditional values, and so forth, which tend to keep the system in its homeostatic, steady state.

A strategy for creating far greater impact is to expose an organizational team to simultaneous training. In the business world this has traditionally meant transporting an administrator and his key subordinates to an out-of-town setting that is conducive to quiet thought and reflection. There, with the help of an outside consultant, they spend a weekend or a few days trying to think through their problems and make plans for overcoming them. Unlike the classroom situation, there is no teacher, and the subjects studied are *their* problems (not those of some unknown third party). Upon their return to the organization, the team is still intact and can continue to try to face their problems as they did during the training session. Since they were all together during training, they are also on the same "wavelength" back in the organization.

The case of a 90-teacher urban elementary school illustrates one practical application of team training. Having recognized that the staff seemed to be having much conflict and confusion in the school, the principal and teachers decided to have a survey made of the school's organizational climate as a useful diagnostic step in the search for more effective organizational behavior. An organizational climate survey was made using both Halpin's OCDQ and Stern-Steinhoff's OCI. When it was time to present the climate data to the faculty for their analysis and study, the principal was quite apprehensive that the findings might be so threatening to the teachers as to be harmful. Reluctantly, the consultants agreed to present the climate data to an existing "steering committee" of teacher representatives, who would then transmit the data to the rest of the faculty.

The consequence was that the faculty was quite suspicious that some information was being kept from them, that they were being treated as second-class citizens, and so on. The problem was solved—with more difficulty than should have been necessary—by finally bringing the entire faculty group together in a pleasant, relaxed setting away from the school for a conference with the consultants, at which the organizational climate data was presented in full and then discussed. Later, in groups of those who had similar jobs, the teachers and school's administrators and supervisors made plans for solving some of the school's climate problems upon their return to the job.

The result was a noticeable brightening of the faculty's outlook and a determination to continue the new-found spirit of inquiry and study of their problems as a regular part of their professional activities. Because their learning experience with the organizational climate data—and the subsequent analysis and planning—had been done in teams, the application of their learning to the school setting was facilitated.

Temporary Systems

A factor that is partly responsible for the slow pace at which organizations adopt new practices and, in general, change, is that organizations simply do not have adequate energy or resources to devote to change processes. The organization's struggle to attain the goals set for it, plus the need to maintain the functioning of the organization as it exists leaves few resources for innovative practices. Time, people, money, and other resources are usually allotted to making present operations work as well as possible and in meeting the continual crises which arise.

It has been pointed out that our conception of an organization is usually that of a permanent system: a church, a school, or a corporation. These are durable, on-going structures. However, in our society we do use a wide variety of temporary systems to serve special purposes.

Miles,[6] lists conferences, games, task forces, research projects, parties, performances of the lively arts, and even carnivals as some of the many kinds of temporary systems for which we find frequent use. Of these, some temporary systems provide expressive outlets for people and a certain respite from the daily grind of organizational life. Others, such as *ad hoc* committees, scientific expeditions, and political campaign committees are created to accomplish particular tasks on a short-term basis. A third type of temporary system is useful for inducing change in a permanent system and can be most effective in putting concepts of organizational behavior to work in schools.

In the illustration given earlier, of the elementary school and the organizational climate survey, it was found that a temporary social system is highly useful in facilitating change. In the school setting during the regular school week, teachers and administrators were so involved in teaching classes, planning, attending conferences, supervising after-school programs, and the like, that there was little time or energy for adequately studying or discussing one of the serious problems in the school: its organizational climate. The temporary system, in this case, was a Saturday conference. It should be noted that the conference was held away from the school in a pleasant, quiet, relaxed setting. The school's teachers and administrators, together with the consultants, comprised the system: parents, school clerks, teachers' aides, and others were not included in the temporary system. These factors, in addition to some specific conference planning and procedures suggested by the consultants, produced a relaxed air of informality and an openness which the faculty had never before experienced as a group.

One of the characteristics of a temporary system is the expectation that it will exist for only a limited time: this fact can be utilized to facilitate attaining the objectives of the system. If it is utilized as it was in this case, to lower defenses and temporarily (at least) to induce new patterns of interpersonal relationship, there will be a greater chance of internalizing

---

[6] Matthew Miles has reported extensive research and experience utilizing temporary systems as change-inducing mechanisms in schools. Much of this section is based on Matthew B. Miles, "On Temporary Systems," in Matthew B. Miles, ed., *Innovation in Education* (New York: Teachers College Press, 1964).

changed behavioral patterns rather than merely learning "about" these patterns.

Temporary systems may be used to bring about changes in the behavior of individuals or of groups; that is, we can focus on one teacher, or a workgroup within the school, or an entire faculty. There are three distinct types of changes that are generally sought by temporary systems: educative, re-educative, and treatment. The organization and functioning of the temporary system is geared to one of these processes:

1. An educative system is designed to provide its participants with knowledge, attitudes, and skills which are new to them.
2. A re-educative system has a more complex task: (a) unlearning or correcting something that the participants have already learned, and (b) then providing educative activities to replace what has been discarded or add to what has been corrected.
3. A treatment system seeks to correct an existing deviancy and to restore a state of health to either individuals or groups.

Figure 10–1, as proposed by Matthew Miles, illustrates five functions which temporary systems can serve and suggests representative kinds of

FOCUS OF ATTENTION

FUNCTION OF THE SYSTEM	Person	Group or organization
Compensation, maintenance	Game Party Vacation, travel	Carnival, office party Recognition banquet
Short-term task accomplishment	Research project Artists' colony	Task force Scientific expedition
Change: treatment	Psychodrama Psychotherapy Social casework	Consultant-organization relationship ("sociotherapy")
Change: re-educative	Sociodrama Human relations training laboratory Teacher training institute Brainwashing	Simulation exercise Survey feedback method Team training
Change: educative	School or college class Golf lesson	Ad hoc committee Educational experiment Utopia

FIGURE 10–1. Temporary systems classified by function. From Matthew B. Miles, "On Temporary Systems," in Matthew B. Miles, ed., *Innovation in Education* (New York: Teachers College Press, 1964), p. 442. © 1964 by Teachers College, Columbia University. Reproduced by permission of the publisher.

temporary systems which are typically used to carry out those functions. Obviously, the practicing school administrator is primarily concerned with temporary systems which are educative or re-educative in nature. It may be readily seen that, in Miles' lexicon, the process being suggested in this book for putting concepts of organizational behavior to work in schools is a re-educative one. However, the range of types of temporary systems which Miles has identified can be helpful to the administrator for selecting those systems which are appropriate to the existing need or goals of his school's faculty.

Data Feedback

Feedback is a characteristic of an open system and has a stabilizing effect on the system. It is often illustrated as a loop, for it returns to the system information which enables it to adapt so as to keep the system in a steady state. Thus, organizations with effective feedback mechanisms tend to adapt to circumstances in their suprasystems and yet remain essentially unchanged. This process is similar to the case of the political aspirant who utilizes opinion polls and grass-roots soundings to check on his "image" and then tailors his next speech to the issues and the point of view that his feedback tells him will help "keep him in the race." The press may soberly discuss the "new" Senator Glockenshpiel while the man himself actually remains virtually unchanged. Feedback used in this way tends to restrict meaningful change in both individuals and social systems.

Change is more frequently attributable to the substantial impact of significant stimuli from the suprasystem than it is to the internal forces of the system itself. A widget manufacturer, for example, will probably tend to make and sell widgets much as he has always done. Feedback from marketing surveys and consumer research may cause the firm to introduce model changes and refinements in their widgets, but the firm will remain essentially widget-oriented and will simply seek to do better what it is already doing. Significant change in the firm usually is traceable to fundamental environmental disturbances such as technological changes which sharply reduce the widget market or the importation of foreign-made widgets at lower prices. So it is in schools. Feedback from countless sources—ranging from test results to violent street protests—constantly tend to cause schools to seek to adapt existing ways of doing things to changing external conditions, resulting in reinforcement of the homeostatic tendency found in all organizations. Because the school or organization is a "domesticated" organization that is somewhat protected from its environment it rarely encounters the drastic caliber of external change that would put it out of business.[7]

But we have been discussing permanent systems. Floyd Mann [8] and others have demonstrated the change-effect on a social system by providing certain kinds of feedback to it via a temporary system. This process was illustrated on a simple level earlier by the case of the elementary school and organizational climate data. In this case, the feedback consisted not of some external expressions of "how the school was doing," but took the form of perceptions from the teachers and supervisors themselves. After gathering climate data from the members of the school's social system, the consultants were able to display these data to the faculty in chart and graph form and describe some of the implications that they seemed to suggest. Faculty members could question and discuss the data in order to compare them to their own perceptions of the climate in the school and why it was so. This kind of feedback activity accomplishes three things:

1. *It reveals consensus.* Those issues or matters of relevance to the system can be identified, which alone can lead to useful behavioral change. For example, if the teachers of a school find that *they, themselves,* perceive a high level of disengagement, questions are sure to be raised: Why? What do the data really mean? What can be done about it?
2. *It reveals discrepancies.* If, let us say, some of the teachers see a high level of disengagement and another group in the same faculty does not agree, most faculty groups will want to know why this is so and what it implies for the operation of the school.
3. *It stimulates participation.* Whether the feedback deals with organizational climate or any number of other facets of the system's functioning, the feedback process involves the members in concerns that are of central importance. The members can identify with the problem and understand that they can make a contribution to its solution. This heightened involvement in itself can be a powerful force for improving the system's performance.

There are many kinds of feedback data which can be obtained and used in order to induce change in this way: feedback dealing with deci-

---

[7] For a discussion of Carlson's concepts of "wild" and "domesticated" organizations, see pp. 147–48.

[8] Floyd C. Mann, "Studying and Creating Change: A Means to Understanding Social Organization," *Research in Industrial Relations,* Industrial Relations Research Association Publication 17, 1957. See also Floyd Mann and Henry Baumgartel, *The Survey Feedback Experiment: An Evaluation of a Program for the Utilization of Survey Findings* (Ann Arbor, Mich.: Foundation for Research on Human Behavior, 1964).

sion making processes in the school, role-perception and role relationship, communication, leader behavior, and many other aspects of organizational behavior. All the foregoing kinds of feedback data can be readily made available with the aid of a skilled, knowledgeable consultant. However, from an organizational behavior point of view, it is probable that in most cases the specific *type* of data that is used in the feedback is less important (at the outset, at least) than how the actual process is handled. Behavioral outcomes are the objective, not merely "knowing about" a problem. Important objectives in utilizing feedback in this way include the involvement of teachers, their concern, increasingly open interaction between them, and their skill in solving group problems. This approach is process-oriented, the first essential of which is to develop the process skills of the participants which, it is hoped, will ultimately result in improved organizational behavior.

To elucidate further, let us describe three simple, widely used techniques of utilizing feedback which deal specifically with group functioning, not with the larger problem of the organizational behavior in the social system of the school itself. However, these techniques illustrate the operational principles that underlie data feedback as a technique.

Discussion groups, decision making groups, and other kinds of groups often face the problem of ineffective or dysfunctional behavior by participants. A widely used technique for tackling this problem is to require that observers record behavioral data as the group goes about its work.[9] For example, an observer could keep track of who talks to whom. A diagram, such as that in Figure 10-2, could be used not only to record the observations but also to help present the information to the group participants. In the particular case illustrated, the number of lines made by the observer on this form indicates the number of statements which were made in the group during a fifteen-minute observation period—which was twenty. Four of these statements were made to the group as a whole; the arrows representing these statements stop at the middle of the circle. Those lines with arrows at each end represent statements made by one person to another which drew a response from the recipient.

We see that one person, Harold, had more statements directed toward him than anyone else, and that he responded or participated more than anyone else. The short lines drawn at the head of one pair of arrows indicates who initiated each remark. Harold, who is obviously the leader, had remarks directed at him which required a response from

---

[9] This discussion of the three observation and feedback techniques is based on Leland P. Bradford, Dorothy Stock, and Murray Horwitz, "How to Diagnose Group Problems," *Adult Leadership*, II, No. 4 (September, 1953), 12–19. Published by the Adult Education Association of the U.S.A., Washington, D. C.

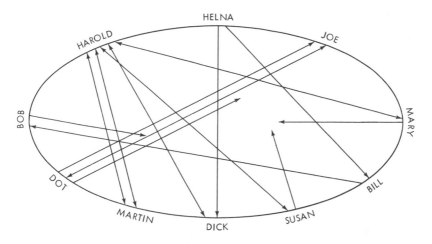

FIGURE 10–2. Technique for collecting data on who talks to whom. From Leland P. Bradford, Dorothy Stock, and Murray Horwitz, "How to Diagnose Group Problems," *Adult Leadership*, II, No. 4 (September, 1953), 18. Published by the Adult Education Association of the U. S. A., Washington, D. C.

four other people. The use of this form requires a full-time observer with no other duties during the exercise.

Categories suggested by Bales [10] in his work on interaction analysis provides a basis for the instrument, as illustrated in Figure 10–3, on which data may be recorded regarding who in the group makes what kind of contributions. This record enables the researcher to quickly note who talked and also what type of contribution was made. At the end of a time period it is thus possible to record the frequency and type of participation by each member.

A third form, somewhat simpler to complete than either of the other two, enables an observer to record in more general terms what happened in the group. (See Figure 10–4.) This form can be used as a checklist by an observer to sum up his observations or it can be filled out by all group members to start an evaluation discussion.

After data has been collected, the second step is feeding back pertinent information to the entire group. Whether the information is collected and reported by the leader or by the observer, it is very easy to hurt the group during the feedback process rather than help it. Considerable skill and sensitiveness are necessary for undertaking this specialized aspect of group participation. The following cautions are particularly pertinent when one provides data feedback to the group:

---

[10] Robert F. Bales, *Interaction Process Analysis* (Cambridge, Mass.: Addison-Wesley Press, 1950).

Member No.	1	2	3	4	5	6	7	8	9	10
1. Encourages										
2. Agrees, accepts										
3. Arbitrates										
4. Proposes action										
5. Asks suggestion										
6. Gives opinion										
7. Asks opinion										
8. Gives information										
9. Seeks information										
10. Poses problem										
11. Defines position										
12. Asks position										
13. Routine direction										
14. Deprecates self										
15. Autocratic manner										
16. Disagrees										
17. Self assertion										
18. Active aggression										
19. Passive aggression										
20. Out-of-field										

FIGURE 10–3. Instrument for recording who makes what kind of contribution. From Leland P. Bradford, Dorothy Stock, and Murray Horwitz, "How to Diagnose Group Problems," *Adult Leadership*, II, No. 4 (September, 1953), 18. Published by the Adult Education Association of the U. S. A., Washington, D. C. (Based upon observation categories discussed in Robert F. Bales, *Interaction Process Analysis* [Cambridge, Mass.: Addison-Wesley Press, 1950].)

1. Be sensitive to what information the group is ready to use—what will be most helpful to the group *now*, rather than what was the most interesting point observed.
2. Don't "avalanche" the group with information. If too much information is given, it can't be used and tends to lead to confusion and feelings of uneasiness. Select only two or three observations which will stimulate thinking and discussion. Let the group ask for more information as it needs it.
3. Don't praise the group too much. Learning does not take place only when the group is told that it is "on the beam." Mentioning accomplishments is desirable as it helps get difficulties faced honestly.
4. Don't punish, or preach, or judge. The observer can't play the role of God. He says, "It was interesting that participation was less widespread today than it was yesterday." He doesn't say, "Some of you dominated the discussion today."

1. What was the general atmosphere in the group?
   Formal _ _ _ _ _ _ _ _   Informal _ _ _ _ _ _ _
   Competitive _ _ _ _ _ _ _ Cooperative _ _ _ _ _ _ _ _
   Hostile _ _ _ _ _ _ _   Supportive _ _ _ _ _ _ _ _
   Inhibited _ _ _ _ _ _ _   Permissive _ _ _ _ _ _ _ _
   Comments: _

2. Quantity and quality of work accomplished
   Accomplishment: High _ _ _ _ Low _ _ _ _
   Quality of Production: High _ _ _ _ Low _ _ _ _
   Goals: Clear _ _ _ _ Vague _ _ _ _
   Methods: Clear _ _ _ _ Vague _ _ _ _
                 Flexible _ _ _ _ Inflexible _ _ _ _
   Comments: _

3. Leader behavior
   Attentive to group needs _ _ _ _ _ _ _
   Supported others _ _ _ _ _ _ _
   Concerned only with topic _ _ _ _ Took sides _ _ _ _
   Dominated group _ _ _ _ Helped group _ _ _ _
   Comments: _

4. Participation
   Most people talked _ _ _ _ Only few talked _ _ _ _
   Members involved _ _ _ _ Members apathetic _ _ _ _
   Group united _ _ _ _ Group divided _ _ _ _
   Comments: _

FIGURE 10–4. Form for recording general atmosphere of the group. From Leland P. Bradford, Dorothy Stock, and Murray Horwitz, "How to Diagnose Group Problems," *Adult Leadership,* II, No. 4 (September, 1953), 19. Published by the Adult Education Association of the U. S. A., Washington, D. C.

5. It is easier to discuss role behavior than people's behavior. "What role did the group need filled at that time?" rather than "That behavior is bad."
6. Go lightly on personality clashes. It is usually better to discuss what helped and what hindered the whole group.[11]

The third step of the data feedback process is diagnosis from the information reported and consideration of what the group and its members will do differently in the future. Usually this process involves a number of steps:

1. The members assess the observations, relate them to their own experience, and test to see whether or not they, as individuals and as a group, agree with the reported data.

---

[11] Bradford, *et al., op. cit.,* p. 19.

2. The group examines the reasons. What caused some event to occur?
3. The group moves to a decision of what to do. What can be done in future similar circumstances? What can individual members do before that time to help? What methods or procedures should be changed? What new directions sought?

This stage is the crucial one if the group is to benefit from its feedback activities. Unless the members can gain new insights into the functioning of the group and can find new ways of behaving, the group will not improve its processes or continue to grow and develop. It is very easy for the discussion to cover only the first two steps in this procedure. The leader and the members must be sensitive to this danger and encourage the group to move to this third step. Although the decisions which are made may be quite simple, agreement on future action sets up common expectations for the next meeting and gives a reason for the evaluation.

The Role of the Consultant

We have suggested here a general outline of a heuristic approach to the practical utilization of behavioral concepts in the school, using simple illustrations to elucidate the concept and show how it can be employed with some specificity. However, the approach suggested here is no "do-it-yourself" project. These techniques cannot be acquired merely through experience by well-intentioned people. Along with team training, temporary systems, and data feedback, an essential component of this approach is a consultant.

A popular notion of consultants is that they are experts who can come into the school, make a study to find out what is wrong, and prescribe corrective procedures. In some technical areas of school administration— perhaps in such areas as finance, record-keeping systems, or schoolhouse design—this may very well be a proper approach for the consultant to take. In dealing with organizational behavior, however, appropriate functions of the consultant will help facilitate the group's learning. Thus, the consultant suggests alternatives, provides technical information when the group requests it, and proposes activities which are designed to stimulate the group to examine its own operations and relationships. It is a sensitive, difficult role, and one for which special qualifications are essential.

Chris Argyris, who was a prominent consultant to business, industry, and the government in the 1950's and 1960's, had this to say about the consultant's qualifications: "Ideally, such an individual should be a competent field researcher, laboratory planner, T-group educator, organizational or small-group theorist who is personally capable of establishing authentic relationships. Admittedly, such an individual is extremely hard to find." [12] The truth is that not only are such exceptionally well prepared consultants hard to find, but the few that are available are in great demand. Many are kept busy at high fees for corporations where their effectiveness has long been recognized and on government-supported projects. Argyris meant, as would many of his colleagues, a behavioral scientist: a consultant not from the field of education but who had a Ph.D. in one of the behavioral sciences. These qualifications suggest the kind of individual who should be sought by the school administrator.

Almost certainly the consultant will be a professor. And more than likely, he will be found in a school of business or industrial administration or perhaps in a school of public administration. Departments of behavioral sciences such as psychology and sociology also have some professors who may be qualified to help. However, the school administrator must recognize that not many of these professors will have the time or the inclination to work in a public school situation on a consulting basis.

One further caution regarding the selection of a consultant must be made. To many outside academe, "a professor is a professor." This view is far too rigid, and the practitioner in search of a consultant should be keenly aware of this. The professorship is a highly flexible role, and the interests, backgrounds, and personal and professional values of professors vary widely. Many excellent professors are not "field oriented," whereas others on the same faculty might be highly effective when working on practical problems. To some extent this was illustrated by the TV interview of a renowned scholar in the field of organizational behavior during a violent student upheaval on his campus in 1968. When he was asked to comment on the significance of the student disorders occurring around him, he looked a bit confused and replied, "I don't know what's happening!"

Fortunately, education faculties—particularly those in educational administration—are slowly but steadily hiring professors who are qualified to help schools in a consultant role. More and more professors of educational administration are emerging who have strong backgrounds in behavioral sciences. Today the educational administration faculty of any first-class university will include a balance of professors: some will have had extensive experience as administrators in schools and will also have acquired considerable depth in the behavioral sciences, and some will be very strong in the behavioral sciences and have more limited experience as school administrators. Such a balance is needed, and the school administrator may find a consultant in either group.

Let us deal briefly with sensitivity training. When the term "con-

---

[12] Argyris, *op. cit.*, p. 284.

sultant" is used in connection with "organizational behavior," many professionals in the behavioral sciences tend to think rather narrowly in terms of so-called *sensitivity training,* which is a specific approach to behavioral training that utilizes specialized techniques for working with groups. The National Training Laboratories, which is an affiliate of the National Education Association, has been the preeminent organization in this field. NTL activities include publications (e.g., *The Journal of Applied Behavioral Science*) which disseminate information on research and practical applications of sensitivity training approaches to organizational problems, and, significantly, on the organization and sponsoring of widespread resident educational programs.

Individuals or groups may undertake sensitivity training at NTL centers and qualified individuals may take advanced preparation to become trainers themselves. Adherents of sensitivity training approaches are intensively preoccupied with the interpersonal behavior of individuals and its effect on the group. In their view, the development of greater sensitivity by the individual to the effect that his own behavior has on others and increasing the effectiveness of the individual's interpersonal skills in group situations are important. The goals of such training are generally associated with the development of greater trust, openness, authenticity, and understanding of interpersonal dynamics. Since the training takes place in group situations, it is frequently referred to as T-group training (a T-group merely being a training group). (See page 164.) Some prefer to call such groups "encounter groups." In recent years the general term "laboratory training" has been gaining popularity for referring to the numerous approaches and their variations which have been developed in this rapidly expanding field. It is beyond the scope of this book to delve deeply into this aspect of putting behavioral knowledge to work in schools. Fortunately, those who are active in applying the techniques of laboratory training to organizations are also prolific writers and the administrator can readily apprise himself of this field by reading some of its literature.[13]

Qualified consultants whose interest includes sensitivity training techniques can, naturally, be very helpful in many school situations. However, unless the particular techniques of this approach are desired for a specific reason, the administrator places needless limits on his search for a consultant if he insists on finding a person with the skills and interests of a competent sensitivity trainer.

---

[13] See, for example, E. H. Schein and Warren G. Bennis, *Personal and Organizational Change through Group Methods* (New York: John Wiley & Sons, Inc., 1965), and Leland P. Bradford, Jack R. Gibb, and Kenneth D. Benne, *T-Group Theory and Laboratory Method: Innovation in Re-education* (New York: John Wiley & Sons, Inc., 1964).

In a working partnership the practicing administrator and the consultant from the university faculty can provide an effective team in their efforts to apply organizational behavior concepts to the school. The administrator and other members of the faculty benefit in terms of improved organizational performance and the enthusiasm that comes with greater satisfaction from the job. The consultant has a great deal to offer: special knowledge and skills which make him a much-needed member of a temporary system that is focused on change. He also has a great deal to learn. One of the genuine hazards of the professorship in education is being cut off from the schools. Far too often, because of licensing requirements or other impediments, there is little participation in the "real" world of the schools except peripherally. Consequently, the practitioner is correct in viewing the professor as one who is withdrawn from the "firing line," although in some cases, this is probably as the professor would wish. When he looks for a consultant, however, the administrator will want to seek out those professors who are not only highly qualified in terms of their own interests and their competence in organizational behavior, but who genuinely see the school as a place where they want to work and conduct research.

It should be emphasized that we are suggesting a *partnership* between the practicing administrator and the university-based consultant. Without such a partnership, the administrator is largely cut off from the skills and the knowledge domain of organizational behavior which are based on research and do not come only from experience. Such a partnership will pair professional colleagues: professional peers who have specialized orientations, skills, knowledges, and experiences to utilize in solving problems of organizational behavior.

Summary

In this chapter, we discussed four problems which limit the usefulness of behavioral science research concepts: (1) the problem of role relationships, (2) the problem of communication, (3) the problem of internalizing, and (4) the problem of generalizing. The role of organizational behavior in school administration was emphasized (1) as being important to a long-range learning opportunity for the entire school faculty, and (2) as being an added dimension of administrative practice, rather than a supplantation of established structural approaches. A heuristic approach to putting organizational behavior concepts to work was proposed which featured *team-training, temporary systems, feedback,* and the use of the *"outside" behavioral science consultant,* and illustrative examples of the simple use of such a system were described.

index